KINGDOM
OF DISORDER

KINGDOM OF DISORDER

The Theory

of Tragedy

in Classical France

John D. Lyons

Purdue University Press
West Lafayette, Indiana

03   02   01   00   99   5   4   3   2   1

∞The paper used in this book meets the minimum requirements of
American National Standard for Information Sciences—Permanence of
Paper for Printed Library Materials, ANSI Z39.48-1992.

Printed in the United States of America
Design by Anita Noble

Library of Congress Cataloging-in-Publication Data
Lyons, John D., 1946–
      Kingdom of disorder : the theory of tragedy in Classical France /
   John D. Lyons.
           p.   cm. — (Purdue studies in Romance literatures ; v. 18)
      Includes bibliographical references and index.
      ISBN 1-55753-160-9 (cloth : alk. paper)
      1. French drama (Tragedy)—History and criticism. 2. French
   drama—17th century—History and criticism. 3. French drama—
   Classical influences. 4. Classicism—France. I. Title. II. Series.
   PQ561.L96 1999
   842'.051209—dc21   98-55267
                                                                 CIP

Contents

Preface

The earth is still fresh on modernity's tomb. The news that we are no longer modern, but postmodern, has reached television and the popular press, and with modernity's retrospective celebrity come its various obituaries. These necrologies, as is customary, start with the time and place of the decedent's birth, give details of growth and major achievements, present the cause of death, and end with some mention of those who owe much to the departed.

Seventeenth-century France looms large in many accounts of modernity's genesis, though to be sure there are those who say she died in childhood. Thus Joan DeJean, in *Ancients against Moderns,* sees the promising, generous, inclusive, and sensitive modern spirit crushed by the better-organized and elitist Ancients during the French Culture Wars that took place during the *fin de siècle* around 1690. A different obituary by Stephen Toulmin agrees in large part on the country and century of modernity's birth, but attributes to his subject a much longer life and a vastly different personality. On this account modernity had a promising start, was gravely injured in 1610 on the right bank in Paris—exactly at the moment when the religious fanatic Ravaillac killed modernity's guardian, King Henri IV—and never recovered her good and generous nature. The modernity of Toulmin's *Cosmopolis* lived well into the middle years of the twentieth century, not inclusive or sensitive at all, but a rather insecure and reactionary character who suppressed diversity and emotion in favor of an idealized "reason."

Fans of romance may already have guessed the factor that connects these rival stories of modernity's birth. It's the familiar baroque plot called "the changeling" or "switched in the cradle." DeJean's Ancients are Toulmin's Moderns! The two accounts, and many others, agree, however, that to understand modernity we need to take a good look at what was happening in French culture, and especially in Paris, in the 1600s.

For John Dryden, writing two-thirds of the way through the century, being "modern" almost required being French. Certainly to write drama and even to speak about it with appreciation meant to know the new twists that the French had given to the theory of drama. Dryden's *Of Dramatick Poesie* has been described as being so close to the 1660 work of the French writer

Pierre Corneille that "his essay almost serves as a substitute for the original" (Gilbert 601). In this "essay" in the form of a conversation, four persons who represent different views on drama argue the merits of antiquity, modernity, the English stage, and the theater of other nations. Both Crites, the champion of antiquity, and Eugenius, who holds modern theater more excellent, refer to the important work of the French moderns in formulating the standards for playwrights. In some cases the key terms are not even translated, but appear in Dryden's work in French, the *Trois Unités,* for instance, or *la liaison des scènes.* Lisideius, another participant in the discussion, even more boldly proclaims the superiority of the modern French not only over the ancients, but—scandalously—over contemporary English writers.

Dryden's Lisideius explains the French playwrights' competitive advantage by pointing to the whole theoretical framework (or "rules") constructed by French critics within the Aristotelian tradition:

> because Crites in his discourse for the Ancients has prevented [*i.e.*, anticipated] me by touching upon many Rules of the Stage which the Moderns have borrow'd from [the ancients], I shall onely, in short, demand of you whether you are not convinc'd that of all Nations the French have best observ'd them? In the unity of time you find them so scrupulous that it yet remains a dispute among their Poets, whether the artificial day of twelve hours, more or less, be not meant by Aristotle, rather than the natural one of twenty-four. . . . in the unity of place they are full as scrupulous, for many of their critics limit it to that very spot of ground where the Play is suppos'd to begin. . . . (Dryden 27)

Dryden's *Of Dramatick Poesie* shows the French to be on the "cutting edge" of the theory of drama and identifies a certain extremism or punctiliousness in the critics and playwrights of that nation. Arranging the dialogue so that French modernity triumphs, Dryden proposes a luminous model for the English stage to emulate, based in very large measure on French skill in writing *about* drama. It is surely through Dryden that a certain view—one might even say, a certain myth—of the French aesthetic has been established in the English-speaking world.

The effect of this same dramatic theory radiated to other countries, where it was greeted in similar terms. In Spain, for instance, Ignacio de Luzán's *La poetica* (1737) shows how the French theorists of the seventeenth century provided the basic framework for discussions of drama on the eve of the Enlightenment. The French, who once learned from the Spanish, now provide Spain *modernización* in tragedy, in the view of Luzán, who links the modernity of the French ideas of theater to the accompanying progress in other areas of their national culture.[1] Similarly, Ranieri de' Calzabigi, writing the preface to the collected tragedies of his friend Vittorio Alfieri, described French tragedy as the best that exists ("il migliore che esista") while pointing to its over-theorization as a defining characteristic and a weakness (Calzabigi 83).

If, then, *modernity* is so frequently linked to seventeenth-century France and if one of the most influential products of that modernity was the dramatic theory that so impressed Dryden, Luzán, and many others, whatever happened to that theory? What became of the texts in which it took form and circulated throughout Europe? In a sense the energizing initial debates have disappeared. More specifically, a certain outline of those debates has been *assimilated* and taken over by so many authors of prefaces, manuals, and books of theatrical history that the original struggle to define a modern poetics of tragedy has been forgotten. There remains an impression of a very tidy, formulaic, and static vision of a highly regulated stage. The aura of the revolutionary reinterpretation of the ancient poetics of tragedy—that cutting edge quality that made writing like a Frenchman so scandalously appealing to Dryden—has been lost.

In the two major opposing accounts of the origin of modernity I mentioned early, DeJean and Toulmin both attempt to renew our understanding of our current, late-twentieth-century situation by revising standard accounts of the shifts that occurred in seventeenth-century France. One of the many crucial differences that separates them (and that makes DeJean's vision the more innovative, yet also the more thoroughly historical) is that one assigns the central place to literary culture and the other to the philosophy of science. How does it happen, then, that such leading figures of scientific and philosophical

modernism as Descartes and Pascal are still widely read, studied, and available in multiple, inexpensive editions while the
writers whose theories are said to have brought about a major
continental transformation in the idea of theater are rarely read,
almost never republished, and, when available at all, only found
in expensive critical or facsimile editions? Apparently the idea
that modernism is most of all a *scientific* movement and attitude has become so deeply rooted that we have forgotten that
in the century of modernism's rise to dominance it was primarily
an aesthetic and literary phenomenon. As DeJean writes,
"progress, rather than science, was the determining factor for
the first Moderns" (*Ancients against Moderns* 15)—in other
words, the seventeenth-century's sense that it possessed superiority of taste came first, and scientific progress was later invoked to buttress this initial cultural achievement.

The most self-conscious and explicit articulation of that belief
in progress was in the important treatises of dramatic theory—
substantially theory of tragedy—and in the polemical publications in the great cultural debate about Corneille's pivotal
tragi-comedy *Le Cid* in 1637. However, between us and that
theory stands a tradition of substitutions, as when Gilbert says
of Dryden that "his essay almost serves as a substitute for the
original." As a result of this tradition, represented for decades
by such twentieth-century classics of scholarship as René Bray's
Formation de la doctrine classique and Jacques Scherer's *La
dramaturgie classique en France,* most readers have assumed
that there *was* something that can be called, in Bray's terms,
"the classic doctrine" of French theater. Of course, there *is* such
a thing: it is the distilled and reshaped theory of how plays should
be written—or should have been written—in the view of such
later authors as Voltaire, Sainte-Beuve, Mercier, La Harpe,
Lanson, Bray, and other scholars and critics who viewed the
theater of the period after 1640 as a "classic" national cultural
treasure. However, this doctrine did not exist in seventeenth-
century France, and even if it had existed it would never have
been described by the contemporaries of Corneille and Racine
as *classique.*

A *modern* theater was the goal of the major writers of dramatic theory in seventeenth-century France, and there were
numerous views of how such a modern French theater could
be created in a Christian kingdom—a theater freed from the

uncouth, inconsistent, callous, and dangerously democratic dramatic models left by the ancient Greeks. In attempting to construct the vision of such a new drama, writers played the game of trying to make the most authoritative ancient theoretical text, Aristotle's *Poetics,* support whatever innovation the French writers planned to introduce. Their stretching and patching of the translated Greek text gives a superficial unity to dramatic theory, since all writers packaged their ideas within Aristotelian terms. While common terminology could make it easier to come to agreement on an overall view of how to write the perfect modern tragedy—the aspiration of all dramatic poetics—common terminology *also* makes it easier to carry on a debate.

This debate, this nonformation of a French classical doctrine in the seventeenth-century, is what I describe in this book, *Kingdom of Disorder.* The Abbé d'Aubignac, author of the first long and systematic French book of dramatic theory, *La pratique du théâtre* (published in 1657, but substantially written more than a decade earlier), describes tragedy in these terms, as the *place ruled by disorder and anxiety* ("c'est là où règnent le désordre et l'inquiétude"). This disorder and anxiety can describe the theory of the new, modern tragedy as well as the world of the tragic characters. The turmoil of ideas, which created an unusually broad audience for works of cultural theory, must have been part of the appeal of the French poetics for contemporaries in other countries as well as in France. The theorists do not speak with one voice nor are they without internal contradictions even within their individual treatises. The radical variations in their views on the "rules," on the three "unities," and on the key concepts of *bienséance* (character decorum) and *vraisemblance* (verisimilitude or plausibility) are so great that the use of similar terminology has led many readers to suppose a consensus that is simply not there. Next to the disorder and uneasiness of the theorists, I consider one theme around which there is, if not unanimity, at least agreement by a majority of the theoretical community: tragedy is shaped according to the needs, prejudices, and feelings of the audience. Though in some sense the tragic world onstage is carefully sealed off from the everyday world in which the spectators live, the fictive tragic world can never be described without constant reference to what the audience believes and what the audience feels. The theory of tragedy is thus a theory of *inquiétude* felt by the audience on behalf of the tragic characters.

Seventeenth-century writers inhabited a cultural world very different from the one twentieth-century readers seem to imagine for that earlier period. We do not imagine, for instance, that a major theorist of tragedy would recommend staging the death of dramatic characters as "beaux Homicides" (La Mesnardière 206) or that the adjective "criminal" is an appropriate one for the hero of a French classical tragedy (La Mesnardière 84). We do not often consider the best tragedy to be the tragedy that wrings the most tears from the audience (La Mesnardière 86; Racine, pref. to *Iphigénie, Théâtre complet* 511), nor would we expect an important theorist and critic to claim that tragedy written in verse is theoretically unacceptable, despite its practical monopoly of the French stage (Chapelain, "Lettre sur la règle des vingt-quatre heures" 126). It would probably not occur to us to state categorically that tragedy cannot include events that happen at night (d'Aubignac 121). In an attempt to bridge the gap between the textual reality of seventeenth-century poetics and our common modern views of it, I have taken as point of departure four groups of concepts important to the seventeenth-century authors and still recognizable (though often in oddly twisted forms) to us—those terms I have already mentioned: "rules," passion, verisimilitude (including decorum), and the unities of action, place, and time.

The authors I discuss are generally well known. For the most part they are authors of treatises on the poetics of theater. Both d'Aubignac and Hippolyte-Jules Pilet de La Mesnardière, author of *La poëtique* (1640), were commissioned by Cardinal Richelieu to write complementary texts on theater. Jean Chapelain is the author in his own name of several short works on dramatic theory, most notably the "Lettre sur la règle des vingt-quatre heures" (1630), and he was the principal author of the mitigated censure of Corneille's *Le Cid,* the *Sentimens de l'Academie françoise sur la Tragi-Comédie du Cid* (1638). Pierre Corneille's career-long meditation on dramatic theory, energized by that censure, culminated in his three discourses on dramatic poetry (1660). Contemporary with the discourses are Corneille's critical examinations (*examens*) of each of his plays up to his *Œdipe* (1659). These *examens* often contain important generalizations about comedy, tragi-comedy, and tragedy. It is no doubt indicative of a change in fashion, a growing skepticism about the usefulness of polemical and theoretical treatises, that Jean Racine limits his published statements about tragedy to the prefaces and dedicatory letters in the printed editions of his plays (1672–91). I make briefer mention of other authors, but I think that it is worth putting to rest at the outset any notion that the long, self-proclaimed poetics have a monopoly on the theory of drama or the theory of tragedy. As I use the term, "theory" of tragedy includes any statement about tragedy that generalizes beyond an individual performance or dramatic work. Bishop Bossuet's denunciations of the sinful nature of tragedy and Marie de Sévigné's comparative comments, in her letters to her daughter, about the merits of Corneille's and Racine's tragedies, for example, include statements of a general nature about tragedy and can rightly be considered contributions to the theory of tragedy in seventeenth-century France. Indeed, it is one of the central features of seventeenth-century modern culture that the theory of tragedy was framed as a subject of interest to a wide public, not limited to scholars, playwrights, or technicians of the theater.

One of the concepts universally associated with French seventeenth-century theory of tragedy is *rule.* Whether it be a college student in a course on the history of theater or an extremely refined critic of French culture, almost everyone who approaches the French culture of this period takes it entirely for granted that tragedy had something to do with *rules*—despite the important work of E. B. O. Borgerhoff half a century ago. Unlike Borgerhoff and Will Moore, who demonstrated the distance of practice from theory, I do not propose a comparative study of the writing of tragedy and the explicit attempts to formulate a theory of tragedy within a system of "rules." Instead, I am interested in the problems inherent to a poetics articulated in terms of rule. In my first chapter, I propose reconsidering the term *rule,* recalling that rules are not only authoritative expressions of imperatives but also a somewhat peculiar and historically localized fragmentation of the technical knowledge of the playwright. By imposing a rule-formulated understanding of Aristotle's *Poetics,* humanist scholars prepared the way for a power struggle between playwrights and theorists. They also gave seventeenth-century France a new way of focusing discussions of tragedy, so that even those who rejected the "rules" learned to express their vision of tragedy within this idiom.

The second chapter considers the twentieth-century misconception that French classical poetics requires tragedy to be a primarily "rational" experience. This mistake is often made when readers confuse the rationality of the "rules" with the requirements of tragedy itself as dramatic experience. In fact, seventeenth-century theory proposes the goal of temporarily depriving theater audiences of their ability to reason. Passionate feeling, rather than careful reasoning, is the theoretical aim of tragedy in this period.

What is tragedy about? That is, what kind of event should take place in the staged tragic story? The third chapter examines verisimilitude (or plausibility), a quality that most theorists seek in the tragic story. In asking for "verisimilitude" in the tragic fiction, theorists aspire to a world of order, one from which both chance and unfitting conduct are absent. Yet how can tragedy occur in such an orderly world—that is, what can go wrong? The theorists plunge into deep contradictions in trying to reconcile their notion of an orderly, modern, monarchical, and Christian tragic aesthetic with their view that tragedy is primarily a demonstration of the punishment of moral vice. The result of their contradictory requirements is that French theorists implicitly reject the Aristotelian "tragic middle" for a *chiaroscuro* world of innocence and crime.

The final chapter deals with the famous or infamous hallmark of French classical theory of tragedy: the "three unities." Far from being merely formalistic or decorative concepts, the prescribed limitations in action, place, and time permit a compromise between the apparently independent reality of the tragic scene and the audience-driven poetics that requires the playwright to think of the audience at every step of creating a tragedy.

In revisiting the original texts that propose competing visions of a modern theater for France—visions that have indirectly for centuries shaped the reputation of French culture—I hope to dispel the widespread notion of a monolithic doctrine, of a set of formulas that would later be executed in the brilliant tragedies of the reign of Louis XIV. The creativity of the theoretical imagination, unfettered by the practical realities of the stage and by the need to please audiences, is no less brilliant and is, as we will see, far stranger.

Acknowledgments

I thank colleagues who have heard and questioned earlier sketches of the present argument—Georges Forestier, Gérard Defaux, Wilda Anderson, Hélène Merlin, Anne Birberick, Kevin Brownlee, Bradley Rubidge, Patrick Henry, Marina Scordilis Brownlee, Steven Rendall, Thomas Pavel, Milad Doueihi, Sylvie Romanowski, and Philip Lewis. I am deeply indebted to my wife, Patricia Lyons, for her patient reading and rereading of portions of the text. I thank Kendall Tarte for help with bibliographic research. I am also grateful for the support of the National Endowment for the Humanities and research leave granted by the University of Virginia.

A portion of the second chapter appeared as "The Decorum of Horror: A Reading of La Mesnardière's *Poëtique*" in *Homage to Paul Bénichou,* edited by Sylvie Romanowski and Monique Bilezikian (Birmingham, AL: Summa, 1994), 27–41. It is reprinted here with the gracious consent of Summa Publications.

Chapter One

Regularity

Articulating the Aesthetic

Regular Theater

Seventeenth-century French culture did not use the term *classicism* to describe contemporary changes in literature and the arts. Instead, critics and theorists used the term *régulier* to indicate the change that occurred in the theater at the time of Corneille. In 1685, Jean Racine, Corneille's younger rival, delivered the customary eulogy of Pierre Corneille ("le Grand Corneille") in welcoming his younger brother Thomas Corneille as his successor in the Académie française:

> vous savez en quel état se trouvait la scène française lorsqu'il commença à travailler. Quel désordre! quelle *irrégularité!* Nul goût, nulle connaissance des véritables beautés du théâtre; les auteurs aussi ignorants que les spectateurs; la plupart des sujets extravagants et dénués de vraisemblance; point de mœurs, point de caractères. (Racine, *Œuvres complètes* 2: 344)

Racine joins Corneille in rejecting the state of irregularity that became perceptible only after "regularity" began. Regularity is, in some way, the state of responding to rules, or, as the French said toward the middle of the century, being *dans les règles*. Of his first play, *Mélite ou les fausses lettres* (1633), Corneille wrote later, "elle n'a garde d'être dans les Règles, puisque je ne savais pas alors qu'il y en eût" (1: 5).

In view of the importance writers like Racine and Corneille attribute to "regularity" or "the rules," it is not surprising that one of the most widespread truisms about French seventeenth-century tragedy is that it was strictly controlled by rules. Yet, in 1660, at the peak of fame as France's greatest playwright, Corneille both confirmed the theoretical importance of the rules and admitted that there was no consensus about what these rules were. In the first paragraph of his *Discours de l'utilité et des parties du poème dramatique,* Corneille wrote of the rules: "Il est constant qu'il y a des préceptes, puisqu'il y a un art, mais il n'est pas constant quels ils sont. On convient du nom sans convenir de la chose, et on s'accorde sur les paroles, pour contester sur leur signification" (3: 117). While emphasizing the importance of what he at times called *règles* and at other times *préceptes,* Corneille pointed out the divergence of views as to the specific precepts that comprise this corpus, thus concisely introducing one of the principal characteristics of seventeenth-century French dramatic theory. On one hand, the term *rule* took on a completely unprecedented importance, for never before had playwrights justified their works by writing about rules of dramatic composition. On the other hand, as Corneille attested, the specifics of these rules and even their existence were in doubt. After all, he admitted that the rules exist only because an art exists, and the existence of the art entails the existence of rules. So the proof of the existence of the rules resembles an act of faith, for such entities are only known indirectly and deductively, as part of a perplexing theoretical activity. It looks as if two of the major playwrights of the seventeenth century agreed that they worked within a theoretical structure called "regularity," yet Corneille (and, as we shall see, Racine also) cast doubt on the validity and specific identity of the rules. What, then, was this culture of regularity as it concerned tragedy? Was it a uniform adoption of the concept "rule" as central to the theory of tragedy? Many readers would miss the nuanced qualification in Georges Forestier's 1992 statement that "Ce qu'on appelle aujourd'hui l'*esthétique classique* est donc un ensemble de codes et de règles" (*Introduction* 10), where the operative word is "aujourd'hui."

It is possible to write plays without rules, as Corneille attested. It is possible also to speak theoretically about drama and other literary forms without invoking the concept "rule"—both in antiquity and in recent times writers have not centered their arguments on the structure or existence of rules. In seventeenth-century France, however, the noble dramatic genre, tragedy, was most often discussed by references to "the rules," even when the participants in literary and dramaturgic debates were determined to disprove the importance of specific rules or of the rules in general. It would be useful to know what a "rule" is and how "the rules" became such an integral part of the theory of tragedy.

Taking Aristotle Apart

The art of writing plays was known and discussed theoretically for at least two thousand years before Corneille. In sixteenth-century France, as in Italy of the fifteenth and sixteenth centuries, in many treatises on poetics, commentaries on Aristotle's *Poetics,* and prefaces and epistles to published dramatic texts, both practicing playwrights and literary theorists had debated how to construct tragedies. The points about which they argued were often the same as the issues raised in seventeenth-century writings about tragedy, mostly because Horace's *Ars poetica* and Aristotle's *Poetics* were the direct or indirect sources: the incidents and space and time parameters of the tragic story, the relationship between the tragic story and history, and the effect of the dramatic performance on the audience. However, subsequent to the great wave of poetic theorizing and commentary in sixteenth-century Italy, thinking about poetic texts took a startlingly different form: poetic theory, and especially the theory of tragedy, was divided into parcels increasingly known as *rules* (*regulae,* or *regole*). French authors of the seventeenth-century discovered a poetics that had already been broken into this articulated form. Knowledge of poetics seemed to Corneille's generation to be practically synonymous with knowledge of rules. In 1660, for the collective edition of his plays, Corneille wrote a series of retrospective critical prefaces called *examens.* It is profoundly revealing that the first words of the *examen* of his first comedy, *Mélite,* concern the "rules."[1] Without preamble of any kind, he hurries to head off a possible misunderstanding on the reader's part, for Corneille knows that the reader will assume a knowledge of "rules," implicitly understood to be the basis both for the playwright's activity of writing and for the informed reader's activity of judging a dramatic work. We have come to take for granted that Corneille's approach is entirely unremarkable within seventeenth-century culture, but we will understand that culture better if we take account of alternative ways of talking about dramatic art. In keeping with the colloquial term *coup d'essai* (a "first crack" at doing something), Corneille could first have addressed his lack of practice or experience in the theater, the absence of models to imitate, or his failure to have been initiated into the tradition of stagecraft by a mentor. Instead he places knowledge about dramatic composition within a tradition of writing *about* composing texts for the stage, a tradition we call poetics.

Yet even within the history of poetics, Corneille's assumption that the expression "les Règles" conveys the totality of the necessary knowledge is peculiar and specific to his time. In keeping with a long tradition, poetics could be seen as a unified but fluid body of discourse bearing knowledge about composition. A poetics without rules is not only entirely thinkable but was entirely current less than a century before Corneille's *examens*. How did it come about that poetics, as presented in Italian and Latin texts, became a series of rules less than a half-century before Corneille's birth in 1606? There are a number of ways to describe this transformation, some easily documented and others much more speculative yet deeply suggestive of a global change in the way the world was viewed in seventeenth-century France.

The sixteenth-century Italian editors and commentators of Aristotle's *Poetics* (published in Latin by Valla in 1498 and first translated into Italian in 1549) were faced with integrating this ancient yet newly available discourse on tragedy with Horace's already well-known *Ars poetica*. The attempt to combine the two very different accounts of poetic composition had many often-noted ramifications for the Renaissance and the seventeenth century, and one of the most important but also most neglected consequences was the division of Aristotle's treatise into the kind of normative unit that had long been extracted from Horace's work. Bernard Weinberg observes that "The *Ars poetica* did not come to the Renaissance as a naked text for which the simplest and most elementary interpretations had to be provided" (1: 72), since the earliest printed editions included two commentaries from late antiquity, one from the second century by Helenius Acron and a third-century commentary by Porphyrion. Acron's commentary initiated a practice that was to have momentous consequences over a thousand years later, for, as Weinberg writes, "One thing that he does (and I presume that he was the first to do it for this particular text) is to distinguish a series of precepts, definitely labeled as such, in the *Ars poetica*" (1: 73). Around 1500, Iodocus Badius goes further toward a total and systematic reduction of Horace's text to a set of separate kernels of knowledge: "whereas the earlier commentators had only occasionally labeled their remarks as 'precepts' [*praecepta*], Badius constantly and invariably supplies a 'regula' at the end of each section of the commentary" (Weinberg 1: 109).

Early in the sixteenth century, then, appeared a model or systematic practice of breaking the Horatian text into parts and then extracting from each part a "rule" that could be expressed independently from the original text. By the time the major commentaries on Aristotle's work were written, this model was established and available to be transferred onto the Greek text. Slightly less than a century before Corneille's *examens,* Bartolomeo Maranta wrote a series of lectures on Aristotle's *Poetics* for the Neapolitan Academy. Maranta announced as his purpose "to reduce to a method the rules and precepts of the poetic art, by means of which the poet may become perfect" ("ad methodum redigere regulas et praecepta artis poeticae . . ." [qtd. in Weinberg 1: 486]). As Weinberg notes, "The attempt to reduce Aristotle's discussion to a set of numbered precepts recalls a similar effort on the part of the commentators on the *Ars poetica,* an effort by this time commonplace. It had not yet, however, gained currency among the students of the *Poetics*" (1: 489). Almost simultaneously with Maranta's lectures, Lodovico Dolce, writing about Ariosto, proclaimed in 1564 that the poet should write in a "regulated" manner ("scriver regolatamente, ornatamente, figuratamente & artificiosamente" [qtd. in Weinberg 1: 174]).

In 1570, writing one of the most influential expositions of the *Poetics, La poetica d'Aristotele vulgarizzata et sposta*—influential in part because it was contradicted vigorously by such seventeenth-century French writers as Hippolyte-Jules de La Mesnardière—Lodovico Castelvetro continued the relentless frag-mentation of Aristotle's text into a "multiplicity of rules" (Weinberg 1: 199–200). It was in the discussions of tragedy particularly, Weinberg concludes, that "the theorists converted much of the *Poetics* into precise rules. In fact, in the history of modern Aristotelianism, the passage from principles to rules took place at this juncture, and if in the later neoclassical period it was possible to speak everywhere of 'Aristotle's rules,' it was because the Italians of the Cinquecento had been the alchemists of this change" (2: 809).

This brief history of the emergence of the "rules" helps bring to the fore an aspect that we usually overlook. Rules are not only the expression of some kind of authority; they are also a particular discursive unit. Many texts are considered authoritative without being structured as a series of rules. Aristotle's *Poetics* could be considered a weighty, even decisive, source of knowledge about how to write tragedy without being articulated as rules. Therefore we should try to understand how the "regulation" of the *Poetics*—the breaking of the ancient text into separate paraphrasable normative units—shaped discussions of tragedy in seventeenth-century France. What are the characteristics of rule-expressed thinking that lead to Corneille's description of his first comedy as not being "within the rules"? He could, after all, simply have said that he was a novice in the dramatic art or that he had discovered other ways to write.

It may help the twentieth-century reader to think of this new tonality in discussion of the dramatic art in terms of the immense changes that are now occurring in the late twentieth century, such as the passage from analog reproduction of sound and image to digital reproduction. The same music is recorded and many of the same criteria are used, at least initially, to judge the success or failure of the recording, but the sound is no longer discussed in the same terms, and gradually the new recording medium—discontinuous, atomized, more easily manipulated yet more distant from physical reality—encourages new artistic concerns and new theoretical descriptions of music. In fact, music itself becomes, in an age of "sampling," a different concept from what it was before.

To describe tragedy in terms of rules required a similar rethinking of the art, a rethinking that may appear, as does digitizing, to move away from concepts like talent, genius, or authenticity toward industrial standards and mass production. In sixteenth-century France there were heated exchanges about the merits of the poet's spontaneous, natural, or supernatural inspiration, on one hand, and the careful mastery of the craft of writing, on the other. In the seventeenth century this discussion continues, but it is transformed by the new currency of a more or less standard "unit" of artistic mastery, the *règle*. A certain checklist of compositional requirements begins to dominate theoretical discussions, and the items on this list begin to exert a power that sometimes seems independent of the concept of art in its wholeness and occasionally forgetful of the result of the assemblage of these rules into a productive dramatic entity.

To return to Corneille's playfully mordant comment—"Il est constant qu'il y a des préceptes, puisqu'il y a un art, mais il n'est pas constant quels ils sont"—we can perceive the semantic root of both art (from Latin *ars*) and articulation (from Latin *artus,* Greek *arthron:* "joint" or "socket"). The issues raised in discussions of the dramatic art, and especially of tragedy, in the seventeenth century concern articulation in the two current senses of that word: to locate joints (that is, points that can be perceived either as sites of separation or of union) and to make something explicit by stating plainly. To articulate the art of composing tragedy by spelling out what is done, or should be done, by the talented playwright means to reject the neo-Platonic appeals to inspiration or furor in favor of the neo-Aristotelian insistence on theoretical discourse. Once writers or a whole community of writers are committed to articulating—both to stating explicitly and to locating the divisions that contain the sockets of the structure—the differences between authors (which specific rules they present) matter much less than that they are participating together in a "regular" discourse. Or, as Corneille puts it, at one time he wrote plays by using common sense, "Ce sens commun, qui était toute ma Règle . . ." (1: 5). Afterward, he rushed into regularity by articulating what had once been contained in the fullness and flow of that common sense.

We have become so accustomed to the concept of "rule" as applied to dramatic theory that it is difficult for us to realize how the introduction of rules modified the way people wrote general statements about dramatic poetry. There are several features of the rule-defined thinking of the seventeenth-century that we should bear in mind. First of all, rules are units that make up a larger entity, such as the seventeenth-century version of an "art poétique." Such a view supposes that a discourse on drama is articulated serially in a number of more or less parallel utterances or clusters of utterances. Second, a discourse on drama containing rules is not of uniform "density" or authority, since some passages state the "rule" itself while surrounding passages explain it, illustrate it with examples, argue for its importance, provide related but nonessential advice about dramatic writing, and so forth. It is tempting to think that this variable density of theoretical discourse derives historically from the major form that neo-Aristotelian poetics took in the Renaissance: commentary on the *Poetics*. The alternation between the ancient philosopher's statement and modern glosses of less authority would lay the foundation for a theoretical discourse of varying weight even when the theorist had broken away from an overt commentary form. Yet comparison between the poetic treatises of the seventeenth century and various texts of Aristotle's *Poetics* shows that Aristotle's text itself is treated as variable in terms of the binding quality of its advice. The fact that between three and five "rules" can be precipitated out of the continuum of the Aristotelian text indicates that much of the *Poetics*—e.g., the advice that the playwright represent "visible deaths, torments, woundings" (Halliwell ed. 43), and so forth—is treated as secondary.

This variation in the density of theoretical texts is a direct consequence of rule-oriented thinking, for the importance of a text like the *Poetics* is no longer sought in the significance of the text as a *whole* but rather is located in the exegesis and appreciation of certain extremely important *parts*. (It is, of course, more than likely that the commentary tradition and Christian exegesis of Scripture prepare the way for articulated reading of texts like the *Poetics*.) The attention given to these parts of the *Poetics* results from a third important feature of rule-oriented thinking: its transcendence of textual origins. The rule is more important than any individual statement of the rule. Once theorists understood the *Poetics* as a text that could be taken apart, they had only a small further step to take to *extract* rules or precepts from the canonical text, which could then recede into the background. When Maranta began to give lists of the rules he found in Aristotle, the ancient philosopher's authority became a kind of "commodity" that could be packaged in different ways through restatement.

In this way an "Aristotelian poetics" separates itself from Aristotle and can ultimately begin to find fault with his thought as insufficiently systematic or rational. D'Aubignac writes that the term "les Regles des Anciens" should not be understood to mean that the authority of the rules comes from their ancient source, since "les Regles du Theatre ne sont pas fondées en autorité, mais en raison" (26). In fact, it is because poetic theorists have a sense of what the rules are that they can locate in Aristotle the most important passages and separate these from the merely useful or the frankly outmoded. At first this may look like a simple illustration of the "hermeneutic circle" or "fore-structure of understanding." We bring to all texts some understanding that allows us to enter the text, even if that initial understanding or projection yields later to some more complicated interaction of preunderstanding and the difference brought by the text. For seventeenth-century poeticians, Aristotle's statement of a rule merely serves to reinforce the already-determined validity of the rule. The goal of poetic theory when it makes use of the earlier *Poetics* is not to restore Aristotle's meaning at the expense of modern theory but to reinforce a particular form of modern theory.

Multiplication, Conflict, and Inflation

Rule-expressed thought operates through a series of divisions that keep multiplying. Not only does the use of rules divide the modern theorist from his ancient predecessors, and the ancient text into parcels, but description of plays according to rules partitions those works so that the plays, like the theoretical text, become a sequence of parts. D'Aubignac and La Mesnardière, among the seventeenth-century theorists, are carrying further a tendency that was already visible among the Italian neo-Aristotelians of a century before. R. S. Crane makes the compelling argument that Francesco Robertello, in his 1548 commentary, shifted the emphasis from tragedy conceived as a whole to tragedy conceived as a collection of "devices which will produce a desired effect upon a specific audience" (qtd. in Weinberg 1: 67). As a consequence, notes Crane,

> since the sense of the total poetic structure is lost, there is
> no longer any possibility of deriving from such a structure
> the criteria for the appropriateness, for the goodness or bad-
> ness, of individual parts. Instead, criteria for each separate
> part will be separately derived by a reference to the char-
> acter of the audience as it specifically affects that part and
> in the light of the utility or the pleasure which that part should
> produce. (Qtd. in Weinberg 1: 68)

Crane is here describing the fragmentation of the tragedy as a work of art, but such a way of reading and describing results from a poetics that is itself already becoming analytic rather than synthetic. In other words, a theory conceived as a collection of *parts* encourages a view of tragedy as a corresponding collection of parts.

Fragmentation of the poetics into rules is closely related to growing disputes over who is in charge of the rules and what their purpose is. As poetics becomes more complex and compartmentalized, it becomes more a field suitable for specialists in textual scholarship. Viewed as a body of rules that have a debatable relationship to one another, the poetics is less obviously an immediately usable instrument for the practicing playwright. An increasingly analytic approach to Aristotle's poetics favors erudite commentators as the possessors of poetic theory.

The dominance of theorists over the rules inflects the purpose of the rules. Are they normative or are they instrumental in a practical way? Is the purpose of the playwright primarily to observe the rules, or are the rules instruments to achieve some other goal, such as the approval of the audience? These two different ways of looking at rules have consequences that can be expressed in quantitative as well as qualitative terms. If the playwright measures success by exact observation of the rules, then the more rules there are, the more difficult it will be to observe them all within a single dramatic work. In this situation, the existence of a large number of rules increases the likelihood of failure. If, on the other hand, the playwright looks on rules as instruments to be used in achieving another aim, then the proliferation of rules may very well facilitate his task by giving ever more precise guidance to solve all the problems he might encounter.

The *Dictionnaire de l'Académie* lends weight to the first of these possible views of rule, the normative or judgmental one. The *Dictionnaire* defines *regularité* as "observation exacte des règles. Il se dit dans la Morale. . . . Il se dit aussi en parlant de quelques arts. *Ce bastiment paroist beau, mais il n'est pas dans toute la regularité possible. cette [sic] Tragédie n'est pas dans toute la regularité où elle devroit estre.*" The relationship between the definition and its illustrations brings to the fore the negative potential of rules. The only two citations illustrating artistic regularity concern the failure of architect and playwright to observe all the rules. Neither of the agents is mentioned, only their work, yet clearly it is the architect and the playwright who have failed to create the appropriate (that is, total) conformity of object to normative rule, and since only total observation of applicable rules can be considered regularity, regularity is almost always measured in negative terms, as falling beneath the goal of *toute la regularité.*

The distinction between being and appearance, between *être* and *paraître*, is a fundamental one for early modern thought. Such a distinction is crucial for Cartesian epistemology with its rejection of sensory perception as the basis for certain knowledge, and it is often a central issue in lyric and dramatic poetry throughout the seventeenth century. Twentieth-century critics have often argued that this conflict is a primary feature of the "baroque" aesthetic.[2] In the Académie's significant choice of citations to illustrate *regularité,* there is a divergence between a building's appearance and its being. It appears beautiful but it *is not* in full regularity, so that the pleasing appearance is in some ways deceptive or misleading. True success lies in observation of the rules rather than in the creation of a certain effect of beauty.[3]

Widespread perceptions of seventeenth-century French culture associate that culture with rules and with reason. In fact, it is tempting to think that regularity and rationality have a good deal in common. Yet it is sometimes difficult to reconstruct the basis in reason for specific rules. It is possible to make irrational rules. And it may be that, past a certain point, a complex system with many rules begins to generate irrational results.

There is nothing inherently irrational about making rules. Indeed, modern rationality has become closely identified with making and observing rules, as manifested in works like Descartes's "Rules for the Direction of the Mind" ("Regulae ad directionem ingenii"), and this articulating tendency of the early-modern and modern periods is simply, to some extent, the working-through of Aristotle's own vigorous division of topics into branching taxonomies.[4] However, all such division of an idea (e.g., the writing of a good tragedy) presents the risk of conflict among the rules in such a way as to lead to an apparently irrational result either from overlap of the rules (if there is no clear understanding of a set of priorities among the rules) or from the omission of some crucial factor. Both dangers lead potentially to the creation of more and more rules. Descartes, for instance, prepared for the possibility of omission in his rules for method (or "préceptes," as he called them) by creating a fourth and final precept "de faire partout des dénombrements si entiers, et des revues si générales, que je fusse assuré de ne rien omettre" (138). In the case of poetic regularity, as Corneille poignantly yet mockingly claims, there are certainly rules (or precepts) but it is not certain what they are.

This state of uncertainty was not only theoretically possible, but historically real. New rules appeared in the course of the seventeenth century. The *liaison des scènes,* which Corneille had described in the *examen* of his comedy *La Suivante,* changed status over the years. Corneille describes this practice of linking scenes by having characters already present on the stage see, hear, or speak to characters arriving from offstage as a "grand ornement dans un poème, et qui sert beaucoup à former une continuité d'action, par la continuité de la représentation; mais enfin ce n'est qu'un ornement, et non pas une règle" (*Discours,* in Corneille 3: 176–77). Yet only a few sentences later, he concedes that audiences are now so accustomed to this *liaison* that "ce qui n'était point une règle autrefois, l'est devenu [*sic*] maintenant, par l'assiduité de la pratique" (3: 177). This rule is not only modern (he points out that the tragedians of antiquity did not always practice this linking, though it would have been easier for them, since their plays had fewer scenes than did later tragedies) but actually becomes a rule, in his view, sometime between 1633 and 1660.

There is, of course, a certain ambiguity in the description of rules as new. If rules are analogous to scientific "laws," then they had always, in some sense, "existed" in successful dramatic practice before they were spelled out and named by theorists. A "new" poetic rule is thus only a newly formulated or "discovered" rule. When a "law" of nature is discovered, it merely describes what has been happening and what will continue to happen—though it does permit people to modify situations such that the circumstances for certain events do not occur. In other words, formulation of the law can modify the behavior of one part of the system, that is, humanity. The result of the "discovery" of a poetic rule, on the other hand, has the potential of modifying the entire system, since this system consists entirely of human agents. As rules appeared they modified theorists' perceptions of existing tragic texts, making what had seemed a good or successful tragedy into a bad or unsuccessful one in theoretical terms.

The uncertainty about rules that is entertained and exacerbated in the course of the century by the multiplication of rules helps foster a potential that exists in rule-expressed thinking much more than in a unified or under-articulated view of art. Rules may collide with each other and create practical and even theoretical contradictions. In a unified view the major goal of an art is expressed forcefully, while the "technical" details necessary for attaining that goal are left to the talent of the practitioner, or to imitation of models, or to some form of instinct or "genius." Once the discourse of poetics is separated into articulated units, it runs the risk of losing strong priorities. Concepts once linked in a causal sequence can be understood as distinct requirements. When Maranta began to present Aristotle's *Poetics* as lists of *numbered* precepts, a model was established for conceiving these precepts or rules as equal in importance. The very act of listing and numbering encourages a kind of heaped up (paratactic) and leveling interpretation of Aristotle's discourse.

The continued "discovery" of rules in the seventeenth century pushes further in this direction for two reasons. The first is that uncertainty about the final structure of regularity prevents consensus about the exact priority of one desideratum over another. New rules can interfere with previously naïve practice or even with another rule—Corneille took delight in elaborating rules in the course of his long career. The other is the sheer weight that a rule acquires by virtue of the controversy surrounding it. The *liaison des scènes,* though by all accounts less important than the *unité de lieu,* can attract enormous attention by the complexity of describing what it entails. While there is general agreement that the overwhelming principle of dramatic representation is verisimilitude, each "rule" that is generated with the long-range goal of assuring verisimilitude can be violated as an independent rule. It would be possible (this is more or less what Aristotle did) to posit that actions should be verisimilar and thus lay out a clear priority but with much left unspecified and discretionary. However, seventeenth-century regularity tends to construct a series of specific rules that are said to be subordinated to verisimilitude but that have no distinct hierarchy among themselves. When these rules become objects of fascinated polemic in their own right, the goal of verisimilar representation begins to fade in proportion to the intensity that the rules take on. In his *examen* of the early tragicomedy *Clitandre,* Corneille claims that, having discovered that there were "rules," he wrote *Clitandre* with the intention of constructing a play conforming to the rules yet utterly worthless ("une [pièce] régulière [c'est-à-dire dans ces vingt et quatre heures], pleine d'incidents, et d'un style plus élevé, mais qui ne vaudrait rien du tout; en quoi je réussis parfaitement" [1: 102]). No doubt Corneille's glance back at this early play should be taken with a grain of salt as to his intention, but the author's claim of insubordination to the concept of regularity points to an insubordination within "regularity" itself. That is, the very fact that one can theorize, as Corneille does here, a play that follows the rules perfectly and yet is worthless, demonstrates a failure of the rules to be properly subordinated (ordered in priority) with respect to a desired goal.

The poetic theorists attempt from time to time to set up some kind of priority among the rules, but do so unsystematically. Assigning priority to a rule seems to be a rhetorical device with limited duration, a way of adding emphasis, discursive italics. These temporary priorities are revealing (we will look at them in detail in the following chapters), but they are often surprising to a modern reader. D'Aubignac says, "La principale regle du Poëme dramatique, est que les vertus y soient toûjours recompensées, ou pour le moins toûjours loüées, mal-gré les outrages de la Fortune, et que les vices y soient toûjours punis,

ou pour le moins toûjours en horreur, quand mesme ils y triom-
phent" (8–9). La Mesnardière claims that "La plus importante
Régle qui concerne le Théatre" is what he calls "*la Simplicité
du Lieu,* ou autrement *sa Nudité*" (419).[5] La Mesnardière sometimes refers to decorum as a rule ("la Régle des *Bien-séances,*
tres-nécessaires sur la Scéne" [293–94]), rather than as a principle, an aim, or a quality. This reduction of the *bienséances*
to a rule makes the relations of priority among the rules still
harder to specify, since *bienséance* or decorum is just one of a
large and growing set of rules.

The Rule as Art Form

Despite Corneille's emphasis on the mysterious and uncertain
rules in the opening of his major theoretical text, we may be
wrong to think of the seventeenth-century theater as bound by
rules in any greater degree than subsequent drama. In some ways
seventeenth-century drama had vastly fewer rules than the dominant late-twentieth-century dramatic form, the television serial.
Manuals for writing screenplays for television or cinema make
the treatises of Corneille's day seem enormously liberal and
approximate. Now the timing of individual camera shots, the
number of seconds recommended for certain kinds of dialogue,
the proper mixture of themes according to target audience and
time of day, and the prescribed sentence structure for dialogue
has advanced to what can be considered quasi-scientific status.

When Corneille begins his major work of poetics by acknowl-
edging the existence of precepts and at the same time by stating that the specific content of these precepts is uncertain, he
reveals an attitude toward regularity that is at the least ambivalent and probably ironic. In a certain sense Corneille resigned
himself to the system of rules after the Quarrel of *Le Cid.* His
tragedies conform in broad terms to the constraints of time,
place, and action, and his prefaces reveal elaborate efforts to
deal with the conflict of verisimilitude and history. Yet most
of all, Corneille reacted to early criticism that he was ignorant
of the rules by seizing the terrain of poetic theory as his own
and producing a poetics articulated in terms of rules but under-
cutting and devaluing regularity in subtle but energetic ways.
If, at the outset of his career, it seemed that the playwright's

creativity was opposed to rules "discovered" or elaborated by
poeticians who were not themselves active playwrights, by the
time of the three *Discours sur le poème dramatique* (1660)
Corneille had seen that rules are not eternal but created. Rather
than endure them, he moved to generate and refine them, suggesting their transitory and sometimes arbitrary nature but using them as a supplementary challenge to his craftsmanship.
The term *règle* often appears in Corneille's writing with a curiously indefinite ontological status, as if marked by quotation
marks and suspended for examination as a hypothesis. In his
important *examen* of *Horace,* he writes, "si c'est une Règle de
ne le point ensanglanter [the stage], elle n'est pas du temps
d'Aristote, qui nous apprend que pour émouvoir puissamment,
il faut de grands déplaisirs, des blessures, et des morts en
spectacle" (1: 839). He observes this "rule" while questioning
whether such a rule exists and affirming that no such rule is to
be found in the writing of Aristotle. In this way Corneille's
theory of poetics can at times become an ironic demonstration
of his mastery of a theory that devalues the very structure of
that theory, the articulation of dramatic composition into rules.

Corneille, then, makes himself at home within seventeenth-
century regularity by occupying it ironically rather than by ignor-
ing it. In his theoretical texts, rules are deprived of authority
and yet presented in exquisite detail, so that, oddly enough,
regularity becomes most fully achieved as an aesthetic concept in Corneille's work. He is the author who sees theory, in
its modern form, as an aesthetic object in its own right and not
solely as an instrument for the composition of tragedy. Corneille prefaced *Horace* with an elaborate dedication to Cardinal Richelieu, in which there is an often-quoted passage about
Richelieu as spectator, a passage that offers an unusual combination of several key concepts—rule, authority, and spectatorship.[6]
It is worth looking at the core of this letter, in which Corneille
uses Richelieu for a major realignment of the aims and the means
of dramatic writing

> nous vous avons deux obligations très signalées; l'une
> d'avoir ennobli le but de l'Art, l'autre de nous en avoir facilité
> les connaissances. Vous avez ennobli le but de l'Art, puis-
> qu'au lieu de celui de plaire au peuple, que nous prescrivent

nos Maîtres, et dont les deux plus honnêtes gens de leur siècle, Scipion et Lélie ont autrefois protesté de se contenter, vous nous avez donné celui de vous plaire et de vous divertir; et qu'ainsi nous ne rendons pas un petit service à l'Etat, puisque contribuant à vos divertissements, nous contribuons à l'entretien d'une santé qui lui est si précieuse et si nécessaire. Vous nous en avez facilité les connaissances [de l'Art] puisque nous n'avons plus besoin d'autre étude pour les acquérir, que d'attacher nos yeux sur Votre Eminence quand elle honore de sa présence et de son attention le récit de nos Poèmes. C'est là que lisant sur son visage ce qui lui plaît, et ce qui ne lui plaît pas, nous nous instruisons avec certitude de ce qui est bon, et de ce qui est mauvais, et tirons des *règles* infaillibles de ce qu'il faut suivre et de ce qu'il faut éviter. C'est là que j'ai souvent appris en deux heures ce que mes livres n'eussent pu m'apprendre en dix ans. . . .
(1: 834; emphasis added)

This passage is generally read as flattery of Richelieu, and even as ironic flattery. It seems difficult to resist a sense of irony, given the enormous contrast between the tone of this passage and Corneille's writings from the Quarrel of *Le Cid* only four years earlier. Yet we should consider that Corneille does many things in these few dense lines. He describes a shift in the aim of dramatic writing that constitutes a new, modern aesthetic distinct from that of antiquity. He moves the source of dramatic rules from scholarly discussion to empirical observation. And he helps define what he means by "rule."

Richelieu is not portrayed here in his historical roles as sponsor of plays and amateur playwright, nor as patron of the Académie française that had so recently, at the Cardinal's urging, censured Corneille's hugely popular tragi-comedy. Instead, the Cardinal-Duke is described as a spectator, the ideal spectator whose reaction is the quintessence of audience response. Corneille persists in placing an audience-centered aesthetic ahead of a scholarly, abstract one. This is really important in view of subsequent habits of describing seventeenth-century theater as bound by codified rules, for Corneille declares outright that only Richelieu's reaction as spectator matters, not books (this presumably includes books published with royal encouragement). In recognizing the "infallible rules" that can be derived from what the playwright reads in the Cardinal's face, Corneille publicly jettisons the intermediaries (Chapelain and the Académie, who had done Richelieu's bidding in the Quarrel of *Le Cid*) whose regulatory efforts are only a mask and a distraction from the real authority of this powerful audience.

In this highly visible statement about the rules of tragedy, Corneille offers the conclusions he has drawn from the Académie's relatively moderate censure of *Le Cid*. Yes, he says, there are rules that a writer of tragedies must use. The reason for using rules is to please the audience—such is their purpose. Rules are extracted (*tirer*) by the observant playwright from the audience's reaction and not from other sources. Corneille thus rejects the Académie as source of knowledge about how to write and remains unrepentant in his empiricism. He has, however, accepted two principles: that audiences are not all of equal importance to the playwright and that the playwright now numbers among his tasks the public statement of dramatic theory expressed in the language of the day, that is, the language of "rules."

One of Corneille's strategies is to multiply rules in such a way that he is always in control of them because he creates many of them. Another strategy, often combined with the first, is to become a strict judge of the "regularity" of his plays after the fact. This is a particularly effective and subversive approach when the play is extremely successful, since Corneille can then show that the play is both in violation of the rules and yet triumphs in achieving the theatrical pleasure that Aristotle set as the purpose of drama. Rather than apologizing for his play against the severity of the rules, Corneille apologizes for the rules against the triumph of his play, thus operating as a saboteur from within the theoretical community. *Clitandre* is an example of this approach among his comedies, and *Horace* among his tragedies.

We have already noted the importance of Corneille's letter to Richelieu at the time of the first edition of *Horace*. In it Corneille takes a stand against the multiplicity of rules. Even more interesting is Corneille's theoretical position twenty years later in his *Examen d'Horace*. Yet to appreciate the author's criticism of his own tragedy, it is important to remember how subsequent literary history has made *Horace* the paradigm of French "classical" tragedy: "*Horace* marks an epiphanous mo-

ment in the history of the theater. In this, Corneille's first 'tragédie régulière.' Classicism, full blown and triumphant, emerges
as the paragon of a new esthetic" (Greenberg, "*Horace,* Classicism and Female Trouble" 66). Another critic writes, "De
toutes les tragédies de Corneille, *Horace* est la plus 'régulière':
la première, et, du propre aveu de son auteur, l'une des trois
seules . . . où il ait 'vraiment observé l'unité de jour et de lieu.'"[7]
If *Horace* marks the triumph of "classicism" as regular theater,
then regularity must be understood as having only an approximate relationship, at most, with the "rules"—Corneille himself was the first to give a detailed published demonstration of
how *Horace* violated the rules in his *Examen* of 1660. Yet much
before the *Examen,* there was an unwritten consensus that
Horace did not conform to the rules. This opinion, expressed
in conversations and letters, explains, according to Georges
Couton, the delay in the first performance of the play: "Est-ce
que Corneille a hésité avant de permettre la représentation? Et
n'aurait-il pas hésité parce que les doctes élevaient de très sé-
rieuses objections qui lui faisaient craindre une nouvelle Querelle du *Cid?*" (note in Corneille 1: 1536). D'Aubignac, in his
Pratique du théâtre, gave a retrospective account of the objections of the theorists and outlined his own proposal for avoiding a violation of the rules: instead of having Horace kill his
sister, she would die by throwing herself on her brother's sword
while he remained passive (68).

Corneille's own theoretical position is different from that
of the contemporary theorists and of the nineteenth- and twentieth-century scholars. In the *Examen* the author gives himself
the advantage over his critics by being one-up on them theoretically. Yes, he concedes, his play violates the rules, but not
in the way they say it does. Having written a successful play
(and by 1660 being the "great" Corneille), *Horace*'s creator is
superior to his "learned" critics as a playwright. His supreme
triumph is the luxury of discovering "hidden" violations of the
rules that the theorists were incapable of seeing because they
had not pondered the implications of Aristotle's *Poetics:*

> C'est une croyance assez générale que cette Pièce pourrait
> passer pour la plus belle des miennes, si les derniers Actes
> répondaient aux premiers. Tous veulent que la mort de

> Camille en gâte la fin, et j'en demeure d'accord: mais je ne
> sais si tous en savent la raison. On l'attribue communément
> à ce qu'on voit cette mort sur la Scène. . . . (1: 839)

A brilliant opening. Corneille sets up his "demolition" of the
theorists with a puzzle. There is a problem with *Horace,* but it
is not what you think, he implies. After refuting the accusa-
tion that Horace's murder of Camille violates a rule—Corneille
casts doubt on the "rule" against deaths onstage and points out
that Aristotle is silent on the issue—the author finds three defects in the play: the suddenness of the murder, the presence
of two "actions" (or plots) rather than one (violation of the
single-action rule), and finally Camille's shift from being a
secondary character to being a central one midway through the
play. Having noted these three defects, Corneille plays the
rulemaker. First, he redefines the single-action rule (or unity
of action) as the rule of the "unity of peril": the hero of a tragedy
should be put at risk (of death) only once in the course of the
drama unless the second risk is an unavoidable consequence
of the first. Second, Corneille promotes a new "inviolable
Rule" that could be called the Rule of Dignity or of Character Importance:

> Camille qui ne tient que le second rang dans les trois pre-
> miers Actes, et y laisse le premier à Sabine, prend le premier
> en ces deux derniers, où cette Sabine n'est plus considérable,
> et qu'ainsi s'il y a égalité dans les Mœurs, il n'y en a point
> dans la Dignité des Personnages . . . et je n'ai point encore
> vu sur nos Théâtres cette inégalité de rang en un même
> Acteur, qui n'ait produit un très méchant effet. Il serait bon
> d'en établir une Règle inviolable. (1: 840–41)

In order to play the game of rulemaker, Corneille sets up
the idea of modern theoretical invention in the first paragraph.
Saying that Aristotle did not prohibit deaths onstage and that
even Horace in his *Ars poetica* did not make a *Règle générale*
about this, Corneille attributes this "rule" to the theoretical
community that has attacked *Horace.* Once he has shaken off
that rule by implying that it did not affect the audience response,
Corneille goes on to much subtler observations that lead to a
new rule with greater empirical validity. He claims that arbi-

trary variations in character importance always produce "a very bad response," whereas Camille's death apparently did not produce such a negative response. So Corneille demonstrates that he is a master at creating modern rules, much better ones than the community of theorists. Yet, at the same time, he casts doubt on the usefulness of all rules beyond the single basic rule of pleasing the audience. After all, the defects he finds in *Horace* are flaws in a well-received play, and he became the preeminent tragic author precisely by writing tragedies like *Horace* that violated the rules he subsequently established.

Corneille locates his authority to debunk and create rules in his ability to test rules through observation of the audience. However, other theorists do not see audience response as a source of authoritative knowledge about rules. La Mesnardière, to the contrary, frequently implies that there is an ancient, even perpetual conflict between the rules and the audience. This leaves the question of the authoritative foundation of rules in limbo. In his *La poëtique,* written after the Quarrel of *Le Cid* and before *Horace,* La Mesnardière never speaks directly about the source of his ability to present rules for tragic playwrights nor does he even defend the authority of the tradition on which he draws. Did Aristotle draw his rules inductively from the practice of the Greek playwrights? La Mesnardière seems to suggest this when he writes that "Ce merveilleux Philosophe ayant observé tous les Poëmes que la Grece avoit admirez, comprit en trois excellens Livres les Preceptes de ce bel Art, de qui les principalles Regles avoient été pratiquées par les Ecrivains illustres" (EE). Why did they follow these rules and with what results? La Mesnardière does not say, but he hints at a mysterious tradition of unknown origin. The tragedians of antiquity followed the rules "encore qu'ils ne les connussent que par certaine tradition parvenuë jusques à eux sans autheur et sans fondement."

Even though La Mesnardière does not explain the authority of the rules, he does see them as conflicting with the wishes of a certain kind of audience, the *peuple.* Tragedy is not meant to amuse the "brutal multitude," who preferred tragedies with happy endings. In declaring that Euripides's tragedies "qui finissent par les malheurs sont infiniment plus parfaites," Aristotle formed the rules against the people's taste:

> Ce jugement solennel prononcé pour Euripide, et contre la
> multitude, fait bien voir que le Philosophe l'a toûjours fort
> méprisée, qu'il ne s'est point arresté à considerer son goust,
> et qu'il n'a jamais estimé qu'elle fust l'objet de ce Poëme,
> puis qu'il en forme les Regles contre les sentimens du peuple.
> (La Mesnardière T)

La Mesnardière sees the rules as an action directed against the
base wishes of the people and as a protective gesture aimed at
preserving the pathos required by the proper sort of audience.[8]
The rules derive their force from the difference between what
they prescribe and what the wrong sort of audience wants—in
both cases the point of contention is a kind of *feeling*. In returning to Aristotle for the knowledge of tragedy, La Mesnardière writes:

> puis que nous voulons sçavoir les principaux axiomes d'une
> Science agreable qui plaist lors qu'elle tourmente, et qui
> n'excite les Passions que pour en calmer les orages, puisons-
> les dans leur propre source, et non pas dans les ruisseaux. (5)

The proper audience of tragedy is an audience that is moved
by a drama composed according to the rules. The authority of
the rules can only be determined by reference to the quality of
the audience—and the argument regresses into an endless circle.
What is certain, claims La Mesnardière, is that common sense
is an inadequate basis for the composition of tragedy:

> je ne me suis point arresté aux opinions extravagantes de
> ces personnes déreglées, qui tiennent que la Poësie n'a pas
> besoin d'Enseignemens, et qu'avec le sens commun on peut
> connoître et produire tous les ouvrages de l'esprit. . . . Ainsi
> nous devons permettre à ceux qui ignorent les Arts, de n'estre
> aucunement touchez des graces que nous y voyons. (TTT)

Regularity is a practice that shapes both audience and author, and for La Mesnardière the commitment to rule as a necessity for making and appreciating tragedy is more important
than any individual rule. Against this shared wish to participate in rule-expressed thought stands the mere common sense
of the "unruly," the *personnes déreglées*. La Mesnardière's commitment to regularity unites the author and the public within

an equal burden of rule, since the rules serve both to produce and to appreciate (*connoître*) works of art. These are, significantly, called literally "works of wit"—a term that sheds the connotations of the more technical and laborious term, *art,* in order to suggest both what is noble and what is not limited to production. Playwrights and public participate in the witty activity of drama, separating themselves from others who have only common sense and are thus deprived of rule. In the absence of an argument for a philosophical authority as foundation for the rules of tragedy, La Mesnardière locates the force of the rules within the elite community of the witty, who use rules to separate themselves from other, inferior persons.

However, d'Aubignac seems to feel that rules need to be grounded in some authority other than the consent of a community of wit. He sees reason as the foundation of regularity and he emphasizes that the attribution of the dramatic rules to antiquity is merely historical accident. In fact, for d'Aubignac reason seems to be particularly characteristic of the modern period. As we saw earlier, he emphasizes that the rules are independent of the authority of antiquity:

> je dis que les Regles du Theatre ne sont pas fondées en au-
> torité, mais en raison. Elles ne sont pas établies sur l'exemple,
> mais sur le Jugement naturel. Et quand nous les nommons
> l'Art ou les Regles des Anciens, c'est parce qu'ils les ont
> pratiquées avec beaucoup de gloire. . . . C'est pourquoy dans
> tout ce Discours j'allegue fort rarement les Poëmes des An-
> ciens; et si je les rapporte, ce n'est seulement que pour faire
> voir l'addresse dont ils se servoient dans la Pratique de ces
> regles. . . . (26)

Throughout this passage, d'Aubignac divides his approach to poetics into two registers. On one level are reason, judgment, the discourse of the poetic theorist, and the rules themselves. On another, distinct and inferior, level are authority, example, and "address" or skill. The first level is modern, and the second ancient. The latter provides raw material for illustration of the concepts elaborated by the former. Therefore, says d'Aubignac, his few references to ancient tragedy are entirely incidental and supplementary to his reasoned articulation of the rules of dramatic practice. As poetician, d'Aubignac not surprisingly rejects imitation itself as a way of writing plays. After all, he maintains his own position by promoting poetics, philosophical reflection on practice, as a surer and more efficient way of learning the craft of the playwright. However, it is worth noticing how the division of theory into rules also projects across the Greek and Latin tragic corpus those shadow traces of rules and examples. The ancient tragedies become interesting as assemblages that are derivative of rules rather than as complete and freestanding dramatic works.

One of the paradoxes of "regularity" in seventeenth-century French poetics of tragedy is that these rules aim at perfecting a structure for the representation of an *irregularity*. Tragic subjects all contain a transgressive action, one that violates a certain set of rules. These are not the rules of poetics but moral or political rules to which poetics must refer both for the choice of dramatic subjects and for construction of character. Do poetic rules *require* that represented actions and characters violate the other rules of society? This is a much-discussed theoretical point in the works of Corneille, La Mesnardière, d'Aubignac, and their contemporaries and one that is never entirely resolved by the community of theorists. It is easy to suppose that the transgressions of tragic heroes are meant only to confirm the existence of a deep structure of order that will be confirmed by the heroes' downfall. However, this global generalization, which would probably be accepted by most theorists of tragedy in the twentieth as well as the seventeenth century, does not give an adequate idea of the tension that exists between the regularity of poetics and the (at least temporary) irregularity of the represented world. We will return to this problem in chapter 3.

The Return of Taste

If there is one single author whose name is associated, at least in the traditional school curriculum, with the "rules" of tragedy in the seventeenth century, that author is Nicolas Boileau. Rarely do readers see anything problematic about giving a satirical poet the position of authoritative voice of poetic precepts, though one could argue that satiric writing prevents the kind of simplification that is present in most statements of literary or grammatical "rules."[9] It is true that Boileau, in addition to writing satires, translated Longinus's treatise *On the Sublime* and wrote a series of reflections on this text.[10] Boileau's *Art poétique* (1674), a partly satirical text itself, actually represents the *decline* in interest in rules among major writers.[11] Far from representing the most authoritative expression of rule-governed poetics, Boileau demonstrates both the assimilation of such a poetics and the impulse to move beyond rules and beyond their refinement and defense in theoretical treatises. Continuing the movement that Corneille exemplifies as early as his dedication of *Horace,* Boileau locates the authority for poetic knowledge in a reflective and communicative audience. While Corneille is a playwright who observes his audience and sometimes identifies himself with it, Boileau speaks most often directly as reader and spectator, and very infrequently as author.[12] In regard to tragedy, Boileau speaks as a kind of transcendental subjective spectator capable of describing his reactions to the stimulus proposed by the poet:

> Le secret est d'abord de plaire et de toucher:
> Inventez des ressorts qui puissent *m'*attacher.
> (169; emphasis added)

Because this ideal spectator expresses himself in imperatives and optative subjunctives (such as "Que le Lieu de la scène y soit fixe et marqué"), *L'art poétique* seems to be a discourse of rules, for the spectator's desires are urgent, authoritative, peremptory, and without appeal. Yet regularity has, in certain ways, been dealt a decisive blow. In the place of the endlessly proliferating and often competing units of theoretical discourse that are the rules, Boileau has introduced a unifying source that resolves all conflicts. The spectator's desire is supreme and takes precedence even over the discourse of poetics itself, for the ultimate imperative, which reduces all else to advice rather than law, is "N'offrez rien au Lecteur que ce qui peut luy plaire" (159).[13]

Both *L'art poétique* and the regularity of d'Aubignac and La Mesnardière seem open-ended, but this open-endedness is quite different in Boileau's "post-regular" text. Rules require other rules to supplement their ever-inadequate specificity, as

Montaigne had already observed over a half-century before.[14]
A "rule" about monologues provokes other potential rules to
adapt the requirement or prohibition of monologues to special
circumstances. Thus the rule puts the burden on the rulemaking
theoretician to respond to the challenges of the practitioner, for
the purpose of rules is precisely to disburden the playwright
of the decisions that are made in advance by the theorist. Boileau, on the other hand, expresses strong desires and enunciates the experience of the spectator. The spectator—even the
ideal, transcendent spectator who speaks in *L'art poétique*—
leaves the solution of emergent problems to the playwright:

> D'un nouveau Personnage inventez-vous l'idée?
> Qu'en tout avec soi-mesme il se montre d'accord
> Et qu'il soit jusqu'au bout tel qu'on la vû d'abord.
>
> (172)

Boileau thus moves from a poetics of rule to a poetics of taste,
locating authority in the public and responsibility in the playwright. Taste need not be justified—at least in Boileau's conception—and can express itself adequately in the imperative,
or even in less polite forms:

> Le Theatre fertile en Censeurs pointilleux,
> Chez nous pour se produire est un champ perilleux.
> Un Auteur n'y fait pas de faciles conquestes.
> Il trouve à le siffler des bouches toûjours prestes.
> Chacun le peut traiter de Fat et d'Ignorant.
> C'est un droit qu'à la porte on achete en entrant.
>
> (172)

Boileau's expressions of taste can easily be confused with
rules. After all, they seem to oblige the writer of tragedies
with a rulelike weight, and they erupt from the body of *L'art
poétique* as a series of articulated desiderata that are reminis-
cent of a stratified reading of Aristotle's *Poetics*. The most
famous couplet of Boileau's text is sometimes cited as the quintessence of the rules for French classical tragedy:

> Qu'en un Lieu, qu'en un jour, un seul Fait accompli
> Tienne jusqu'à la fin le Theatre rempli.
>
> (170)

This is the utterance through which the "three unities" invented by neo-Aristotelian poetics reach most readers. Not only do we often read this passage as a rule, but Boileau actually uses the term *règle* two verses earlier in a way that pulls together French nationalism, rationalism, and regulation:

> Un Rimeur, sans peril, delà les Pirenées
> Sur la scene en un jour renferme des années.
> Là souvent le Heros d'un spectacle grossier,
> Enfant au premier acte, est barbon au dernier.
> Mais nous, que la Raison à ses regles engage,
> Nous voulons qu'avec art l'Action se ménage.

(170)

What Boileau has done, in effect and no doubt intentionally, is to reduce the complexity of the rules of place, day, and action to a simple, colloquial formula that collapses the lengthy and problematical arguments of d'Aubignac and Chapelain to exactly twenty-four syllables, thereby eliminating the problems that poetic theorists only succeeded in multiplying once they started inspecting the assumptions and entailments of scenic representation. When Boileau's formula is juxtaposed with the arguments of the treatises, the antitheoretical character of his poem becomes obvious and even brutal. The "three unities" should be observed because they correspond to French taste, not because they are a universal ontological requirement of dramatic performance. Even reason itself is not given here as a universally compelling faculty, for it distinguishes the French from their neighbors and rivals in Spain. Therefore while the French are "reasonable" and the Spanish "unreasonable," reason itself, paradoxically, does not require a process of reasoning. The French spectator does not have to struggle through a series of proofs to arrive at the conclusion that changes of place are impossible in tragedy. Instead the French spectator possesses this conclusion of reason as spontaneously as taste. Hence the reasons underlying the unities need not be articulated, nor indeed do the "unities" need to be stated separately from one another. Boileau reverses the whole poetic enterprise of his seventeenth-century French predecessors through an energetic process of condensation, concentrating on results in place of means. In his celebrated formulation, the unities themselves are presented as fused with the goal of holding the spectator's attention throughout the performance.

A further example of Boileau's impulse to reverse the regulating movement of French poetics is his brief but significant reference in chant I to Pierre de Ronsard's poetics of the previous century. Contrasting Clément Marot's poetics with Ronsard's, Boileau makes another of his rare uses of the term *règle:*

> Marot bien-tost aprés fit fleurir les Ballades,
> Tourna des Triolets, rima des Mascarades,
> A des refrains reglez asservit les Rondeaux,
> Et montra pour rimer des chemins tout nouveaux.
> Ronsard qui le suivit, par une autre methode
> Reglant tout, broüilla tout, fit un art à sa mode:
> Et toutefois long-temps eut un heureux destin.
>
> (160)

There are two variants on *règle* here, one apparently conveying a favorable evaluation and the other linked to a severe condemnation. Marot had "refrains reglez"—measured refrains. This seems to be a positive view of Marot's work, contrasting with the disorder Boileau perceived in earlier poets in whom he found "mots assemblez sans mesure" (119). On the other hand, Ronsard, "Reglant tout, broüilla tout" (160). The word *reglant* looks here as if it refers to the articulation of poetic theory into rules, and the expressions "une autre methode" and "un art à sa mode" reinforce this interpretation. Boileau seems to be claiming that Ronsard's excessive drive toward regularity through explicit poetic method led to a muddle. The verb *broüilla* ("to jumble") suggests not merely confusion but the breakdown of large entities, which previously maintained their own internal structures, into fragments that can be mixed together into an entropic mass. By repeating *tout,* Boileau implies that Ronsard's striving for regulation of everything is what drove poetics beyond some desirable limit, after which the method had the opposite, harmful effect of a breakdown. It seems plausible to infer that Boileau is arguing in favor of some middle way, between the extremes of the opposite *tout,* in which there is both less confusion and less regulation.

An immediate counterargument seems to arise to the anti-regularity stance Boileau takes in connection with Ronsard. A few verses later in chant I is the well-known passage on François de Malherbe, "Enfin Malherbe vint. . . ." Malherbe, according to Boileau, "reduisit la Muse aux regles du devoir" (160). Noteworthy, besides the vagueness of this expression itself (far less specific than Boileau's desiderata for tragedy in chant III), is the fact that this reference to Malherbe's work comes only twelve verses after the mention of Ronsard's "method" and in sharp polemical contrast to this earlier poetics. Malherbian poetics are depicted here as an assimilated model. Malherbe's "laws" ("Tout reconnut ses loix") are embodied in his verses themselves rather than in a series of published rules or theorized method. The rules, in d'Aubignac and La Mesnardière, were meant to replace imitation as the means to master dramatic writing. In direct contrast to the anti-imitative approach of these earlier seventeenth-century theorists of tragedy, Boileau recommends that new poets take Malherbe's verses as model for their work ("Marchez donc sur ses pas, aimez sa pureté, / Et de son tour heureux imitez la clarté" [160]). La Mesnardière and d'Aubignac had systematically preferred regularity to dramatic tradition, explicit theorized rules to the replication of earlier tragic models. For these theorists of tragedy, rules intervene to separate the modern tragic author from his precursors, both recent and ancient. By rehabilitating imitation, Boileau returns to the tradition of the poet as master craftsman, learning by studying the work of his predecessors rather than poetic theories.

Boileau's *Art poétique* appeared a year after Racine had been elected to the Académie française. The playwright was at the peak of his success. The author of *Andromaque, Britannicus,* and *Phèdre* appears to many modern readers the quintessential "classical" French playwright, whose tragedies seem to incorporate the rules of tragedy with such success that the rules achieve the naturalness, *le naturel,* that is the height of cultivation rather than the rush of spontaneous inspiration. There is no doubt that in his plays Racine does routinely adopt certain broad parameters of what we now consider classical dramaturgy: from the first words of the play until the last, fewer than twelve hours seem to pass, the characters' actions seem to be related to their emotional preoccupations or their political habits, and the action that appears onstage can be said roughly to happen in one "place." Yet the question of what role

the "rules" play in Racine's theory of tragedy is a very different matter, since in one case we are dealing with practice and
in the other with theory, a series of interlocking statements that
give some account of practice. Although he did not write an
extensive statement of poetic theory as did Corncille, Racine's
prefaces give an intriguing picture of his complex position
on regularity. Racine locates himself as tragic poet as free of both
regularity and irregularity, as able to use rules for polemical
purposes but beyond rules in the creation of his plays. He assigns
rules to the world of pedants and critics, a world that is opposed
to the more powerful alliance of patrons and poets. He is clearly
of his time, that is, typical of the early to middle reign of Louis
XIV, in restoring the importance of taste and of the *cœur* in
appreciating the quality of a tragedy. Likewise, he is close to
Boileau in emphasizing genius and imitation of the ancients
over rules, particularly when those rules are conceived as the
rational advance beyond the practice of antiquity. In this last
regard Racine resolutely turns against the classical modernism
of a d'Aubignac or a La Mesnardière.

One might ask: but if the events of Racine's plays can take
place in the same time it takes to act them onstage and if everything happens without a change of sets, isn't Racine following the rules? In terms of the *theory* of tragedy we have to
answer, maybe not. One might well arrive at a way of writing
a tragedy because such a practice seemed to be the best imitation of esteemed models, or seemed to coincide with contemporary fashion, or responded to audience taste, or seemed to
be the best way to express a given idea or emotion. If Racine
divides *Phèdre* into five acts and Victor Hugo in 1830 divides
Hernani into five acts, are both following the rules? The Romantics, in writing pantoums (like Baudelaire's "Harmonie
du soir"), were obliged to follow the rules of the pantoum,
yet few speak of the Romantics as having cultivated "rules."
Two writers could produce similar texts, yet one might describe
the text as the outcome of following rules and the other might
describe it as an embodiment of a certain taste, perception, or
impulse. In *practical* terms, the difference may be of no importance whatever, but in *theoretical* terms it is crucial. For
the purposes of the present study, it is not the construction of
Racine's tragedies that is most pertinent, but the kind of gen-

eral statements he made about tragedy and its relation to the idea of rules.

In 1668 Racine published the first text in which he addressed the issue of poetic rules. In dedicating his third play, *Andromaque,* to Henriette d'Angleterre, the playwright appeals to Henriette against the judgment of his critics:

> pourvu qu'il me soit permis d'appeler de toutes les subtilités de leur esprit au cœur de VOTRE ALTESSE ROYALE. . . . Et nous qui travaillons pour plaire au public, nous n'avons plus que faire de demander aux savants si nous travaillons selon les règles. La règle souveraine est de plaire à VOTRE ALTESSE ROYALE. (*Théâtre complet* 129)

The rules belong to a self-accrediting, marginal, uncreative group to which Racine certainly does not want to belong. There is no reason to assume that he is merely flattering Henriette d'Angleterre and through her, her amorous brother-in-law, the king. He enunciates a theoretical position that is far from original but still significant in the poetics of the time: pleasing the audience—however that audience be defined and limited—is more important than following a set of rules elaborated by the community of poeticians.[15]

Shortly afterward, in the "Au lecteur" to his sole comedy, *Les plaideurs* (printed in 1669), Racine again attacks the preoccupation with poetic rules conceived independently of the emotional impact on the audience: "Ceux mêmes qui s'y étaient le plus divertis eurent peur de n'avoir pas ri dans les règles et trouvèrent mauvais que je n'eusse pas songé plus sérieusement à les faire rire" (*Théâtre complet* 193). The perception that there *are* rules or that there *should be,* independently of any precise specification of what those rules are, hinders audience reception of the comedy. Racine implies that this is the reaction of an ignorant audience, alienated from its own spontaneous response to drama by a confused sense that someone, somewhere, must know something about the theory of comedy that they do not know. The precise attribute of regularity that afflicts these spectators is the authority of rules rather than the quality of fragmentation and proliferation that so concerns d'Aubignac and Corneille. Yet the rules (it is significant that the term appears in the plural, with all that it implies of innumerable and unlimited requirements) have become a fetish, in the Freudian sense: they are required for the experience of pleasure (yet this requirement is seen by the observer as irrational, as an alienating supplement to the "basic" or "natural" conditions of pleasure), they take the place of an authority or potency that has been removed and carried off, and the spectator—the potential subject of pleasure—would have difficulty explaining the source of their efficacy. These spectators cannot experience directly their own laughter except through this missing and obscure thing, *les règles.*

In view of Racine's statement of "the sovereign rule" of pleasing Her Royal Highness in 1668, it comes as no surprise that this worried audience that has lost its spontaneous ability to enjoy its own laughter is a Parisian audience, *la ville* rather than *la cour,* an audience of minor aristocrats and bourgeois. Those with real power, who have no need to apologize for their reflexes or to conceal them, do not imagine that there are rules somewhere that should intervene in the experience of comedy. Real authority transcends the phantasm of rules and tinges the comedy with the glamour of the court:

> Quelques autres s'imaginèrent qu'il était bienséant à eux de s'y ennuyer et que les matières de palais ne pouvaient pas être un sujet de divertissement pour les gens de cour. La pièce fut bientôt jouée à Versailles. On ne fit point de scrupule de s'y réjouir; et ceux qui avaient cru se déshonorer de rire à Paris furent peut-être obligés de rire à Versailles pour se faire honneur. ("Au lecteur" of *Les plaideurs, Théâtre complet* 193)

Although the audience of rule fetishists has not been "cured" and is not able to experience comedy in a spontaneous way, these reluctant laughers have another indirect route to reach pleasure (or at least to simulate it, as they had earlier simulated boredom) by imitating the laughter of Their Royal Highnesses.

What is most important about Racine's description of regularity is that this obscure and haunting sense of a body of prescriptions for the writing and for the reception of comedy strikes those who are without political authority, do not write plays, and have, most of all, no knowledge of the "rules," whatever these might be. As Racine describes the role of rules in the cultural imagination of his time, they are in sharp opposition to real authority. In this respect Racine's thought seems very close to Pascal's description of symbolic substitutes for authority, substitutes that, for an enlightened observer, serve to reveal the weakness of those who bear them:

> Le chancelier est grave et revêtu d'ornements. Car son poste est faux et non le roi. Il a la force, il n'a que faire de l'imagination. Les juges, médecins, etc., n'ont que l'imagination.
> (*Pensées,* fragment 121)

Unlike Pascal, however, Racine seems to imply, at least for comedy, that a natural response is possible, that is, that human nature is not so obliterated by culture as to be out of our reach. What is important is to remove the imagined regularity so that audiences can respond directly to the play.

Racine continues two years later, in the preface to *Bérénice* (1671), to urge audiences to abandon the mediating fiction of rules and to trust their own reactions to plays.

> Ils ont cru qu'une tragédie qui était si peu chargée d'intrigues ne pouvait être selon les règles du théâtre. Je m'informai s'ils se plaignaient qu'elle les eût ennuyés. On me dit qu'ils avouaient tous qu'elle n'ennuyait point, qu'elle les touchait même en plusieurs endroits et qu'ils la verraient encore avec plaisir. Que veulent-ils davantage? Je les conjure d'avoir assez bonne opinion d'eux-mêmes pour ne pas croire qu'une pièce qui les touche, et qui leur donne du plaisir, puisse être absolument contre les règles. La principale règle est de plaire et de toucher. Toutes les autres ne sont faites que pour parvenir à cette première. Mais toutes ces règles sont d'un long détail, dont je ne leur conseille pas de s'embarrasser. Ils ont des occupations plus importantes. Qu'ils se reposent sur nous de la fatigue d'éclaircir les difficultés de la poétique d'Aristote, qu'ils se réservent le plaisir de pleurer et d'être attendris.
> (*Théâtre complet* 325)

Once again the "rules" appear as an empty set, for the public Racine describes does not know what they are but assumes that they must prohibit the kind of play just seen and enjoyed. The imagined negative rules seem to be a projection of the spectators' view of themselves and of their pleasure, since they do not consider themselves authorized to enjoy. Racine does not make a direct attack against the existence of the rules but rather removes them from discussion, minimizing their importance, and consigning them to the work of technicians. In doing so, he also collapses poetic theory into poetic practice, denying to poetics the status of an important public discourse.

When Racine states, in terms strikingly similar to Boileau's contemporaneous demand, that the principal rule is to delight and to move, he is really articulating the rule that ends all rules.[16] Rather than a multiplicity of important and equally valid and constraining specifications for dramatic creation, the rules as Racine describes them have no intrinsic or absolute value but only a relative and derivative one in relation to the single true requirement of a play: *de plaire et de toucher.* Racine, like Boileau, is countering more than a century of theory of tragedy. He is setting himself against readings of Aristotle that fragment and level the philosopher's comments about drama into a series of competing injunctions. Instead Racine subordinates theory to the experience of tragedy and subsumes the entire poetics of tragedy into a single unified block of knowledge. While retaining the vernacular term *rules,* he reduces this concept to (mere) detail in very pejorative terms, insisting on the tedium, the hairsplitting, and the antihumanistic nature of the technical study of poetics. True, Racine is no doubt sarcastic throughout this passage, and he no doubt considers his work as expert in these matters to be at least as important as the "more important concerns" of the theater public. Yet the effect is no less to withdraw the practice of the playwright from theoretical discourse and to disarticulate poetics in the sense of replacing a nebula of rules with a single rule.

For Racine the issue of rules is a matter of a power struggle but also of what we could call a "pleasure struggle." The rules of tragedy are propounded by a group of nonplaywrights attempting to control the work of practicing dramatists. Yet the function of the rules—as the critic whom Racine savagely attacks, toward the end of the preface to *Bérénice,* admits—is to prevent pleasure. Thus the rules, in the plural, violate the single rule that Racine recognizes, to delight and to move: "Il se plaint que la trop grande connaissance des règles l'empêche de se divertir à la comédie" (*Théâtre complet* 326). The body of poetic theory, no longer divided into multiple rules, becomes once more a whole discourse with nuances and gradations, but this discourse is withdrawn from the public and reserved to playwrights.[17]

It is hardly surprising, then, that Racine avoids the term *règle* in addressing the public in prefaces and letters. Outside the heavy, insistent, and even sarcastic repetition of the word in the preface to *Bérénice, règle* is either absent or only used once or twice in prefaces. It appears neither in the dedicatory letters nor in the prefaces of *La Thébaïde* or *Alexandre le Grand,* nor in either of the two prefaces to *Britannicus,* nor in the prefaces to *Mithridate, Iphigénie,* or *Esther.* Racine certainly was aware of the significance of his choice to stress or to omit mention of the rules. The word appears nine times in the preface to *Bérénice* (1671), yet in the 1670 preface to *Britannicus* there is not a word about the rules, and a year after *Bérénice* the playwright speaks of the *règles* only once. Clearly Racine knows that critics use the "rules" to control the plays' reception by Parisian audiences and he does not want to concede validity to this way of speaking about tragedy. Rather than play the Cornelian game of running circles around critics and theorists by multiplying rules, by creating them, and by applying them to his own tragedies in preemptive strikes, Racine acknowledges the importance of technique and art while denying that this art can be broken into a series of criteria independent of the tragedy itself.

On the other hand, Racine does make use of the concept of rules when he finds a way to use the critics' weapons against them. For instance, in the first preface to *Andromaque,* he derides the critics who maintain that he should have remade the heroes of his play, "qu'on réformât tous les héros de l'antiquité pour en faire des héros parfaits" (*Théâtre complet* 130). Since the rules are the currency that circulates among critics, Racine appeals to the rules to make himself seem without responsibility and powerless to re-create the heroes as he chooses: "Je trouve leur intention fort bonne de vouloir qu'on ne mette sur la scène que des hommes impeccables mais je les prie de se souvenir que ce n'est point à moi de changer les règles du théâtre" (130–31). Such scruples do not always bother him. For instance, in accounting in its preface for the title of *Athalie* (1691), he writes, "j'aurais dû dans les règles l'intituler Joas;

mais la plupart du monde n'en ayant entendu parler que sous
le nom d'Athalie, je n'ai pas jugé à propos de la leur présenter
sous un autre titre" (641).

In place of rules, Racine proposes a knowledge of Aristotle's
Poetics and Horace's *Ad Pisones* together with an understanding of ancient theatrical models and of ancient taste. This may
seem to be the same thing as what was known as *les règles,*
but Racine's approach is pointedly different. For participants
in the game of rules (Chapelain, Corneille, d'Aubignac, and
others), the rules are in part, as we have seen, *extracted* from
Aristotle's text and in part created by modern poetic theorists.
Rules are a recent product that presents an ambivalent view of
ancient tragedy and of the society that gave rise to tragedy. In
fact, La Mesnardière and d'Aubignac (and even Corneille) make
it clear that one of the advantages of the rules is that they prevent French playwrights from making the mistakes that abound
in the work of ancient dramatic authors. Perhaps most important in Racine's denigration of the rules is his lucid recognition of the implicit assumption that knowledge of the rules can
replace firsthand knowledge of the Aristotelian text.

Contrary, then, to what we might suppose, Racine's rejection of the rules is a way of proclaiming his fidelity to Aristotle
and, more important, to the work of Aeschylus, Sophocles,
Euripides, Seneca, Menander, and Terence. In regard to the
reception and appreciation of tragedies and comedies, Racine
repeatedly stresses the taste of the audience as the decisive factor,
taste that is not improved but rather spoiled by the specter of
rules. In regard to the writing of plays, he emphasizes the imitation of ancient playwrights. In practical terms, the staged result
might be the same, but the theoretical path to that result is
conspicuously different—and this theoretical path reveals
the wholly different spirit of Racine's aesthetics. Rather than
explain his dramatic construction in terms of the unity of action and the attendant qualifications on that unity, Racine speaks
of "cette simplicité d'action qui a été si fort du goût des anciens" (preface to *Bérénice, Théâtre complet* 324). Likewise,
in describing the use of the chorus in *Athalie* (1691) he does
not refer to a rule about scenic linking but rather recalls the
plays of ancient tragedians and bases his creation directly on
their works without making a detour through the rules: "J'ai

aussi essayé d'imiter des anciens cette continuité d'action qui fait que leur théâtre ne demeure jamais vide" (preface to *Athalie, Théâtre complet* 696). In this case both the resultant staging and the theoretical account are different from comparable texts of his contemporaries, for neither the use of choruses nor justification by direct imitation of ancient plays was current in the seventeenth century.

Racine's brief but revealing statements about the theory of tragedy (and of comedy) discomfit common assumptions about seventeenth-century regularity. While he explicitly embraces such concepts as verisimilitude, continuity of action, decorum (*convenance*), and the middling moral quality of heroes, he distances himself energetically from the *règles,* particularly insofar as these are part of a body of knowledge available to those who have no experience writing plays and no direct knowledge of Aristotle's text. In opposition to the rules, he asserts the importance of a single rule, the rule of delighting and moving the audience.

Twentieth-century views of French classical tragedy and the contemporary theoretical discussion surrounding it are at variance with the texts of poetics that remain from the 1600s. The question of the importance and function of the "rules" is asked and answered quite differently by Corneille, Racine, and their contemporaries, and by post-Romantic critics and theorists. From the many recent accounts, three can serve here as an example of major divergences: René Bray's synthesis of *la doctrine classique,* Paul Valéry's description of a classical aesthetics of arbitrary constraint, and Catherine Kintzler's recent account of Corneille's and d'Aubignac's poetics as anticipating a Kantian transcendental theory of a possible reality.

René Bray's 1926 "classic" synthesis of the theory and criticism of seventeenth-century France, *Formation de la doctrine classique,* promotes the idea of a single, unified, comprehensive, and obligatory literary doctrine controlling writers of dramatic and lyric poetry following the prescriptions of La Mesnardière. For Bray, all literary concepts of the period exist solely in the form of rules. Eight years after the armistice that concluded the First World War, he describes the seventeenth-century poet as a soldier: "Pour remplir sa mission, il doit obéir à la règle, et en obéissant à la règle, il est sûr d'atteindre son but" (99).

For Bray, the major confrontation of the century is between the antiquated partisans of poetic liberty—typified by the sixteenth-century Pléiade—and the expositors and observers of the rules. After 1640, "le mouvement est achevé. On ne conteste plus guère la souveraineté des règles. L'artiste est le prisonnier d'un code immuable" (106). Bray never distinguishes competence from obedience, concept from rule, nor rule as practice from "rule" as imperative requirement.[18] In other words, Bray never ponders the implications of the term itself, the possibility of multiple understandings and uses, including popular, critical, or subversive reappropriations. The military analogy directs his reading of all theoretical and critical texts even when he provides fairly informative summaries of Corneille's strategy of ironic inflation, about which Bray says that the playwright "chicane sur leur interprétation [des règles] et sur leur application" (109). This sounds hard to reconcile with the image of the faithful soldier following an immutable code, yet once he sets up the idea that all contemporary literary and dramatic concepts are rules, Bray is no longer able to read theoretical texts as other than some form of *chicane,* quibbling. To practice unity of scenic place is for Bray to follow the rule of unity of place; the rest—whatever Corneille might say—is merely Norman deviousness. Bray's direct or indirect influence on almost all manuals and school editions is immense and durable, though some discomfort with the reduction of all dramatic theory to "rules" appears from time to time in the quotation marks surrounding the term.[19]

Bray's book appeared five years after the first publication of Paul Valéry's essay "Au sujet d'Adonis" (1921) in which the poet and critic gave a kindred but more philosophically complex account of "la doctrine classique." Not basing himself on theoretical texts of the period, Valéry instead formulates an intuitive or sympathetic reconstruction of that doctrine. Valéry takes La Fontaine's poem *Adonis* as the point of departure for a meditation on the literary culture of the seventeenth century seen as sharing a common devotion to arbitrary constraints, *règles.* Like Bray, Valéry does not see seventeenth-century literary culture as founded on an understanding of what will move and please audiences, nor is he concerned with accurate representation of any external reality. Instead, poetic success is a kind of virtuoso achievement of producing verses within severe limitations that are entirely outside the control of the poet. History seems to Valéry to show the dominance of this "espèce d'obstination qu'ont mise les poètes de tous les temps . . . à se charger de chaînes volontaires." He asks "D'où vient cette obéissance immémoriale à des commandements qui nous paraissent si futiles?" (477). Mentioning Racine as belonging to this same aesthetic, Valéry does not even bother to seek an empirical justification for the rules. Instead of being a codification of practices that seem to bring success with readers, a political imposition, or prescription for conveying a deep moral truth, the rules for Valéry are valuable because they cause the poet to produce a difficult, objective, aesthetic experience: "Les exigences d'une stricte prosodie sont l'artifice qui confère au langage naturel les qualités d'une matière résistante à notre âme, et comme sourde à nos désirs" (480).

The rules that interest Valéry are, of course, mostly the conventions of meter and rhyme, but the aesthetic basis of his description of La Fontaine's work can be used to argue for the conventional, arbitrary quality of all French classical literature with its observation of "règles anciennes." What is central to Valéry's view of the classical aesthetic is, first of all, the centrality of rules perceived as arbitrary and conventional, and, second, the voluntary submission to a constraint perceived by the poet as external both to his own desire and to that of his public. Valéry's view of rule would have seemed absurd to d'Aubignac and to La Mesnardière.

A radically different conception of "rule" in seventeenth-century dramatic theory is that of Catherine Kintzler in her systematic *Poétique de l'opéra français de Corneille à Rousseau.* Kintzler totally rejects the concept of convention as the basis for French classical rules. Taking verisimilitude to be the central concept of dramatic regularity and reading d'Aubignac and Corneille through Kantian concepts, Kintzler gives a remarkable revitalized vision of the crucial term that lead to such extensive discussions in early modern poetics:

> Du réel, le théâtre n'empruntera certes pas la banalité, l'anec-
> dotique, la superficialité; la fiction esthétique, pas plus ici
> qu'ailleurs, ne se donne comme réplique de l'observable,

> elle se pense plutôt comme révélation du vrai. Le rapport
> de la poésie dramatique à l'idée d'un réel, sa mondanité n'ont
> rien à voir avec une reproduction, elles sont de l'ordre du
> réglage. L'autonomie du monde théâtral ne montre son indé-
> pendance que par les lois qui gouvernent ce réglage. De
> même que le monde réel, la poésie dramatique est assujettie
> à des lois qui la contraignent, et qu'il n'est pas au pouvoir
> du poète de modifier. . . . La résistance que le monde drama-
> tique offre au poète, et qui fonde l'attente poétique du specta-
> teur, doit pouvoir se dire, lorsqu'on veut en fournir une
> expression théorique, sous la forme d'une *régularité*. (134)

Kintzler centers her account of dramatic rules on the creation
of a model world that is not merely analogous to the world of
seventeenth-century science, but *identical* to that theoretically
constructed world: "c'est la nature régulière, mathématisable,
et abstraite de la science classique" (105). No rules that apply
to dramatic representation count for Kintzler, only rules or
natural laws that apply to the separate world of the tragic fiction. This exclusion of any poetic precept that is not derived
from the idea of a verisimilar tragic fiction is motivated by her
central aim of justifying the "marvelous" or supernatural world
of opera within the poetics of tragedy. Her solution to the problem of accounting in purely rational terms for the operatic world
is to transform theorists of tragedy, playwrights, and (theoretical)
spectators into transcendent subjects, into the "I" of the Cartesian *cogito*. Whether or not this is an accurate vision of the
spectator as conceived by classical poetics is a question we will
consider in subsequent chapters.

The result of this approach is to restrict the concept of regularity to the structures governing the fictive world created within
theater. In other words, Kintzler is concerned only with the
creation of a hypothetical model of a fictional world, a model
that would be similar to, and in fact almost indistinguishable
from, the world of a scientific philosopher such as Descartes
when he created a theoretical world in his *Mundus*.[20] As a result Kintzler must reject any "rule" that refers to the nonfic-
tional world of the theater itself, including the audience,
political forces, and physical structures. For instance, the
theory of tragedy tries to determine whether or not characters
should be killed within sight of the audience, but Kintzler finds

this to be a matter unrelated to regularity simply because the rules do not deal with audiences.

For Kintzler, then, the authority of the rules and the concept of regularity itself derive from a transcendental philosophy of the theater as alternative reality. Regularity therefore has nothing to do with conventions or axioms because these suppose the existence of a community outside this alternative reality. To think of rules as axioms permits a modernistic or postmodern pluralism in theater, admits Kintzler,

> Mais l'axiomatisation de la théorie des fondements du théâtre véhicule aussi des obstacles. Elle est responsable notamment du fait que bon nombre de nos contemporains projettent ce modèle axiomatique sur le théâtre de l'âge classique. Une telle projection, selon laquelle tout est réductible à une relativisation historico-sociologique, aboutit par exemple à l'incapacité de penser le théâtre merveilleux . . . autrement que sous le concept de convention. (135)[21]

Conventionality, however, is not only a twentieth-century projection onto the early modern. We have already seen that Corneille, at least, thinks of certain rules as conventions. When he describes the *liaison des scènes* as having become a rule, he plainly points to the audience's shift in expectations as the source of the rule's authority. Playwrights later in the century, in his view, now have a tacit agreement with the audience (a convention) that scenes will be linked by interaction between characters who are already onstage and those who are entering.

Kintzler aptly describes seventeenth-century poetics as requiring the construction both of a fictive world and of a fictive audience, but fails to describe both the instability that is attributed to that audience and the divergence between what happens in the fictive world and what appears to the spectator.[22] Yet "rules" in poetics were not turned exclusively toward the creation of an autonomous coherent world but included expectations and needs attributed to the public that varied with time. Regularity concerns both the mimetic creation of a fictive world and all that modulates, facilitates, and hinders the audience's perception of that world as a source of pathos.

Corneille's comment about the "rule" requiring the *liaison des scènes* indicates that the rule was created during his lifetime and must be observed, not by virtue of any internal, logical necessity of the dramatic world but because audiences are used to it. For Corneille, the closest literary approximation of an independent possible world similar to that of a scientific model of nature is not the dramatic world but the world of the novel (*le roman*). Events in the novel may occur without reference to the needs of the spectators, but tragedy must be organized in such a way that probability is sacrificed to the requirements of staging (3: 163). The writer of a tragedy must supply corrective or supplemental causes to displace events so that they fit onstage and within the time allowed, but this displacement or rearrangement takes place precisely because the author is not representing a purely autonomous world but only one that appears autonomous. The world of tragedy, as theorized by Corneille, d'Aubignac, and others, is a world governed by a *hidden cause* (that is, hidden to the fictive characters who inhabit that world): the satisfaction of the spectator.

Any account of the regularity of seventeenth-century theory of tragedy that does not take into account the nebula of rules that concern the relationship between the spectator and the fictive world has an immense advantage: such a refined and reformed theory can be coherent and rigorous. However, it needs to sacrifice the ambivalence, variety, and complexity of the seventeenth-century French texts about tragedy. The following chapters attempt to give a sense of the paradoxes generated by a culture of regularity. By "culture of regularity" we mean here the habits of a society that framed what it did and what it said with a consciousness of multiple, proliferating, normative statements about how literary and artistic production should be carried out. The culture of regularity affects those who claim to know the rules, those who believe there are rules but profess not to know what they are, and those who argue against the rules or even against the whole concept of rule. Whether or not contemporary statements of rules had or have any relevance for the writing and appreciation of tragedy, the numerous texts that debate the rules are an important part of the society that produced and viewed French classical tragedy, or as the contemporaries of Corneille and Racine called it, *la tragédie régulière.*

Chapter Two

Passion in the Age of Reason

Passion above All

According to the dramatic theories of the seventeenth century, the principal purpose of tragedy is to produce in the spectator or reader overwhelming emotion, driving the spectator beyond the control of reason. Following the emotion of the character, or "Personne theatrale":

> [the spectator] s'afflige quand elle pleure; il est gay lors qu'elle est contente; si elle gémit, il soupire; il frémit, si elle se fasche; bref il suit tous ses mouvemens, et il ressent que son cœur est comme un champ de bataille où la Science du Poëte fait combattre quand il lui plaist mille Passions tumultueuses, et plus fortes que la Raison. (La Mesnardière 74)

This theoretical insistence on an obligatory, transcendent emotion is difficult for modern readers to appreciate and to accept. One reason for our difficulty is the confusion in purpose and in audience that dramatic theorists entertain and that scholarly and critical discourse perpetuates. On one hand, poetics as a type of discourse addresses itself to readers identified either as philosophers, as cultivated and reflective critics, or as practitioners of the specific arts that philosophers have chosen to describe and regulate. On the other hand, the practitioners of these various arts—for example, the authors of tragedies—will address themselves to a clientele of nonspecialists whose needs and interests are different and perhaps completely opposed to those of the practitioner. In considering the advice given by d'Aubignac, La Mesnardière, and others to writers of tragedies, we perceive a growing insistence on formulas, guidelines, definitions, and limitations—all directed toward a deliberate, craftsmanlike, and, in sum, rational approach to writing drama

43

for both theatrical and printed distribution. Thus, compared to the sixteenth-century debates about inspiration and individual temperament, these later poetic arts can accurately be called rationalist. In terms of this professional audience, we can accept Bray's insistence that the classical aesthetic is based on "le culte de la raison" (191). However, the audience of classical theater—as opposed to the audience of theoretical discourse about theater—is theorized quite differently from the group of professionals whom the theorists hope to guide. The theater audience is expected to seek emotional stimulation (or manipulation). For this aim to be achieved, the work of the playwright—with his cleverness, his formulas, his mechanisms, and his plans—must be concealed in order to permit the spectator to have an experience that departs totally from the deliberate and controlled crafting of the play. It is accurate to say that dramatic theorists promote a kind of war on reason in terms of the effect on the audience during the dramatic performance and the kind of experience and character represented in the dramatic fiction.

The different distribution of reason and emotion between the producers of tragedy, on one hand, and the audience of tragedy, on the other, is conceived by seventeenth-century writers as part of a widespread strategy of *using* emotion to achieve aims defined by reason. French thought of this period is characterized by its positive evaluation of passion once the latter has been directed properly, and an acceptance of passion either as a healthy aspect of the human condition (the Cartesian position) or as an inevitable part of this earthly life for the vast majority of men (a view represented by the Oratorian Father Jean-François Senault). The writer of tragedy does not compose in the throes of passionate inspiration, carried away by profound identification with the dramatic characters and their plight. Instead, whether guided primarily by Aristotle's text, by rules articulated by sixteenth- and seventeenth-century theorists, by empirical observation of audience response, or by careful imitation of previous tragic texts, the playwright imagined by La Mesnardière, d'Aubignac, and Corneille is a dispassionate technician. The viewer of tragedy, on the contrary, is carried away during the performance by passionate identification with the tragic characters. No doubt the very best of readers and viewers are eventually able to reflect on their experience and on the artifice that caused it—such a public furnishes the readership for texts such as Corneille's "examens"—but almost all contemporary theorists consider a tragedy a failure if it permits the viewer to stand back and to consider the tragic events in rational terms.

It is probably no coincidence that Cardinal Richelieu, who was patron of playwrights and poetic theorists as well as harsh critic of Corneille during the Quarrel of *Le Cid,* stands as a model of the split between cool reason on the side of the writer and melting passionate surrender on the part of the audience. Such an aesthetic distinction can also be a rhetorical and political one. In the letter to Richelieu that opens the Oratorian's treatise *De l'usage des passions* (1641, only three years after the Académie's *Sentimens* on *Le Cid*), Father Senault describes the Cardinal as an exceptional human being by virtue of his utter lack of emotion:

> Vous employastes vostre force contre vous-mesme, et pour vous preparer à conduire des sujets et à vaincre des rebelles, vous declarastes la guerre à vos Passions, et vous fistes regner aussi absolument la Raison dans vostre ame que nostre Monarque dans la France. . . . C'est un malheur déplorable que les Princes pensent à vaincre leurs ennemis, et ne songent pas à vaincre leurs Passions. (1–2)

To rule others it is imperative to have utter self-control, but it is a great advantage to have as adversaries people who are highly emotional and unable to conceal their emotions. Richelieu's face, says Senault, never changes under the influence of fear or anger. Yet the Cardinal is entirely aware of the most hidden inclinations of others:

> Vous lisez leurs intentions dans le fonds de leurs cœurs, et le Ciel qui vous a fait part de sa lumière, vous a donné la connoissance de leurs plus secrettes pensées. . . . Vous les gagnez [ceux qui vous abordent] par leurs passions, et elles vous servent de chaisnes pour les prendre et pour les arrester. Plus puissant que nostre Hercule Gaulois, qui ne tenoit les hommes attachez que par les oreilles, vous les tenez enchaisnez par les cœurs, et vous les conduisez selon vos desirs et selon nos besoins. (7)

Senault is unambiguous about the hierarchy of reason and emotion, and his treatise is evidence that, outside of the experience of tragedy, there really is a "culte de la raison"—in the full, paradoxical sense of that expression. The reason of the dominant Cardinal is not only praised as a faculty but described in its quasi-theatrical manifestation: "vostre [visage] qui ne change jamais, est une preuve asseurée de la paix dont vous jouyssez, et de la victoire que vous avez remportée sur toutes vos Passions" (3). However, it is equally important that the Cardinal's subjects have emotions on which he can draw, pulling the chains that control their deepest feelings. According to Senault's dedicatory letter, the unequal distribution of reason and passion is a fortunate circumstance because it favors orderly government. The subjects' lack of self-control facilitates control by the Cardinal.[1]

Although Senault does not write about the theater, his opening comments on Richelieu and the passions illustrate the uneven distribution of reason that is fundamental to the theory of tragedy in seventeenth-century France. Reason is reserved to the playwright, who composes with all deliberation. The spectator must be deprived of reason during the play in order to experience the anguish, fear, suspense, anger, desire, and terror of the dramatic characters.

This crucial theoretical distinction between the reason of the tragic author and the unreason—temporary though it be—of the spectator has been all but ignored in most scholarship and in school manuals and editions. Surely few teachers insist that their students consider French classical tragedy as directed, in theory, toward the primary purpose of de-intellectualizing life and of reducing the reader to spasms of uncontrollable sobbing.[2] Yet, if we take the theorists seriously, this is indeed the aim of tragedy. To cite another vigorous statement of the dominance of passion, consider d'Aubignac's statement:

> personne ne vient presque sur la Scéne qui n'ait l'esprit inquieté, dont les affaires ne soient traversées, et qu'on ne voye dans la necessité de travailler, ou de souffrir beaucoup; et enfin c'est où règne le Démon de l'inquietude, du trouble et du desordre; et deslors qu'on y laisse arriver le calme et le repos, il faut que la Piéce finisse, ou qu'elle languisse. ... (305)

It is difficult for scholarly discourse to emphasize emotion. It runs against the intellectual, rationalist values of the institution, against the very vocabulary that scholars and even students bring to discussions of literature. Psychology or psychoanalysis deal, in part, with emotions or with drives, instincts, and pulsions, yet both of these disciplines not only distance emotion as object of study but prefer to speak metonymically of emotion by treating its causes, the context in which it is expressed, the values that emotions generate or convey, and the social structures that have been established to prevent the expression of emotion.[3] Literature is often presented as valuable for its ability to analyze emotion, to classify it, to demonstrate its manipulation in the service of political or ideological structures. More often than not, instructors warn students that an emotional response is not appropriate for university-level studies and that a reader's emotions are, at the most, a first step in discovering the social construct from which we should try to free ourselves.

Although certain reader-response critics have encouraged exploration of emotions in readers, little of this work—with the notable exception of Christian Biet's *Racine, ou la passion des larmes*— has been directed toward French classical tragedy.[4] On the contrary, a *locus classicus* of our scholarship is the truly impressive and perhaps too persuasive analysis of Racine's style by Leo Spitzer, who argued that Racine endeavored constantly to attenuate emotion and to restrain passionate reaction with "cold rationality."[5] It may, of course, be the case that seventeenth-century French drama appears less emotional in its intended effect than later texts to which we (but not authors like d'Aubignac or La Mesnardière) can compare it. Reading the seventeenth-century theorists allows us to measure the distance between what many have come to value in seventeenth-century tragedy and the *theoretical* discourse that the classical period produced about dramatic poetry.

The theorists probably come closer to reaching consensus on the issue of emotion than they do for any other concept. They demand that three effects be represented onstage and produced in the audience: greatly increased emotion, the paralysis of reason or judgment, and the consequent disruption of language.

Passion, the very term used to describe the state of the dramatic characters and the state to be produced in the audience, signifies a type of excess. The dictionary of the Académie (1695 edition) defines *passion* in traditional scholastic mode as "Mouvement de l'ame excité dans la partie concupiscible ou dans la partie irascible."[6] More significant, as is usually the case for dictionaries of the time, is the set of illustrative uses: "Grande passion, forte passion, passion violente, passion véhémente, ardente, dereglée, furieuse, aveugle, estre maistre de ses passions, la passion l'emporte . . ." [etc.]. The dictionary associates passion with literary, and especially theatrical, texts, commenting that the word "se prend aussi, Pour l'expression et la representation vive des passions que l'on traite dans une piece de theatre, ou dans quelque autre ouvrage d'esprit." It is this *representation vive* of passion that is almost universally ignored by modern critics and teachers of tragedy.

Means or End?

The requirement that tragedy represent characters in the throes of passion and that the tragic text produce intense emotion in the spectator or reader is related to the ancient and celebrated *topos* of catharsis or purgation. The term *related* is a vague one, appropriate for the difficulty that French theorists had in determining how to understand, to use, or to evade the Aristotelian concept while maintaining the notion of emotional excess as tragic aim. Interestingly, perhaps, the Académie française, the body that should be most alert to literary denotations of common words, did not see fit to define *purgation* in terms of its use in the *arts poétiques* and does not associate *purger* with emotion. This is all the more revealing in that the dictionary of the Académie *did* define *passion* as an object of literary representation. This is suggestive of the widespread understanding that drama both simulated and stimulated emotion much more effectively than it carried out its Aristotelian mission of purging emotion. Nonetheless, in order to understand the extent to which the French classical emphasis on pathos surpasses our customary academic presentation of the "rules," it is important to set forth the difference between the excess of passion and the "officially" acknowledged role of emotions within the neo-Aristotelian framework.

The terms imposed by translations of Aristotle's *Poetics* convey a quantitative concept of emotion (*purger, modérer*), treating emotion as a substance subject to the topic of "more" or "less," but seventeenth-century theorists move far beyond the cathartic reduction to set a wide range of emotional excess at the center of tragedy. Although neither Corneille nor Racine, the two practitioners whose texts have been institutionalized as the definitive canon of classical tragedy, endorse the theory of purgation, all theorists, including the two major tragic authors, acknowledge that pity and fear in some way are traditionally supposed to improve the moral disposition of the audience and all make some reference to catharsis, either as "purgation" or as "moderation" of passion. Corneille quotes Aristotle's single mention of catharsis (*Poetics,* chapter 6): "par la pitié et la crainte elle purge de semblables passions" (3: 142). La Mesnardière also cites the *Poetics:* "l'imitation réelle des malheurs, et des souffrances, qui produit par elle-mesme la Terreur et la Pitié, et qui sert à modérer ces deux mouvemens de l'Ame" (8). "Pity" and "fear"—also known as "compassion" and "terror"—are the two accepted emotions that are to be produced in the audience.

There are two quite different ways of theorizing tragic catharsis in the seventeenth century, although few theorists are very clear about this issue and occasionally make statements incompatible with their primary emphasis. The first approach uses pity and fear to regulate other emotions. In this account of catharsis, pity and fear are instrumental or "meta-emotions" insofar as they are above the various other emotions that they serve to control, moderate, or otherwise subordinate. This instrumental view of pity and fear as desirable emotions in the audience's experience of tragedy seems to be the most widespread view among theorists, and is set forth notably by d'Aubignac and La Mesnardière. The second way of theorizing catharsis takes pity and fear as objects, as the targets of tragedy's cathartic effort. André Dacier and René Rapin are the principal theorists who describe tragedy as reducing or eliminating pity and fear rather than as using these emotions to further ends. Neither of the two seventeenth-century conceptions of catharsis resembles widespread twentieth-century attempts at understanding this obscure concept. One typical recent scholarly attempt to elucidate Aristotle's meaning is "a powerful release of emotion which has a salutary effect on our emotional (and hence our ethical) disposition" (Halliwell ed. 191). This modern view, emphasizing *release* of emotion and very reasonably supposing that tragic purgation resembles medical procedures of the same name, leads us to believe that an excess of emotion is discharged during the theatrical experience and that this discharge is the pleasant and healthful process known as purgation. In the seventeenth century, surprisingly, the discharge of excessive emotion did not constitute purgation.

The clearest statement of the instrumental view of emotions is given by Corneille in his first *Discours:* "purgation des passions par le moyen de la pitié, et de la crainte" (3: 122). This formulation presents Aristotle's statement about the effect of tragedy in slightly different terms from the version given in the second *Discours* and quoted above. It leaves no doubt that pity and fear are the *means* rather than the objects of purgation. Corneille interprets Aristotle as teaching that the audience is meant to feel pity for characters whose emotions lead them to unhappiness and fear for the spectators themselves if their desires lead them to commit certain acts (Corneille 3: 149). La Mesnardière emphasizes that fear is the direct instrument of moral improvement:

> On juge bien . . . que la Crainte est proprement l'effet que la Tragédie doit produire dans les esprits lors qu'elle expose de grans crimes; et c'est absolument pour tirer de cette Passion le fruict que nous venons de voir, qu'elle introduit quelquefois des Héros qui sont fort coupables. (26)[7]

In this view, pity and fear are not decreased or discharged but increased during the reading or viewing of the tragedy and afterward as well. Fear is excited selectively in members of the audience, and the residual fear that accompanies the spectator after the end of the play improves the spectator's conduct:

> faisant voir le chastiment d'un adultére, il faut de necessité qu'elle [la tragédie] effraye le vicieux, coupable du mesme crime, et que par là elle l'oblige à se retirer d'un vice qu'il voit sévérement punir. (La Mesnardière 26)

According to Chapelain, the public should leave the theater with "crainte" (*Sentimens* 361).

In describing pity and fear as instruments, theorists had the problem of explaining the value of pity. Corneille gave a logical reading of Aristotle's pair by seeing pity as a step in the production of fear:

> La pitié d'un malheur où nous voyons tomber nos sem-
> blables, nous porte à la crainte d'un pareil pour nous; cette
> crainte au désir de l'éviter; et ce désir à purger, modérer,
> rectifier, et même déraciner en nous la passion qui plonge à
> nos yeux dans ce malheur les personnes . . . (3: 141)

On the other hand, Corneille admits that fear alone can lead to moral improvement without pity but that pity cannot have any "purgative" effect without fear. *Le Cid* serves as an example of the highly instructive fear without pity (the case of Don Gomès, father of Chimène, whose envious pride, according to Corneille, awakens no pity but certainly discourages us from following his example) and of the spectator's pity for the two lovers without fear of falling into their situation (3: 148). Corneille very lucidly sees that this whole line of interpretation leads not toward purgation but toward instruction by example, making fear the supreme dramatic emotion.[8] At any rate, Corneille admitted that he considered purgation simply "une belle idée," and not an effect that had ever occurred as a result of any tragedy.

Unlike Corneille, La Mesnardière had no systematic explanation of the relation of pity to purgation. Instead, he had two apparently incompatible, or at least, separate views of pity and fear. The first requires the moderation *of* pity and fear, and is mentioned only twice—once in a direct quotation from Aristotle (above) and once in a discussion of why terror and not horror is the legitimate tragic emotion.[9] This view, never developed or explained, is clearly not the instrumental but the objective view of pity and fear. However, the instrumental approach is the one that dominates La Mesnardière's writing, and he splits the two emotions apart and assigns a utilitarian function to fear alone. Fear of suffering the fate of a bad character is a useful, morally improving emotion, but we cannot pity such criminal characters (107–08). On the other hand, pity is a sweet and pleasant emotion that tragedy should create for the sake of pleasure alone.[10] Here purgation breaks down and yields to a competing view of tragic emotion, the belief that emotion is simply a source of pleasure. In this division between the morally useful emotion of fear and the enjoyable emotion of pity, the Aristotelian fusion of the two emotions into a single experience is dissolved. La Mesnardière, like Corneille, admits that pity and fear may very well function separately and that both are not required for a tragedy:

> La Tragédie a deux Objets, qui sont d'exciter la Pitié, et de provoquer la Terreur en des Sujets separez, si un seul n'en est pas capable; ou de produire ces Passions dans une seule Avanture, si elle en est susceptible. (143)

The second major explanation of tragic purgation holds what could be called the "objective" view, that pity and fear are bad emotions, at least in excess, and that tragedy reduces them. This is "objective" in the sense that pity and fear are the objects, not the means of purgation. They must be driven out. As René Rapin writes in his *Réflexions* (1674), "La tragedie rectifie l'usage des passions, en modérant la crainte et la pitié, qui sont des obstacles à la vertu" (23). In Rapin's view we are too easily moved to pity and squander that emotion on objects that do not deserve it. The representation of truly pitiful spectacles would harden us so that we feel pity less often, just as fearful sights could harden us to feel much less fear:

> la tragédie [se sert des] avantures les plus touchantes et les plus terribles que l'histoire peut luy fournir, pour exciter dans les cœurs les mouvemens qu'elle prétend, afin de guérir les esprits de ces vaines frayeurs, qui peuvent les troubler, et de ces sottes compassions qui peuvent les amollir. . . . (Rapin 98)

Tragedy does not seem to purge pity or purge by pity but really, as Rapin says earlier, to "rectify" the use of pity. How this rectification occurs is fairly obscure. At times, as in the last quotation, Rapin seems to call for stimulation of fear and pity in situations where the emotion is not justified so that the mind (*les esprits*) will lose the tendency to become stimulated in this way. The intense emotional excitement, for which playwrights seek the most extreme subjects, may use up and deplete the store of these emotions. Such a view could be called "purgation" in the strict sense, because it would remove emotion from the personality. However, in other passages Rapin calls for tragedy to help spectators to store up emotions and not waste them on unworthy objects, and to

> ménager leur compassion pour des sujets qui la méritent. Car il y a de l'injustice d'estre touché des malheurs de ceux qui méritent d'estre misérables. On doit voir sans pitié Clytemnestre tuée par son fils Oreste parce qu'elle avoit égorgé Agamemnon son mary: et l'on ne peut voir mourir Hippolyte par l'intrigue de Phedra sa belle-mère, dans Euripide, sans compassion: parce qu'il ne meurt que pour avoir esté chaste et vertueux. (98)

This is the opposite of purgation, since it teaches us to hold in, to store up compassion (as the very economical verb *ménager* says) rather than allow it to flow forth at the wrong moments. The experience of tragedy is not aimed at the increase or decrease of emotion itself but at training whatever part of the mind or heart controls the outflow or withholding of the emotions. In training the emotions, tragedy brings them into conformity with moral standards, preventing pity for evildoers. Rapin's account of tragic pity, however eccentric and even mean-spirited, has the advantage of giving pity a role that is not secondary and subordinate to fear. On the other hand, Rapin, like Corneille and La Mesnardière, continues to theorize tragic plots that are based either on pity or fear but not both. However, in distinguishing occasions for withholding and expending compassion, Rapin gives a case of a blameless hero who meets a miserable end, thus presenting a situation that La Mesnardière thinks an abomination and Corneille thinks likely to revolt the audience. By sharpening the spectator's ability to withhold pity from "unworthy" characters, Rapin breaks down what was and still is widely considered a major characteristic of tragedy, a rich mixture or amalgam of emotion in the spectator's response to the play's characters. Rapin thus hastens the decline of the tragic story by arguing against plots that may cause us to feel pity for characters despite their moral failings. In this way he announces the coming of eighteenth-century theatrical forms such as the *drame* and the *comédie larmoyante*.

André Dacier's translation and commentary on Aristotle's *Poetics* (1692) is another major text that presents the "objective" treatment of pity and fear as emotions to reduce or eliminate.

Although his translation of the key phrase in chapter 6 of the Greek text permits a broader, instrumental interpretation of the role of these emotions ("[tragedy] par le moyen de la compassion & de la terreur modere & corrige nos passions" [5a]), he returns to the passage to specify that tragedy "acheve de purger en nous ces sortes de passions, et toutes les autres semblables" (79). Conceding, with apparent reluctance, that the passions cannot be entirely removed from the soul (*déracinées*), Dacier admits that the issue of how exciting pity and fear can purge these emotions is problematic. His solution is close to Rapin's, for Dacier sees tragedy as hardening the spectator to these emotions, desensitizing people for future experience of unhappiness and fear, "en nous rendant ces mêmes malheurs familiers, car elle nous apprend par là à ne les pas trop craindre, & à n'en être pas trop touchez quand ils arrivent veritablement" (81). Where Rapin sees tragedy as preparing us to be arbiters of conduct when we are spectators of tragedy or of life, Dacier seems to envisage the audience's own experience of fear and self-pity. Seeing the misery of tragic characters "dispose les plus miserables à se trouver heureux, en comparant leurs malheurs avec ceux que la Tragedie leur represente" (82). Tragedy aims at making the audience happy, not because justice was done—as La Mesnardière and d'Aubignac hold—but because the audience is better off than the characters. This account of the dramatic experience could very well be considered a kind of "purgation," since we use up our pity and fear on the characters, but Dacier does not actually resort to terms for depletion, evacuation, or exhaustion in his explanation. Instead he sketches a much more rational or distanced processing of the dramatic experience. In leaving the theater, at least, the audience must be able to step back in some way from the plot in order to place their own lives and the life of the tragic character in a comparative, evaluative structure. The spectators will still have, within their souls, pity and fear, but they will see that these emotions are not justified in most circumstances. The result is a kind of economy of the passions, an attempt to re-calibrate human nature so that it comes closer to the ideal Nature from which both original sin and the corruptive degeneration of human institutions have alienated us.[11]

In Rapin and Dacier we see a retreat from the view that the tragic emotions—pity and fear—can themselves be instruments for moral improvement. Unlike Corneille, for example, who proposes the sequential experience of pity, fear, and improved spectator conduct, these later theorists do not develop the direct benefits of the emotions but instead stress the judgmental faculty by which we learn when to permit the emotions to be excited and to attach themselves to specific conducts. In the work of the later theorists, the foundations are being laid for the moralization of theater in *drame* and other eighteenth-century theatrical genres. Pity and fear, no longer excited by the paradoxes of complex moral situations, are to be directed separately at worthy objects after the apprenticeship of "vaines frayeurs."

From Horror to Pleasure

A third emotion that theorists of tragedy associate with tragedy is horror. The loose term *associate* is ample enough to include the directly opposite views of Bishop Jacques-Bénigne Bossuet and La Mesnardière. The former thinks that horror is exactly what the playwright should try to get the spectator to feel (if a Christian drama were possible—and Bossuet rejects all theater as a moral abomination), while La Mesnardière holds horror in utter contempt and denounces theorists who claim that horror, like terror (or in place of terror), is a legitimate tragic emotion. Bossuet writes,

> Quelle erreur de ne savoir pas distinguer entre l'art de représenter les mauvaises actions pour en inspirer de l'horreur, et celui de peindre les passions agréables d'une manière qui en fasse goûter le plaisir? Que s'il y a des histoires qui, dégénérant de la dignité d'un si beau nom, entrent, à l'exemple de la comédie, dans le dessein d'émouvoir les passions flatteuses; qui ne voit qu'il les faut ranger avec les romans et les autres livres corrupteurs de la vie humaine? ("Maximes et réflexions sur la comédie" 178)

In this view, the Christian is expected to feel repugnance for evil because evil is ugly in itself rather than to fear, for fear belongs to a nonmoral or immoral view of experience. Fear is caused by the demonstration of the earthly consequences of evil, which therefore appears as simply unwise conduct rather than as a violation of a transcendent divine ordinance. Yet there is another and even more powerful theoretical distinction implicit in Bossuet's views. Terror requires a certain identification of the audience with the characters, while horror suggests a radical refusal of identification. The fact that Bossuet thinks of horror, rather than fear (or terror), as an emotion that should properly be inspired in the audience is an indication of his rejection of Aristotle's *Poetics* as an apology for drama. Horror does not allow the spectator to identify with the characters and "taste" their pleasure or pain. Instead, the kind of non-Aristotelian or even anti-Aristotelian theory of representation that Bossuet outlines here aims at keeping the spectator outside the character's experience—a radical separation that anticipates Berthold Brecht's principle of estrangement of the audience. Bossuet wants the audience to find revolting the very acts and emotions in which the character finds pleasure. Therefore, in this Christian account of dramatic experience, to sympathize or empathize with the characters' pleasures and temptations as a precondition for fearing the necessary misfortune (or punishment) that ensues is too high a price and too great a risk in view of the dubious didactic value of drama.

By far the most elaborate discussion of horror as an audience emotion appears in La Mesnardière's *La poëtique,* where the theorist's vigorous efforts to deny tragic legitimacy to horror indicate how strongly the latter emotion was cultivated by stage writers in the early part of the century. The theorist is clearly fighting against a taste that he considers so widespread that he needs to mount a sustained attack against the legitimacy of horror. It is characteristic of La Mesnardière to try to ennoble tragedy and its audience, since his book, *La poëtique,* reacts against Castelvetro's popularizing commentary on Aristotle. Looking for ways to limit the audience of tragedy to princes and the aristocracy, La Mesnardière invokes the widespread system of values that sets the mind over the body and certain feelings above others—Descartes did this much more systematically and with more sophisticated physiology and anatomy nine years later in his *Passions de l'âme* (1649). In this perspective, terror is more noble, less closely linked to the body and its reflexes than horror.

Horror, on the other hand, has always been linked to the body. From the Latin *horrere,* "to bristle," to the definition of *horreur* in the *Robert,* "Impression causée par la vue ou la pensée d'une chose affreuse, et qui se traduit par un frémissement, un frisson, un mouvement de recul . . . ," horror designates the body's rather than the mind's reaction to some perception. The way horror is paired discursively in seventeenth-century writing leads quickly to the conclusion that particular kinds of visual stimuli lead to this physical reaction. Spectacle, as the domain of vision, has a privileged relationship to horror in the phrase *spectacles d'horreur* (the title of Jean Pierre Camus's popular 1630 collection of stories). D'Aubignac censures "ces Spectacles pleins d'horreur" (73) and La Mesnardière writes of certain actions in tragedies as *"Spectacles horribles . . . qui exposent à nos yeux des Actions detestables, qui nous font transsir d'horreur à l'aspect de leur cruauté"* (202; emphasis added). The particular kind of sight that produces horror is clear from the expression that Voltaire denounced as a cliché, "le carnage et l'horreur."[12] Horror is associated with carnage, with the injury and dismemberment of bodies. The perceiver's reaction is almost a form of empathy, communication from body to body that bypasses the veneer of civility or the specific narrative motivation of the physical assault that is witnessed to produce the physical symptoms of a personal involvement as participant.

Plays of the early seventeenth century included copious incidents of staged violence, including assault, dismemberment, and cannibalism. "Le goût du sang et des cadavres," as Jacques Scherer calls it, not only dominated much of the reign of Louis XIII, but resisted early attempts to remove such sights from the stage about the time of *Le Cid* (*La dramaturgie classique* 415). It is difficult for us to recall how widespread this practice was and therefore to account for the preoccupation—even the obsession—with carnage and horror in the theoretical writings of midcentury. Duels and combats are mild compared to the horrors catalogued by La Mesnardière, the theorist most absorbed by this issue: "les mouches s'attachent au corps . . . & sucent le sang de ses playes" (98), "les Gibets & les Roües . . . le spectacle des corps qui nagent dans leur propre sang . . ." (419), "Tantale y rostit ses enfants . . ." (222).

One of the major problems of theorists trying to impose greater decorum—the verisimilitude of characters—on French tragedy was the origin of tragedy itself as the historical legacy of a very different culture. Tragedy could not be rid of horror except to the extent that the physical enactment of certain crimes might be removed from the stage itself. In the plot and the words of the characters, horror remained as the basis of tragedy:

> Car il ne faut pas demander que les Personnes theatralles soient absolument vertueuses. La Scene reçoit les Tantales aussi bien que les Iasons, les Medées comme les Hecubes, les Phedres comme les Alcestes: Et puis qu'elle expose à toute heure de meschantes actions, & que les infidelitez, les incestes, les parricides & d'autres crimes de ce genre sont ses sujets ordinaires, il faut par necessité qu'elle admette des meschans, & qu'ils y paroissent revestus au moins de quelque partie de leurs mauvaises habitudes. (La Mesnardière 222)

There is a double problem here, wound together in this list. On one hand there is the relation between the tragic subject (or represented event) and its historical or fabulous basis. On the other, there is the relationship between the culture of seventeenth-century France and its bonds to the past, both classical and postclassical.

The struggle for decorum is, in part, a battle of modernity against the horror of antiquity.[13] D'Aubignac notes the role of ancient practice in shaping what is meant by tragedy: "parce que les Tragédies ont eu souvent des Catastrophes infortunées, ou par la rencontre des histoires, ou par la complaisance des Poëtes envers les Atheniens, qui ne haïssoit pas ces objets d'horreur sur leur Theatre . . . plusieurs se sont imaginés que le mot de *Tragique* ne signifioit jamais qu'une avanture funeste et sanglante . . ." (143). The project of seventeenth-century poetics was not to replicate but to correct the tragedy of the ancients. As La Mesnardière proclaims boldly, "nous n'avons pas entrepris de . . . montrer de quelle sorte ont écrit les vieux Tragiques, mais de . . . faire comprendre comment ils ont deu écrire" (219). The struggle against horror was an attack therefore on the history of tragedy, on its theory and practice, but also on history itself in the sense of an account of political events. Horror was contained in the "rencontre des histoires" as well as in the taste of the Greek audience. The terrifying paradox, for the modern—that is, seventeenth-century—mind facing the ancient requirements of tragedy was that the *personae* of tragedy had to be princes and kings and yet the actions of tragedy had to be serious faults, mistakes, or crimes. These elements seemed incompatible, for whether the prince was mistaken or criminal (and thus logically or justly punished) or whether the prince was the victim of actions (and thus insufficiently strong or astute to avoid social disorder and harm), boundaries were crossed that, for the contemporaries of Richelieu or Louis XIV, threatened the confidence in the structure of society itself.

The "Spectacles pleins d'horreur" that d'Aubignac describes as impermissible for his contemporaries are very specifically violence done to kings: "nous ne voulons point croire que les Roys puissent estre meschans, ni souffrir que leurs Sujets, quoy qu'en apparence maltraittez, touchent leurs Personnes sacrees, ny se rebellent contre leur Puissance, non pas mesme en peinture; et je ne croy pas que l'on puisse faire assassiner un Tyran sur nostre Theatre avec applaudissement, sans de tres-signalées précautions . . ." (73). Horror therefore calls into question the very body of the king and traces the boundary where social disorder passes into physical disintegration. The other principal social structure that is affected by horror is the family, whose disaggregation is made manifest by the misuse, penetration, dismemberment, and incorporation of bodies—incest, parricide, cannibalism. These, the "sujets ordinaires" of Greek and Roman tragedy, must in some way be deflected, covered, repressed for the modern audience.

Yet even in the middle and late seventeenth century, horror and tragedy were frequently associated. A dictionary illustration of the figurative use of the word *tragédie* includes the revealing sentences "Il se jouë quelquefois d'horribles tragedies en ceste cour-là. il [sic] s'y est joüé une sanglante tragedie" (*Dictionnaire de l'Académie*). Furetière illustrates the use of the word *horreur* with the sentence "La Tragedie doit exciter de l'*horreur,* ou de la pitié, selon Aristote." This frank admission of tragedy's aim to excite horror encountered opposition in one of the major texts of dramatic theory in the seventeenth century, La Mesnardière's *Poëtique,* in which the author pronounces himself strongly against horror in tragedy, distinguishing horror from terror and pity, the desirable emotions. Engaging in a lengthy philological argument, La Mesnardière proclaims that Aristotle designated terror and compassion the passions of a perfect tragedy, "sans jamais parler de l'horreur, ce sentiment odieux, & fort inutile au Theatre" (22).

Because La Mesnardière gives more attention to horror than do other major theorists of tragedy, it is worth considering at length the problems horror poses for his view of tragedy and the definitions and restrictions he sets forth. He follows Aristotle's lead in attempting to define tragedy largely on the basis of the emotions awakened in the spectator. Citing Aristotle's claim that tragedy should produce *eleos* or *phobos,* which he translates as *compassion* and *terreur,* La Mesnardière comments that terror is useful because it inspires repentance: "la juste Terreur excitée dans les esprits par les peines des criminels, produit un effet profitable, par le repentir qu'elle inspire aux vicieux" (22). This description of the useful emotion, *phobos,* distinguishes the effect produced in the mind from the presumably physical suffering inflicted on criminals. A series of relays is established between the physical and the mental or spiritual, and *phobos* is attached to this "higher" faculty. A second distinction made implicitly by La Mesnardière is that between the past and the future. In the case of the criminals, both their misdeeds and their apprehension for those misdeeds are past, whereas the *vicieux* who watch or hear of the punishments have either not yet committed the crimes to which they are inclined or have not yet been caught. The fear awakened in them would be forward-looking and useful in preventing crime. These distinctions, though implicit in La Mesnardière's first approach to the problem, are important for the understanding of his complaints about the translation of *phobos* into *horror* by Aristotle's Latin interpreters. *Horror,* according to La Mesnardière, means "Crainte & Horreur," whereas Aristotle meant only to signify *crainte* (33). La Mesnardière thus pushes horror away, though without explicitly defining it, while he promotes fear as a useful spiritual and didactic concept: "la sagesse commence par la crainte du Seigneur." La Mesnardière's task of purifying *phobos*/fear of its associations with the repulsive, sensualistic, and physical horror is not an easy one. Over several pages he complicates his task by admitting that the Greek poets misuse their own language by confusing horror with a "follie semblable à l'Enthousiasme" (24). He admits further that

Aristotle uses the verb *phrittein* "qui signifie *frissonner* . . . qui exprime le Frisson attaché à certaines fiévres, & d'où sans doute est venu le *Frigere* des Latins, qui a fait nostre mot François." *Phobos* makes us shiver, but is not the "sentiment meslé de dégoust, de mépris & d'aversion" designated by *horror*.

In this tangle of distinctions, La Mesnardière resorts next to a moral criterion. Horror is provoked in the spectator by a scale of ethical values: "nous ressentons proprement ce que nous appellons Horreur, lors que nous voyons commettre une cruauté detestable, une infame trahison, ou quelque semblable bassesse, qui offense nôtre esprit sans épouvanter nôtre cœur" (25). Horror affects the mind or *esprit* of a spectator but does not produce fear. The type of affect induced by horror is somewhat unclear. Horrible spectacles *offend* the mind, whereas earlier they are said to provoke disgust, scorn, and aversion. It would be clear to La Mesnardière's readers that horror as moral offense and as disgust is based on the refinement of the viewer's sensibility and moral standards, since the opening comments of the *Poëtique* are explicit in stating that only those of elevated social station can appreciate tragedy, which the people will never understand (N–P). Utility and pleasure—*le profit et la volupté*—are one for the refined spectator. Horror is therefore both disagreeable to such a person and ethically offensive. Terror, on the other hand, is highly desirable. La Mesnardière counsels to

> bien émouvoir la Terreur; Et si la Fable qu'il expose, finit par la punition de la Personne detestable, il doit dépeindre en ses supplices de si effroyables tourmens, & de si cuisans remors, qu'il n'y ait point de Spectateur coupable du mesme crime, ou disposé à le commetre, qui ne tremble de frayeur lors qu'il entendra les plaintes, les cris & les hurlemens qu'arrachent des maux si sensibles au criminel qui les endure. . . . Pour représenter ces tourmens, qu'il s'imagine vivement les douleurs d'un Ixion attaché sur une roüe, & celles d'un Promethée enchaisné sur un rocher, où un Vautour affamé lui vient déchirer les entrailles. . . . (99–100)

The boundary—difficult as it is to recognize in the sensory manifestations—between the horrible and the terrible is drawn with a view to the situation of the aristocratic audience. Terror should induce repentance in the vicious; it should "épouvanter

61

notre cœur." The events represented in tragedy should frighten princes: "Les Princes doivent seuls estre effrayez des disgraces de leurs semblables, qui sont sévèrement punis pour leurs méchantes actions . . ." (N). Horror is not fear, argues La Mesnardière, and therefore will not alter the conduct of the prince. It does not hold forth an idea of what is going to happen to him. Horror is, then, in a sense, provoked by events without historical significance, since horror does not awaken the comparative and mimetic response through which princes learn to avoid falling into the crimes of similar princes. This, rather, is the effect of tragic terror.

La Mesnardière's difficulties in defining and containing horror reveal, however, that this concept is indissolubly linked with spectacle. Horror is provoked "lorsque nous *voyons* commettre une cruauté detestable . . ." (25; emphasis added). Second, horror marks the boundary of some form of tolerance, the point at which repulsion replaces desire or temptation. Third, horror is not connected to the *interest* of the spectator in the sense that he or she has something at stake. Terror or fear (*phobos*) proposes some interchange between spectator and spectacle, offers, that is, some chance that what is seen happening might happen in turn to the viewer. In this respect we could read La Mesnardière's horror as offering an aesthetic experience to the extent that the aesthetic, a category not invoked by thinkers of La Mesnardière's time, offers a disinterested experience of perception. Although La Mesnardière does not speak of the "aesthetic," he does situate horror beyond both the pleasurable and the useful, thus conferring on it a quality that resembles the "aesthetic distance" of later criticism. Indeed, La Mesnardière's horror is akin to the sublime of the later seventeenth century.

Distancing horror and disconnecting it from the spectator's own fate does not mean removing the physical destruction that may be associated with horror. We should be careful not to confuse La Mesnardière's position with what we retrospectively define as appropriate in French classical theater. It would be easy to assume that he simply banished violence from the stage. Instead, he classifies deaths, or "Spectacles funestes," into three types: generous, horrible, and hazardous spectacles. All three involve the staged representation of some potentially mortal action. La Mesnardière actually recommends that death be enacted onstage when it is *généreux*. For instance, he praises

"la mort d'un jeune Prince, qui aprés mille regrets capables d'arracher des larmes des cœurs les plus insensibles, se tuë genereusement auprés du corps de sa Maitresse" (206). Likewise, it seems proper to him that in Seneca's *Phaedra,* the queen should die onstage: "peut-on la voir mourir auprés du corps de ce Prince par un supplice volontaire, sans concevoir de la Terreur qui corrige puissamment les ames incestueuses de l'inclination qu'elles ont à ces detestables Amours?" (207). His impassioned defense of staged deaths leads him to praise enactments of suicides, death by lightning, ax-murder, and the crushing of children. Defending the ancients against Castelvetro, La Mesnardière writes:

> nous lui découvrirons Que des dix Poëmes tragiques que les Latins nous ont laissez, il en détruit les six plus beaux, où la Scene est ensanglantée. Phedre s'y tuë dans *l'Hippolyte* en la presence de Thesée, & de tous ceux qui la contemplent. Megare & ses deux enfans sont écrasez aux yeux du Peuple dans *l'Hercule furieux.* Le desespoir d'Iocaste ensanglante le Theatre dans *la merveilleuse Edipe.* Hercule expire sur la Scene au sommet *du mont Œta.* Une Mere dénaturée massacre l'un de ses enfans à la veuë de tout le monde.... (208)

Such murders and suicides are supposed to be agreeable to the spectator for mimetic reasons; they provide examples for reenactment: "Il faut sans doute avoüer que les meurtres de cette espece n'ont rien qui ne soit agreable, ni mesme qui ne soit utile; & qu'ils ne mettent dans les ames que des exemples vertueux d'un repentir plein de justice, qui merite d'estre imité pour le moins dans les sentimens, puis qu'on n'en doit pas imiter les genereuses actions" (La Mesnardière 207).

La Mesnardière tempers his fervor for staged murders for practical and ethical reasons. One practical reason to avoid murders onstage is that it is sometimes difficult and dangerous to carry them out. Hazardous spectacles risk the lives of the actors (202). A second practical reason for not staging such scenes as the crushing of Megara and her children is that the machinery for death and torture may be more comical than tragic: "On ne met point au Theatre les espées, les gibets, les roües, le feu ... il est tres-difficile d'imiter ces bourrelleries sans que la feinte en soit grossiere, & par consequent ridicule" (205).

The other grounds for banishing certain murders from the stage can be termed ethical, and are joined to La Mesnardière's campaign against horror: "ne pouvant fournir que des exemples detestables de parricides & de meurtres accompagnez de cruauté, il n'excite dans les esprits qu'un transsissement odieux & une horreur desagreable, qui surmontent infiniment la Terreur & la Pitié qui doivent regner l'une ou l'autre . . . dans une parfaite Tragedie" (204). In contrast to the *généreux* spectacles of murder and suicide, which offer models of noble conduct, horror overwhelms the pity and terror that are based on what we would call identification. Horror paralyzes the beholders, makes them *transis*. It seems that horrible spectacles appeal solely to our sense of the present rather than permitting the mental imitation of beautiful murders in which we project them into our own first-person future. The playwright's challenge is not so much to eliminate horror totally from tragedy as to place it at an appropriate remove in order to temper horror's precedence over the other emotions.

La Mesnardière's preoccupation with horror seems to lead him into gratuitous multiplication of examples of the kind of act that is repulsive enough to provoke this emotion: "cette Mere qui trempa les mains dans le sang de ceux qu'elle avoit engendrez . . . l'execrable Atrée ne rostit pas ses Neveux à la vue des Spectateurs. Pyrrhus . . . n'a pas assez d'impudence pour égorger en plein Théâtre la pitoyable Polyxene . . ." (204–05). Many of these examples concern visual representation as opposed to verbal representation of horrible acts in theatrical narrative. He blames Seneca for having placed Medea's infanticide onstage rather than offstage, yet La Mesnardière does not question the necessity for the acts themselves to be part of the tragic plot. He therefore reinforces the idea that horror is a fundamental component of ancient tragedy. Horror, it seems, cannot be eliminated, but by being placed out of sight it can be removed both from our presence and our present. The horrible deed that occurs offstage returns only in the past (and the past tense), relayed by a character. The character is exposed to the horrible and may feel horror, but the spectator does not. This arrangement for relaying the information about the horrible event without provoking revulsion lends support to what Spitzer called the "klassische Dämpfung."

Yet, however much relegating horrible acts offstage may attenuate this paralyzing effect, it seems impossible to theorize about tragedy without repeatedly encountering horror. La Mesnardière lists horror as one of several emotions that can be used in tragedy: "l'horreur, l'amour, la jalousie, l'ambition, l'envie & la haine, & d'autres pareils mouvements, peuvent encore estre employés dans nostre Poëme tragique" (104). Toward the end of *La poëtique,* La Mesnardière seems to be sufficiently troubled by his own recurrent appeal to horror to feel that he must redeem the emotion somehow. It seems that there are, after all, two kinds of horror, one good and one bad. Good horror confirms the spectator in his or her sense of superiority. This horror is "une Passion qui nous fait abhorrer le vice par une haine constante, vertueuse, & qui nous plaist; à cause que nous sçavons bien que nous sommes fort raisonnables dans un si juste sentiment" (324). The other horror is the familiar paralysis that is, throughout, associated with disgust, "un mouvement plein de dégoust & d'aversion, qui offense & blesse nôtre ame, pour peu qu'elle soit généreuse; pour ce qu'elle ne peut souffrir ni l'excés de la perfidie, ni celui de la cruauté qui causent ce transsissement" (324). Not surprisingly, both forms of horror reveal the spectator's condition of moral virtue and good taste. The distinction seems to be primarily a matter of the spectator's pleasure at the revulsion he or she feels. We can even suppose that the two kinds of horror are the same horror expressed in different ways, since it is a pleasure to have sufficient *générosité* to be offended. The second horror is the price to pay as proof of one's taste. The issue that remains open is what is bearable yet sufficiently *méchant* to provoke the audience's abhorrence.

The line between the acceptable and the excessively horrible is even harder to maintain when La Mesnardière describes as exemplary of good tragedy a crime that has all the qualities elsewhere censured: atrocity, blood, parricide, cruelty, and odiousness. Describing Euripides's *Electra,* La Mesnardière praises the perpetrators' description of their atrocity in killing their mother:

> Aprés avoir raconté comment la Reine leur Mere ouvrit sa
> gorge devant eux pour émouvoir à pitié ceux qu'elle avoit
> mis au monde; Aprés avoir repeté les Raisons qu'elle avança

> pour condamner leur dessein, les prieres qu'elle fist pour
> détourner leur cruauté, le pardon qu'elle demanda pour adou-
> cir leur fureur: Bref aprés avoir retouché les pitoyables cir-
> constances d'une action si barbare, ils éxagerent eux-mesmes
> l'atrocité de ce forfait, pour se rendre plus odieux et moins
> dignes de compassion. (232)

The praise La Mesnardière heaps on this example is partly justified by the conversion of horror into terror. If horror is the immediate revulsion felt by the wellborn for atrocities, then the
repentance of Electra and Orestes demonstrates the passage from
an immediate, temporally present experience to a past-and-
future-oriented act of fear and shame. Looking now upon the
act they have committed, they fear the consequences of their
act for the future. This temporalization can be seized in the terms
honte and *terreur,* the sentiments that now dominate them. La
Mesnardière accentuates the shift in time, the stark contrast
between the son's and daughter's feelings before and after their
deed: "Ils sont enfin si effrayez de leur sanglante execution,
qu'ils ne peuvent supporter la seule veuë de ce corps qu'ils
cherchaient avec tant d'ardeur avant que de l'avoir tué . . ."
(232).

Horror, as disgust and aversion, appears as the reverse and
complement of corporal desire. Horror is reverse eros. Like the
erotic, the horrible is fixated on the body, and in tragedy both
horror and eros are in some way placed outside the bounds of
"normal" physical relations. In *Electra* Orestes and Electra
ardently seek the body of their mother, which is partially un-
dressed for them before they dismember it. After their mother's
death they still relate to her physically in an abnormal way.
Excessive interest in her body, which they will mutilate, gives
way to excessive revulsion for that body. Like eros, horror concerns viewing bodies and the effect that view has on the physical
sensations of the viewer. What makes Euripides's work acceptable to La Mesnardière is the movement beyond that fixation
toward fear, *phobos.*

Orestes and Electra serve as mediators between horror and
terror in two ways. First, they experience horror themselves at
sights and acts that would provoke horror in any *généreux* spectator. By experiencing this sentiment themselves, within the
world of the tragedy, they seem to discharge a function of dis-

approval that otherwise would have been passed on to the audience. Horror seems acceptable and even praiseworthy when it is *performed*. Therefore, within the tragic spectacle, it is rather the *horrible* than *horror* itself that should be banished or at least contained.

A modern reader—as, perhaps, also a seventeenth-century reader—can surely be forgiven for not always being able to distinguish in the *Poëtique* between good terror and bad horror. There is a certain unpredictability to the classification. Although one can find consistency in the *a posteriori* arguments by which La Mesnardière justifies the category in which he places his examples, it seems unlikely that one could learn from the *Poëtique* to determine in advance how other examples would fit. La Mesnardière himself trips up occasionally, by ending descriptions of terror with a phrase like "mais sortons de ces horreurs."[14]

It does not seem far-fetched to suppose that, despite La Mesnardière's repeated attempts to deny it, horror is the fundamental tragic sentiment. Indeed, precisely because it is fundamental, La Mesnardière tries to find ways to preserve horror within a didactic, Horatian view of tragedy. As a result, the erotic and horrific fixation on bodies, on their members, and on blood has to be connected to the instructional purpose that recuperates these acts for historical knowledge. If La Mesnardière had been able to dispense altogether with horror, he would not have had to devote so much of his text to terror nor would he have invented the categories of good horror and of the *spectacles généreux*. In order to enjoy the spectacles of carnage and of cruelty in tragedy, La Mesnardière creates his elaborate and confusing system of relays through which horror is converted to terror within tragedy rather than being passed directly to the audience. In this way an ethical framework is created to veil horror in a kind of translucence so that it can be enjoyed while absolving the audience from any responsibility for the acts committed before them.

Much of the difficulty of describing horror in a consistent manner comes from the *a priori* definition of the tragic audience as limited to princes. Because the spectator as well as the *personae* of tragedy are wellborn and politically important and because the usefulness of tragedy consists of teaching applicable lessons to such an audience, an emotion that transcends class distinctions is suspect from La Mesnardière's point of view. La Mesnardière never specifically denies that the common people may feel horror, but it is clear that they cannot feel tragic terror. Terror requires the spectator to identify sufficiently with the dramatic character to fear that the same fate awaits him or her. The common people therefore have nothing to fear from the fate of princes or princesses. Horror also, at times, seems to be related to class. The wellborn are repelled by certain spectacles because of their highly refined sensibilities. Could horror be described as the noble recognition of a common humanity in which nobility yields to a class-free penchant for destruction? Or is it rather a recognition of the way the conduct of princes, with its privilege of violence subject only to the fragile regulation of self-control, must appear to the masses?

What distinguishes La Mesnardière's approach to the conservation of horror in an age of politeness is his willingness to represent spectacles of death and other physical degradation onstage. He does not recommend routinely the technique of visual concealment that characterizes most of Cornelian and Racinian theater. La Mesnardière attempts instead to use nonvisual screening procedures to frame horror into an ethically acceptable form. In the process of doing this, he emphasizes its importance for a seventeenth-century sensibility, and thus invites us to look again at the tragedy of the period. Tending to ignore the horrible, twentieth-century readers accentuate the relays or mediators that are carefully placed near the horrible, but not necessarily in such a way as to conceal it altogether. Whether it be the needle that Dorise thrusts into the eye of her assailant in *Clitandre,* the wound through which the valor of the deceased Don Gomès speaks to his daughter Chimène in *Le Cid,* or the bloody grass that testifies to the complete physical destruction of Hippolytus in *Phèdre,* acts or sights that can be expected to awaken disgust and aversion are common in seventeenth-century theater. This horror is an aspect of classical drama that deserves more substantial recognition.

Another important emotion (the term is, perhaps, too broad) required of tragedy by French classical theorists, as well as by Aristotle, is pleasure. Aristotle had stated that "the poet ought to provide the pleasure which derives from pity and fear" (46).

We all are aware of the debates concerning the purpose of tragedy during the seventeenth century and know that few theorists openly proclaimed the pleasure of the spectator as the goal of tragedy.[15] However, all major theorists considered pleasure necessary for tragedy to reach its aim, even if that aim was instruction or moral improvement. Even the dour and blunt Dacier writes "nous détruirons ce faux préjugé, que tout ce qui plaît est bon" and that he will replace it with the true precept "que tout ce qui est bon plaît, ou doit plaire" (6a). Racine implicitly sets forth a certain kind of pleasure as being of the essence of tragedy when he writes of "cette tristesse majestueuse qui fait tout le plaisir de la tragédie" (preface to *Bérénice, Théâtre complet* 324).

Pity and fear are supposed to be stimulated in spectators, with the goal of creating a third emotion, pleasure. In fact, however, this tripartite scheme does not advance understanding of exactly what spectators were feeling and how these different emotions are related to one another. The actual emotional impact of tragedy on the audience was not analyzed in terms of the *type* or quality of emotion but rather in terms of its *quantity*. Here emotion disrupts the language of the theorists just as it will disrupt the language of the characters in tragedy. Racine frequently makes comments that show how the quantitative replaces other descriptive standards. As early as the preface to *La Thébaïde,* he writes that the catastrophe of his own play is "un peu trop sanglante; en effet, il n'y paraît presque pas un acteur qui ne meure à la fin: mais aussi c'est la Thébaïde, c'est-à-dire le sujet le plus tragique de l'antiquité" (*Théâtre complet* 11). The excess of blood, the excess of death, is justified by the quantity of "tragicness." There is a relation between the *trop* of the accumulated deaths and the superlative *le plus tragique* that results from those deaths. Racine does not specify the emotion produced, because the emotion appears indescribable except to say that it is tragic, and the tragic requires excess in some way.[16] Racine repeatedly affirms that tragedy not only requires emotion but "la violence des passions," which he mentions twice in the preface to *Bérénice* (324, 325). Again Racine associates uncontrollable weeping with the essence of tragedy in the preface to *Iphigénie,* when he writes "Mes spectateurs ont été émus des mêmes choses qui ont mis autrefois en larmes le plus savant peuple de la Grèce, et qui ont fait dire qu'entre les poètes, Euripide était extrêmement tragique, *tra-gikotatos,* c'est-à-dire qu'il avait merveilleusement excité la compassion et la terreur, qui sont les véritables effets de la tragédie" (*Théâtre complet* 511). Despite the concluding return to the strictly traditional duality (pity and fear), it is significant that Racine twice resorts to quantity to describe the role of emotion in tragedy. First, the emotion produced by the fable of Iphigenia is gauged as overwhelmingly strong because the most learned people of Greece could not refrain from weeping. Somehow, Racine implies, it would take a stronger emotional provocation to get Athenians to weep than it would to produce the same reaction in another, less learned (or intellectual) people. Second, the extreme tragic quality of Euripides's work is linked to that playwright's ability to produce emotion in the audience.

Racine, however, is far from being the only author who emphasizes the amount and strength of audience emotion that tragedy should elicit. La Mesnardière promotes passion under the general term "Troubles de l'Ame" as the "premiere beauté de la Poësie Dramatique . . . *Ce sont des sentimens pleins de tristesse et de douleur, dont nôtre ame est agitée à la réception des Objets que le Poëme lui fournit, soit par l'oreille, ou par les yeux, quand il fait voir ou qu'il raconte quelques Actions pitoyables*" (70; italics in original text). Georges de Scudéry claims that "Le Poete . . . se propose pour sa fin, d'esmouvoir les passions de l'Auditeur, par celle des Personnages" (*Observations sur le Cid* 75). Chapelain also writes that "les passions violentes bien exprimées, font souvent en ceux qui les voyent une partie de l'effect, qu'elles font en ceux qui les ressentent veritablement. Elles ostent à tous la liberté de l'esprit . . ." (*Sentimens* 414). The performance of the play onstage should not be required for the tragedy to reach its goal of making the audience weep. La Mesnardière, perfectly Aristotelian in setting the plot or tragic subject above all other aspects of the tragedy, chooses emotion as the touchstone of the quality of a tragic plot:

> j'estime avec Aristote, qu'un Ouvrage est imparfait, lorsque par la seule lecture faite dans un cabinet, il n'excite pas les Passions dans l'Esprit de ses Auditeurs, et qui'il ne les agite point jusques à les faire trembler, ou à leur arracher des larmes. (12)

Far from offering a more distant, reasoned, and controlled response to the tragic plot, the reading experience serves as an example of the pure essence of tragedy in its affect, reaching beyond the theatrical contrivances to dethrone reason by the power of the plot alone.

We saw, above, that pity, fear, and pleasure are the "official" emotions of tragedy. These are not the only emotions mentioned in the treatises on tragedy, but they are the principal ones that the tragedy was supposed to provoke in the audience. In addition, both the characters and the audience are usually presumed to have many other emotions. The cathartic purpose of tragedy is aimed, in the view of most theorists, at emotions displayed by the dramatic characters and concealed by the audience: anger, pride, ambition, jealousy, envy, hatred, and sexual desires are among those assigned to tragic characters. If the "official"—though not necessarily the theoretically favored—purpose of stimulating the emotions of the audience is to purge the audience of certain emotions, then it is very important to try to understand the relation between the characters' emotions and those of the spectators.

One widespread theoretical model holds that purgation takes place because the characters and the spectators have the same emotions. Many spectators, as this theory claims, secretly wish to kill a member of their family or to seduce or rape their daughter, mother, son, father, or sibling. Seeing the enactment of their sinful desire and witnessing the consequent punishment produces fear in such members of the audience. This dominant model of tragic purgation of emotion stresses fear—in fact, despite the almost incantatory repetition of the phrases "pitié et crainte" and "compassion et terreur," there are few explanations of how pity causes a morally improving emotional purgation.

In a passage quoted earlier from La Mesnardière, we saw that the audience was meant to include persons with a disposition toward vice; this is the proper spectator for tragedy, since only in such a spectator can tragedy have its cathartic effect of frightening "le vicieux, coupable du mesme crime" (26). An important word here is "coupable," which Corneille replaces with "capable" in arguing that purgation, if it worked, would result from uprooting (*déraciner*) the vices that are latent in our disposition, not displayed in our acts (3: 145). Corneille, trying to find some theoretical basis for the conception of a tragedy that is mimetic of elements of collective unconscious or of collective latency, does not require the audience to have felt the passions that are to be purged but only to recognize their possibility. La Mesnardière, on the other hand, insists on the passions that have reached the conscious or semiconscious level in the spectator, without fearing to limit the audience for tragedy. As he observes, depraved spectators outnumber "les ames les plus parfaites, qui sont fort rares dans les villes" (20).

In the course of the century, the movement from "coupable" to "capable" is quite plain in the theory of tragic instruction. Racine goes even further than Corneille in the preface of *Phèdre,* that turning point that marks the extreme limit of any attempt to reconcile profane tragedy with official Christian morality. Or rather than a movement from guilt to capability, Racine holds out a vision in which "capable" and "coupable" are the same:

> Les moindres fautes y sont sévèrement punies; la seule pensée du crime y est regardée avec autant d'horreur que le crime même; les faiblesses de l'amour y passent pour de vraies faiblesses; les passions n'y sont présentées aux yeux que pour montrer tout le désordre dont elles sont cause; et le vice y est peint partout avec des couleurs qui en font connaître et haïr la difformité. (*Théâtre complet* 578)

In this view, spectators and characters share the same passions to the extent that they have *any* passions; passion itself is bad since it creates disorder. Racine balances between showing the intrinsically repellent aspect of passion through the staging of horror (a position similar to Bossuet's) and showing the extrinsic effect of terror brought about by the punishment of characters with whom the audience can identify.

Both Racine and Corneille refer to the punishment that follows violations of the law and thus link this crucial component of seventeenth-century catharsis theory to its political foundation. Poetry, and most of all, dramatic poetry, has been cyclically under attack since Plato, and, as Corneille observes, Aristotle invented catharsis in a political gesture and "a voulu trouver cette utilité dans ces agitations de l'âme, pour les rendre recommandables par la raison même, sur qui l'autre [Plato] se fonde pour les bannir" (3: 146). Catharsis serves as an inversion mechanism, turning the very thing that makes tragedy bad, good. In doing so, however, as we can see in seventeenth-century theory, the term *agitations de l'âme* has two radically different meanings. What we can call the pre-Aristotelian meaning, in Corneille's view, is a direct mimetic propagation from the characters to the spectators. In direct propagation, the emotional experience of theater was mimetic in an apparently reversed fashion, a mimesis in the second degree. The actors imitated bad actions, and the audience was stirred emotionally to imitate the actors. Scudéry alleges that in Plato's day the pleasure of mimesis was enjoyed without regard to good or bad morals:

> il arrivoit de là, que les esprits des Spectateurs, estoient des-
> bauchez par cette volupté; qu'ils trouvoient autant de plaisir
> a imiter les mauvaises actions, qu'ils voyoient representées
> avecques grace, et ou nostre nature incline, que les bonnes,
> qui nous semblent difficiles. (*Observations sur le Cid* 81)

This direct propagation model of the dramatic experience is countered by the cathartic model through which the instrumental emotions of pity and fear invert the desirable into the fearful. Rather than experience with the tragic character an incestuous passion, the spectator is meant to be terrified by the result and leave the theater with an inverted disposition. Using this model, we can see that it matters little what emotions the characters represent—ambition, jealousy, hatred, desire—since they will all be ground up and composted in the cathartic mechanism that can generate only two emotional states, pity and fear.

The concept of the "agitations de l'âme" that Corneille locates in the Aristotelian defense of tragedy really consists of two concepts, the Platonic propagation of passion and the Aristotelian inversion of passion. Corneille himself did not subscribe to the idea of catharsis. His comments on *Le Cid* persuasively show that spectators apparently did not leave the theater having experienced the conversion of the emotion of passionate love into sheer terror at the thought of falling in love (3: 146). The experience of *Le Cid* was an intensely emotional one for the spectators, all theorists agree, but it did not provide catharsis.

Instead, *Le Cid* serves as an excellent example for the partisans of an antitragic, anticathartic view of drama, notably Bossuet, who returns to a direct propagation model of dramatic emotion:

> que veut Corneille, dans son *Cid,* sinon qu'on aime Chimène,
> qu'on l'adore avec Rodrigue, qu'on tremble avec lui lorsqu'il
> est dans la crainte de la perdre, et qu'avec lui on s'estime
> heureux lorsqu'il espère de la posséder? Si l'auteur d'une
> tragédie ne sait pas intéresser le spectateur, l'émouvoir, le
> transporter de la passion qu'il a voulu exprimer, où tombe-
> t-il, si ce n'est dans le froid, dans l'ennuyeux, dans l'insu-
> portable, si on peut parler de cette sorte? ("Lettre" 124)

In this remarkable passage, Bossuet writes one of the most elo-
quent evocations of the doctrine of dramatic illusion, so dear
to Chapelain, La Mesnardière, and d'Aubignac, while discarding
altogether the Aristotelian or neo-Aristotelian doctrine of catharsis. "Fear" only appears in this account when the dramatic
character feels fear, and the spectator otherwise is played like
an instrument by the gifted playwright. Bossuet's depiction of
the spectator's emotional experience resembles closely, in a
more effective style, La Mesnardière's enumeration of the one-
to-one emotional communication of character to audience: "il
s'afflige quand elle pleure; il est gay lors qu'elle est contente"
(74). Far from limiting himself to the two official, instrumental emotions, the dramatist runs through a complete gamut. The
third major theoretical emotion of Aristotelian poetics, pleasure, appears in the negative here in Bossuet's description, as
its absence—"le froid . . . l'ennuyeux"—and Bossuet displays
his distress at this admission that he is aware of dramatic pleasure.
Bossuet and Corneille seem to have a very similar view of dramatic emotion, since both believe that the spectator identifies
with the character and feels at least some of the same emotions.

Like the early Racine and like La Mesnardière, Bossuet also
sees the excess of passion and the absence of reason as qualities of tragedy:

> les discours, qui tendent directement à allumer de telles
> flammes, qui excitent la jeunesse à aimer, comme si elle
> n'était pas assez insensée, qui lui font envier le sort des
> oiseaux et des bêtes, que rien ne trouble dans leurs passions,
> et se plaindre de la raison et de la pudeur si importunes et
> si contraignantes . . . ("Lettre" 126)

The experience of inversion, through which the flames of passion become hell's flames, simply never takes place in Bossuet's

view. The Port-Royal moralist author Pierre Nicole agrees entirely with this assessment of tragedy and theater in general as an *école de vice* (219), where the spectators lose their civilized inhibition in regard to passionate love. They leave the theater ready to experience the "désordres horribles" of love:

> il n'y a rien de plus dangereux que de l'exciter, de la nourrir, et de détruire ce qui la tient en bride. . . . Or ce qui y sert le plus est une certaine horreur que la coutume et la bonne éducation en impriment, et rien ne diminue davantage cette horreur que la comédie et les romans, parceque cette passion y paroît avec honneur, et d'une maniere qui, au-lieu de la rendre horrible, est capable au-contraire de la faire aimer; elle y paroît sans honte et sans infamie; on y fait gloire d'en être touché; ainsi l'esprit s'y apprivoise peu à peu; on apprend à la souffrir et à en parler; et l'ame s'y laisse ensuite doucement aller, en suivant la pente de la nature. (221)

Working within the climate of the antitheatrical movement so forcefully championed by Bossuet and Nicole, Racine made a last attempt to give a utilitarian and Christian foundation to the emotional experience of tragedy. In the preface to *Phèdre,* Racine does not count on a cathartic mechanism that uses the raw onstage emotion as an instrument for purging the audience in some way. Rather than invoke catharsis, Racine simply extends the direct propagation model of emotional response, supposing that the audience experiences *exactly* what the characters experience. In this theory, the characters must themselves have some sort of conversion that will prefigure and guide the improved moral dispositions of the spectators. Phaedra, as heroine, "est engagée, par sa destinée et par la colère des dieux, dans une passion illégitime, dont elle a horreur toute la première" (*Théâtre complet* 577). It is highly significant that Racine should use the term *horror* rather than *terror* or fear in this account. Horror is quite different from fear and does not depend on structuring the plot so that the evil are punished. While Phaedra and Hippolytus *are* guilty and punished, the fear syllogism that most theorists propose (the hero was a parricide; he was punished ∴ I hate my father; I will be punished) depends on a series of events from which a pattern can be derived for future application. This view divides the two instrumental emotions temporally: the character's acts are past and provoke the spectators' pity for the character; the spectators' actions are projected into the future and we feel fear for ourselves (Corneille 3: 149).

Terror is thus projected forward from the guilty act and belongs entirely to the audience. Horror is a visceral reaction, which both character and audience can feel. Rather than being purged of that emotion, in Racine's account, we fill ourselves with it in imitation of Phaedra, who has it "toute la première." An emotion that La Mesnardière tried vigorously to remove from the experience of tragedy returns to replace terror later in the century in both Racine's and Bossuet's descriptions of tragic emotion.

Suppressing Reason, Disrupting Language

With the possible exception of Corneille (and, oddly, Scudéry), the theorists insist heavily on eliminating reason from tragedy, both in the tragic world onstage and in the auditorium. Whether passion is a good thing, as La Mesnardière (74) and d'Aubignac (298) consider it, or a bad thing, as Bossuet ("Lettre" 130 ff.) judges it, emotion raging out of control characterizes tragedy. Most theorists not only accept the dominance of emotion over judgment but provide precise instructions to the playwright to avoid the intrusion of reason. Therefore, reasoning activity by the characters should be avoided as well as anything that can cause the spectators to begin to think. Among faults of the first type—characters who are too rational—are the inclusion of deliberative meetings, maxims, or other direct didactic utterances, and types of characters given to intellection, such as philosophers. Within the tragic plot the triumph of reason over passion is as theoretically unacceptable as the triumph of vice over virtue:

> le Theatre doit estre instructif au public par la seule connoissance des choses representées, et j'ay toûjours remarqué, qu'on ne souffre pas aisément sur le Theatre qu'un homme égaré du droit chemin de la vertu, rentre en son devoir par de beaux preceptes qu'on luy vient débiter: on veut que ce soit par quelque avanture qui le presse, et qui l'oblige de reprendre des sentimens raisonnables. Nous ne souffririons point qu'Herode se répentist de l'Arrêt prononcé contre sa femme sur des remonstrances qu'un des sept-Sages de Gréce luy viendroit faire, mais on est ravi de voir, qu'apres la mort de cette Reyne, son amour le bourelle, qu'il luy ouvre les

yeux, et le porte dans un repentir si sensible qu'il soit sur
le point d'en perdre la vie. (D'Aubignac 319)

D'Aubignac takes pleasure in showing the defeat or weakness
of reason in its attempts to modify human conduct. Precepts,
mediation, philosophers—these intrusions recall the character
to his right mind, spoiling the effect of overpowering emotion
that "ravishes" the spectator as it crushes the hero.

La Mesnardière also argues against *sentences* and *Apo-
phthegmes* because these forms are not compatible with the
emotional state of tragic characters. Such utterances "étans des
conceptions tranquilles et qui ne partent que d'une ame qui est
maitresse de soy, jamais les Passions violentes, fort communes
au Théâtre, ne doivent parler ce langage . . . puisqu'un mouvement rapide est toujours aussi éloigné d'un raisonnement pai-
sible et capable de former ces judicieuses Sentences, que le Ciel
l'est de la terre" (217–18).

The banishment of maxims, a definite shift in theoretical
direction between Jean de Mairet's preface to *La Silvanire*
(1631) and La Mesnardière's *Poëtique* nine years later, shows
the increasing insistence on the disruption of language as both
symptom and vehicle of emotion. This disruption is a symptom
of emotion, since the characters speaking, as La Mesnardière's
says, "ne doivent parler ce langage," the language of reason,
if they are to appear caught in the grip of emotion. It is also a
vehicle of emotion, since the audience is expected to incorporate the emotion by contact with the emotion of the characters
so that we love Chimène with Rodrigue, for example. If the
characters begin to reason or deliberate, the audience detects
reason at work and no longer believes that they are truly caught
in emotional turmoil; the staging of reason provokes in turn
the reasoning of the spectator, who ceases to be wrapped in
the illusion of the fictive situation and begins instead to consider the characters' words as mere *text*.

Deprived of reason, the spectator cannot fight off—does not
want to fight off—the effects of passion. Nicole says that during a dramatic performance, spectators are out of their minds—
this is his metaphor, not in the modern casual sense but in the
sense that the self-critical faculty is paralyzed by the hypnotic
fascination of what is happening onstage: "l'esprit y est tout
occupé des objets exterieurs, et entierement enivré des folies

77

que l'on y voit représenter, et par-conséquent hors de l'état de
la vigilance chrétienne, nécessaire pour résister aux tentations,
et comme un roseau capable d'être emporté par toutes sortes
de vents" (223). This is not an eccentric observation by someone ignorant of the theater of his time—Nicole knows Corneille's tragedies and his critical *examens* well. Nicole is in
agreement with the major dramatic theorists about tragedy's
effects, but he deplores the effect that they work so inge-
niously to produce.

Reason must vanish, then, from among characters and
spectators:

> Or nous devons concevoir que les Passions violentes sont
> à nôtre Entendement ce qu'est une vapeur épaisse à nôtre
> Imagination, et ce qu'est l'agitation à l'eau qui nous sert
> de miroir. (La Mesnardière 337)

The mimetic process, as we have seen, is extended by the classical theorists to make the audience an imitation of the fictive
world, and when the reflection in the water—the most ancient
of figures for mimetic representation—is agitated, then we too
must be agitated, distraught, cast in the image of our image.
Hence, the critics repeatedly condemn excessive correctness
or reasonableness in the speech of distressed characters. Examples of this condemnation range from Chapelain's censure
of Chimène, who "paroist trop subtile en tout cét endroit, pour
une affligée" (*Sentimens* 404), to d'Aubignac's blanket prohibition of instructional "Lieux-communs," since the character
"n'est pas dans la moderation convenable pour les penser, ny
pour les dire" (321).

Dramatic rhetoric must be controlled by the overarching concern to conceal the creative workings of the playwright, who
will usually be guided by reason, in order to make all speech
the product of a disordered mind. Yet, as in all classical theory,
vraisemblance intervenes to prevent the representation of the
real and to substitute in its place an artistic ideal of emotional
disorder:

> on doit avouer que ce desordre dans les paroles d'un homme
> qui se plaint, est un defaut qui affoiblit les marques exte-
> rieures de la douleur, et il le faut reformer sur le Theatre,
> qui ne souffre rien d'imparfait: C'est où les manquemens

de la nature, et les fautes des actions humaines doivent estre
rétablies. . . . (D'Aubignac 345)

Because the representation of emotion is only a means of provoking emotion in the audience, fidelity to the symptoms of
real emotion is unnecessary.[17] The "external marks" of suffering that we see in everyday life are, of course, imperfect because the sufferer is not an actor and does not aim to produce
the impression of distress, grief, or rage. Instead, emotional
trauma as we wish it to be, that is, insofar as it awakens the
required emotion in the audience, will replace emotion as it
occurs outside the theater. This emphasis on representing passion in such a way as to produce passion (rather than to imitate its everyday appearance) is in keeping with all the theorists'
advice to prevent the audience from switching into a critical,
distanced evaluation of the representation. The representation
of believable emotion is not an end in itself but rather a means
to stimulate the audience's emotion. For this reason deliberative and didactic discourse must be avoided, particularly late
in the play, since it "cools down" the theater and does not move
the soul (309, 315).[18]

It is one of the recurring paradoxes of seventeenth-century
dramatic theory that in order for representation to be adequate
it must be excessive. Not only is real emotion insufficient, but
conscious acting-out of emotions must *aim* at excess in expression and must avoid the proper degree and kind of expression.
This is the way the quantitative definition of passion as excess
(rather than as a single quality or type of emotion) shapes the
theory of dramatic language. In describing the figures of speech
that suit the emotions, d'Aubignac generally insists on their
variety (a form of quantity) rather than on the appropriateness
of specific tropes:

> Encore faut-il que les figures soient bien variées . . . attendu
> qu'un esprit agité ne demeure pas longtemps en méme as-
> siette. . . . [C]'est une agitation d'esprit qui n'a point de
> bornes, et qui va bien plus loin que le juste mouvement de
> la douleur, de la colere ny du desespoir. (344)

La Mesnardière also approaches the expression of emotion by
pushing language beyond its norms, though perhaps *beneath*

would be more appropriate than beyond. Afflicted characters should be incapable of refined speech, and their expression should tend toward the pre- or subverbal:

> que l'Acteur les anime [represented actions] par une expression réelle de gemissements et de pleurs dans les endroits où ils sont propres, s'il veut que le Spectateur le récompense par des larmes, qui sont le plus noble salaire que demande la Tragedie. (86)

Thus, for La Mesnardière both actor and spectator strain against the barrier to feeling imposed by structured language, and the success of classical tragedy in its primary mission of stirring feeling is demonstrated by the escape from language. Although d'Aubignac demands that dramatic language be more highly embellished than ordinary speech and La Mesnardière insists instead on the bare, colloquial, simple, and unaffected quality of the speech of emotionally afflicted characters (353),[19] both call for the excess of emotion to appear to disrupt the structures of discourse, creating a departure from a theorized "norm" in order to enact and signify emotional disturbance. Thus figures of speech must be assembled disparately rather than pursued (in d'Aubignac's view) to indicate a degradation of the character's discursive abilities. La Mesnardière more radically insists on the passage from word to sound (*gemissements*) as well as on the nonrational standard for tragic success (*larmes*). French, he argues further, is deprived of one of the principal tools for breaking down rational discourse, the use of *clameurs,* that is, the *accens pitoyables* of Greek exclamations: *io io, pheu pheu, ai ai, ee ee, ma moi,* and others (377).

In view of La Mesnardière's insistence on the breakdown of rational discursive forms in the representation of passion, it is not surprising that he argues in favor of *stances.* Just as ordered, clever, highly ornate language is acceptable only when it is spoken by "indifferent" characters—that is, characters who are not emotionally affected by the play's events—so also La Mesnardière finds that metrically uniform speech, subjected to "la contrainte des vers," is appropriate to "les choses indifférentes" but "les [choses] passionnées" cannot be subject to the same demand for order. Rather than presenting the use of *stances* as an ornament (as does d'Aubignac)[20] that requires time and preparation on the part of a character and is therefore an increase in constraint, La Mesnardière views this variation in meter as a breakdown not merely of discursive habit but of the control of reason itself:

> les Passions véhémentes parlent impétueusement, et elles peuvent bien sortir des proportions mesurées d'un langage /
> égal et uni, puis qu'elles sortent fort souvent des Régles de la Raison mesme. (400)

In a long development on the relation between the phonetic and prosodic form and the impression made by language on the imagination (presumably, that of the spectator or reader), La Mesnardière tries to reproduce within his description the disruptive and disordering effect of metrical changes in *stances,*[21] implying that this auditory miming of emotional agitation supersedes the semantic import of the words that form the verses. As a result, language disappears as lexical construction, leaving a disorderly accumulation of sounds or even simply of metrical alternations. Thus, within the phonetic substance itself as nonrational channel of communication, La Mesnardière abandons what we would recognize as semiosis in favor of an indexical approach to drama. Perhaps this is an early anticipation of Antonin Artaud! Closer to hand, there is an evident parallel between La Mesnardière and d'Aubignac. The disorder that the latter requires of figures, the former demands of sound itself.

Among all these stipulations of disorder, there is one discursive mode or figure—Pierre Fontanier will much later classify it among the "prétendues figures de pensée"—that d'Aubignac identifies as the great tragic rhetorical form, "entre toutes, l'Imprécation sera jugée certainement Theatrale, à cause qu'elle procède d'un violent transport d'esprit" (353). Imprecation is not usually set very high among rhetorical figures; in fact, it is more likely to be considered an error than an ornament. Reversing the usual hierarchy, d'Aubignac shows that violence, rather than judgment, is central to drama and that the success of dramatic, and especially of tragic, discourse can be located in the destruction of aesthetic and rational order.

However carefully prepared, however rationally arranged, French classical tragedy is meant to represent characters in moments of extreme emotional turmoil and to create sympathetic and even empathic emotional response in the audience. Thus the dramatic experience is far from Bray's vision of an aesthetic guided by "le culte de la raison," for we are, rather, in that place "où règne le Démon de l'inquietude, du trouble et du desordre."

Chapter Three

The Tragic Story

What should happen in a tragedy? What kind of story should be presented, what series of events should occur? What should be the relationship between the actions in a tragedy and prevailing ethical norms? These are central questions for the French theorists of tragedy as they were for Aristotle. The seventeenth-century French approached these questions by making verisimilitude, *vraisemblance,* a central concept for discussing the fictive world of the tragic characters. By verisimilitude they meant a relationship between what happened in the tragic plot, on one hand, and what sort of events were *expected* by the play's audience—or rather, what sort of events were expected to be expected by the play's audience. After all, the theory of verisimilitude creates two sets of "stories": one is enacted on the stage (the tragic story, also called the "subject" of tragedy), and the other is an ongoing story that theorists attribute to the collective opinion of the audience, a set of norms variously described as what should happen, what is believable, what can be imagined with pleasure, what usually happens, and what certain types of people would do under certain circumstances.

Verisimilitude: The World Corrected

D'Aubignac introduces verisimilitude as

> le fondement de toutes les Pieces du Theatre, chacun en parle et peu de gens l'entendent; voicy le caractere general auquel il faut reconnoistre tout ce qui s'y passe; en un mot la Vraysemblance est, s'il le faut ainsi dire, l'essence du Poëme Dramatique, et sans laquelle il ne se peut rien faire ni rien dire de raisonnable sur la Scéne. (76)

The degree of verisimilitude of a dramatic plot is a measure of the conformity of the plot to what the audience is assumed to expect. In setting out to resolve the problem of how to relate the two sides of this equation, the theorists had to describe both the fictive world of tragedy and the spectator's worldview, a worldview that seems often to be far from what a real seventeenth-century theater audience might have experienced as everyday reality. Although it is tempting to translate the French terms *vraisemblance* and *vraisemblable* as plausibility and plausible, respectively, the danger of these more contemporary terms is that they can allow us to forget that *vraisemblance* was very much a "term of art" for the poeticians. Plausibility suggests that a plot could be evaluated in terms of its simple believability, its correspondence to what the audience could suppose would happen in the everyday world. This would be very foreign indeed to the theory of tragedy for the French classical authors. Although d'Aubignac, La Mesnardière, Corneille, and the others occasionally use the term *believable* (*croyable*) to assess an event or a character's acts in a tragedy, the "belief" in question is a kind of theoretical construct of what an ideal spectator might believe rather than a description of an ordinary audience reaction. Verisimilitude, a word that has a slightly stilted, technical sound to it, has the advantage of reminding us that the theory of the tragic story is creating two models simultaneously—a model world for the stage and a model audience for the theater.

Although the terminology is technical, what is at stake is crucial and easily understood: on one hand the overwhelming majority of theorists demanded that the tragic story be verisimilar, and on the other, the most articulate theorist and the only successful playwright to discuss the question, Pierre Corneille, declared that the tragic subject must *not* be verisimilar. On one hand, then, is a formula for writing that prescribes a tragic story consistent with audience expectations and on the other, a demand that the events of a tragedy defy and challenge such expectations. On one hand d'Aubignac's affirmation that "Il n'y a donc que le *Vray-semblable* qui puisse raisonnablement fonder, soustenir, et terminer un Poëme Dramatique" (77) and on the other Corneille's vehement claim that truly great tragic subjects must be based on events that are "au-delà du vraisemblable" (3: 118).

Since verisimilitude is not an empirical study of what audiences really expected but a model of expectations created *for* the audience, it is important to see the difficulties that are latent in the model's definition. The concept of verisimilitude entered the theory of tragedy as a result of Aristotle's distinction between the task of the poet and that of the historian:

> the poet's task is to speak not of events which have occurred, but of the kind of events which *could* occur, and are possible by the standards of probability or necessity. For it is not the use or absence of metre which distinguishes poet and historian (one could put Herodotus' work into verse, but it would be no less a sort of history with it than without it); the difference lies in the fact that the one speaks of events which have occurred, the other of the sort of events which could occur. (*Poetics,* ed. Halliwell, chap. 9, 1451a)

Aristotle's negative description of what the poet should do (*not* to write of what has happened, *not* to be like the historian, a difference that is *not* in the surface format of the text) has many avatars in the seventeenth century. Seventeenth-century theorists struggle with the fact that most ancient tragic stories are attributed in some way to widely accepted accounts of the past. In other words, tragedy seems to have a relationship to history that is far from being a denial of history. Instead, tragic stories seem to represent a limited repertory selected *from* history. La Mesnardière recommends that the tragic story be based on an incident from history:

> Il faut encore, s'il est possible, que ce soient des Actions fort remarquables dans l'Histoire, & qui soient connuës de plusieurs; afin que le Spectateur ne soit pas si empesché à en comprendre le fons, qui vient de l'Historien, qu'il ne lui reste de l'esprit pour en considerer l'ordre, l'agencement & la conduite, d'où dépend la gloire du Poëte. (17)

Yet history, from which the playwright may or should derive his subject, is inferior to poetry. As La Mesnardière says, paraphrasing Aristotle:

> Pource . . . que le Poëte imitateur du Philosophe, attache ses contemplations aux choses universelles, et qu'il se plaist de les écrire selon qu'elles doivent estre; au lieu que l'Historien

> s'arreste au détail des affaires, et qu'il raconte simplement
> les actions particulieres ainsi qu'elles ont été faites, tantost
> bonnes, tantost mauvaises. (35)

There is a carefully articulated duality running throughout La
Mesnardière's version of Aristotle's text: universal/particular,
contemplate/stop, should be/were. Juxtaposing "contempla-
tions" to "s'arreste" might seem an arbitrary pairing were it
not for the obvious soaring freedom and elevation implied by
contemplation, far from the limited, broken shuffle of the historian's preoccupation with detail. Such preoccupation is re-
inforced by the choice of "affaires" for event, suggesting activity
considerably beneath the nobility of tragedy or epic. The historical variation of deeds, "sometimes good and sometimes bad,"
suggests a random quality to the events studied by history—a
randomness or indifference attributed to the historian and that
the tragic author is apparently meant to reject.

The "universal things" that are appropriate for the poet are
clearly not derived from empirical study, the study of the par-
ticulars. Events as they have happened are beneath poetry.
Rather, things as they should be, in La Mesnardière's phrase,
or things as they should have been (*ont deub estre* [Scudéry,
Observations 76]) are the matter for drama.[1] We might assume
that the verisimilar belongs to a pattern underlying and explaining history, a pattern that is manifest in history to the scholar
capable of assuming the proper distance and level of abstrac-
tion. What *usually* happens—the frequency of relations between
two events interpreted as cause and effect—would therefore
constitute the verisimilar. This is a very possible reading of
Aristotle's recommendations in his *Rhetoric* (1393a). However,
French classical verisimilitude is not based on the kind of historical generalization we might undertake on the basis of the
Rhetoric, because tragic stories are extremely *infrequent* in history. The first part of the playwright's work, locating a verisimilar story, is "la plus difficile; pource qu'à y bien regarder
on treuve fort peu d'Actions dans l'étenduë de l'Histoire et de
la Fable receuë, qui soient propres d'elles-mesmes pour faire
le Poëme tragique" (La Mesnardière 15). If verisimilar events
are what usually happens, then there should be a plentiful supply
of them in history. La Mesnardière's position on the paucity
of tragic events seems puzzling, though, of course, we might

recall that verisimilitude is not the only requirement of the tragic story. Yet the tragic story is *infrequent* in history, and this observation is enough to establish that the verisimilar, in La Mesnardière's view at least, is not definable strictly in terms of a pattern of frequent occurrence. A tragic combination of events and persons does not happen often, yet the tragic plot must be verisimilar. On the other hand, things that happen frequently are not necessarily verisimilar. D'Aubignac notes:

> Il est possible qu'un homme meure subitement, et cela souvent arrive; mais celuy-là seroit mocqué de tout le monde, qui pour dénoüer une Piece de Theatre, feroit mourir un rival d'apoplexie, comme d'une maladie naturelle et commune, ou bien il y faudroit beaucoup de preparations ingenieuses. (77)

An event that happens often, then, belongs to the grouping where what has happened often and what is possible are lumped together—this is in itself an extremely revealing combination. Why should something that is simply *possible* be put into the same category as things that happen often? It would be easy to make two separate categories here, since an event that is "possible" may never have happened, while that which "souvent arrive" seems to belong to the category of the ordinary, the usual, or even the probable. Yet for d'Aubignac, an event that is possible and happens often can be assigned—in certain cases, anyway—to the *non*verisimilar. D'Aubignac gives the key to the distinction between the verisimilar and the nonverisimilar by contrasting what happens in ordinary life and what happens in a story. In ordinary life, death by apoplexy has nothing unusual about it. Death by apoplexy is only objectionable as part of a play, where the character's death is somehow too convenient and also too sudden. The category of the verisimilar seems, then, to belong to our way of looking at stories rather than our way of looking at life. What is accepted in life is not necessarily acceptable in a story. The story framework, the consciousness that we are talking in particular about a stage play, seems to generate a level of suspicion and critical awareness that we do not have about everyday life. These implications of d'Aubignac's "apoplexy-test" of the plot fit together with La Mesnardière's disdainful comments about the historian's recording of the random details of life: life is not verisimilar.

It is not apparent whether something is verisimilar or, on the contrary nonverisimilar, until we begin to think in terms of poetic composition. Neither simple experience nor the recording (or constructing) of life by the historian can serve as guides. Instead, following d'Aubignac's example, we can argue that the perception of verisimilitude is generated by the requirements of the theorized plot structure. Such a structure overrides any appeal to what usually happens. We cannot even identify the verisimilar with events that have an exceptionally high level of probability, since verisimilitude, according to most seventeenth-century theorists of tragedy (following Aristotle), accepts events that are not only improbable but absolutely *impossible*. Magic and divine intervention can be codified within the verisimilar even in the absence of any experience of such events outside of drama:

> [L]es choses impossibles naturellement, deviennent possibles
> . . . la vray-semblance du Theatre n'oblige pas à representer
> seulement les choses qui arrivent selon le cours de la vie
> commune des hommes; mais qu'elle enveloppe en soy le
> *Merveilleux,* qui rend les evenemens d'autant plus nobles
> qu'ils sont impréveus, quoy que toutesfois vray-semblables.
> (D'Aubignac 77)

In this view the verisimilar cuts across the distinction between the possible and the impossible, following Aristotle's dictum that "au regard de la poésie on doit préférer l'impossible croyable au possible incroyable" (recommended by Corneille 3: 169). D'Aubignac adds another elusive term to the discussion here, the *marvelous,* which seems in this context to be a pleasurable surprise available within the set of verisimilar (and naturally impossible) events, provided that the occurrence is not foreseen by the spectators.

The consensus view of French classical theorists is that drama —and most of all, tragedy—is not controlled by the laws of nature as they are available through scientific study or through everyday observation ("la vie commune des hommes"). To argue that "impossible" occurrences can be accepted in tragic stories is to suppose that the distinction between impossible and possible is known to the playwright and to the theorist; if this distinction were unknowable, they would not be able to evaluate plots and to classify them in the four pertinent classifications: the believable impossible, the believable possible, the unbelievable impossible, and the unbelievable possible. Implicit in the promotion of the believable impossible over the unbelievable possible is the idea that playwrights and theorists are more alert to these categories than are spectators of tragedy, since if a spectator were aware that something was impossible it seems unlikely that the spectator would find it believable.

This distinction between the theorist's vision and the spectator's runs through all discussions of verisimilitude, since the distanced, thoughtful professional rejects the "true" as unworthy of tragedy, while the spectator, swayed by the presence of the actors and the emotion of the moment, should on the contrary perceive the dramatic incident as true, not as verisimilar. Paradoxically, the audience must not be aware of the "poetic" (that is, invented) nature of the story but must instead believe that the events onstage come from poetry's rival, history. The demand for this sense of historical truth is so great, in La Mesnardière's view, that *La poëtique* recommends avoiding totally invented subjects for partially historical ones. Totally invented plots, writes La Mesnardière, should be left to tragi-comedy and novels, "car il est du tout impossible qu'une Fable de cette sorte excite bien la Compassion; qui ne peut estre provoquée que par le triste spectacle des Infortunes veritables, ou du moins qu'on estime vrayes" (43). At first glance it seems that La Mesnardière simply has little faith in a modern French playwright's abilities to produce fictions that seem "true" and that will sweep the audience into emotional participation, but the failure to use historical material is also cited as a major failing of the ancient Greeks:

> l'Histoire de Thébes est si manifestement fausse en la plus-part des Avantures qu'elle nous fait passer pour vrayes, qu'il est fort aisé de juger que les plus belles Tragédies que les Anciens ayent admirées, ont des fondemens fabuleux, inventez, & mesme incroyables. (42)

The list of faulty tragedies includes Aeschylus's *Prometheus,* Sophocles's *Women of Trachis,* and four lost tragedies.[2] While the verisimilar is defined against the everyday and against history, historical events find their way into the repertory of tragic stories. Somehow these events must be filtered or "corrected" by verisimilitude before being represented onstage. In this way the verisimilar can be restored to history, provided that the true events of the past are rearranged to conform to a better, more orderly vision of the world:

> la vray-semblance . . . sert aussi à donner aux choses que dit le poète un plus grand air de perfection que ne pourroit faire la vérité mesme, quoique la vray-semblance n'en soit que la copie. Car la vérité ne fait les choses que comme elles sont; et la vray-semblance les fait comme elles doivent estre. La vérité est presque toujours défectueuse, par le mélange des conditions singulières, qui la composent. (Rapin 41)

The verisimilar appears, in general, to be an elusive quality, neither historical nor entirely nonhistorical, neither belonging to the everyday world of the audience nor somehow entirely foreign to the audience. Its difficulty is both revealed and compounded by the theorists' tendency to define it negatively, by what it is *not,* as well as their tendency to forget how they have defined it. So that d'Aubignac sometimes forgets that he has rejected things that happen often and demands that tragedy be based on "ce qui se fait le plus communément" (121).

Yet the theorists sensed problems with verisimilitude as a foundation for tragedy and adopted with enthusiasm the four types of verisimilitude elaborated by the Renaissance Italians: general, particular, ordinary, and extraordinary. A striking feature of this refinement is that it adjusts verisimilitude by pushing toward the outer limit, since the theorists themselves are deeply puzzled and ambivalent about verisimilitude. So they use the four-part scheme somewhat as Ptolomaic astronomers use deferents and equants to repair a fundamentally flawed system.

General verisimilitude covers actions according to certain general types of persons or situations—"ce que peut faire, et qu'il est à propos que fasse un roi, un général d'armée, un amant, un ambitieux, etc."—while particular verisimilitude describes individuals whose actions vary from those of other members of their category: "ce qu'a pu ou dû faire Alexandre, César, Alcibiade compatible avec ce que l'histoire nous apprend de ses actions" (Corneille 3: 166). Ordinary (or common) verisimilitude is the quality of what happens "plus souvent, ou du moins aussi souvent que sa contraire." Extraordinary verisimilitude accounts for "une action qui arrive à la vérité moins souvent que sa contraire, mais qui ne laisse pas d'avoir sa possibilité assez aisée, pour n'aller point jusqu'au miracle ..." (3: 168). The scheme that derives from these categories includes ordinary and general verisimilitude (e.g., what a lover would do most often, or at least as often as he would do the opposite, to paraphrase Corneille) and on the other extreme extraordinary and particular verisimilitude (e.g., what Alexander would do if he were not behaving as he usually did). Since a verisimilar action may be historically or scientifically impossible, and, for d'Aubignac, encompass the marvelous, including things that can only be done "par puissance divine, ou par magie" (77), the limits of the verisimilar model of tragic story are so elastic as to be useless.

While the quest to create a freestanding model of the verisimilar, one that does not require constant reference to the audience, seems to fail, appeals to specific real audiences do not seem to work much better. Late in the century, Rapin gives the concise statement "Le vray-semblable est tout ce qui est conforme à l'opinion du public" (39), yet this opinion was decidedly untrustworthy from a theoretical perspective. Just as "what happens" in life requires correction to be verisimilar, what "the public believes" is impure and uninformed. In reacting to the comment that common sense would be sufficient basis for setting up the tragic story, d'Aubignac writes:

> j'en demeure d'accord: mais il faut que ce soit un sens commun instruit de ce que les hommes ont voulu faire sur le Theatre, et de ce qu'il faut observer pour en venir à bout: car supposons qu'un homme de bon sens n'ait jamais veu le Theatre, et qu'il n'en ait méme jamais oüy parler, il est certain qu'il ne connoistra pas si les Comediens sont des Roys et des Princes veritables, ou s'ils n'en sont que des phantosmes vivans. . . . il faudroit certes qu'il en vist plusieurs et qu'il y fist beaucoup de reflexions pour connoistre ce qui seroit vray-semblable, ou non. (79)

This comment shows two interwoven and confusing movements in d'Aubignac's view of versimilitude. The first and

most apparent is his commitment to the belief that the spectator in his natural, uneducated state cannot be the source of theoretical insight into what makes an event verisimilar. Spectators
really cannot give reliable and useful information about what
is verisimilar, both because spectators who are not familiar with
the theater apply everyday, nontheatrical standards rather than
theatrical, poetic ones and because spectators, as human be-
ings, are sinful and depraved. They may therefore not describe
the world with the degree of correctness that verisimilitude requires. Just as the fiction presented onstage should avoid uncorrected history and ordinary life, the theory—or fiction—of
the spectator must include the opinions of the ordinary person
only to the extent that these opinions have been revised. As
Chapelain writes for the Académie on the occasion of the *Cid*
debate:

> nous ne dirons pas sur la foy du Peuple, qu'un ouvrage de
> Poësie soit bon parce qu'il l'aura contenté, si les doctes aussi
> n'en sont contens. Et certes il n'est pas croyable qu'un plaisir
> puisse estre contraire au bon sens, si ce n'est le plaisir de
> quelque goust depravé comme est celuy qui fait aymer les
> aigreurs et les amertumes. Il n'est pas icy question de satis-
> faire leslibertins [*sic*] et les vicieux qui ne font que rire des
> adulteres et des incestes, et qui ne se soucient pas de voir
> violer les loix de la Nature pourveu qu'ils se divertissent.
> Il n'est pas question de plaire à ceux qui regardent toutes
> choses d'un œil ignorant ou barbare, et qui ne seroient pas
> moins touchés de voir affliger une Clytemnestre q'une Pene-
> lope. (*Sentimens* 360)

While d'Aubignac is less inclined than Chapelain, Scudéry, and
La Mesnardière to denounce the moral corruption of mankind,
he shares their refusal to accept the uncorrected opinion of the
public. When d'Aubignac makes a statement defining verisimilitude as "l'opinion et le sentiment ordinaire des hommes"
(76), this expression must be understood within the technical
context of his treatise.

A second important theme in d'Aubignac's description of
the perfectly naïve spectator is his oddly negative evaluation
of the spectator's impression that what is happening onstage
is real, true. It seems that the play succeeds *too* well. The com-
monsensical man may well assume that the actors onstage are

real kings and princes and may not realize that he is only see-ing actors. Oddly enough, what d'Aubignac considers a fail-ure in this case is the highest form of success according to most theorists, including d'Aubignac himself in other contexts. Chapelain wrote that the spectator should not be able to per-ceive any difference between the stage presentation and real-ity: "Je pose donc pour fondement que l'imitation en tous poèmes doit être si parfaite qu'il ne paraisse aucune différence entre la chose imitée et celle qui imite, car le principal effet de celle-ci consiste à proposer à l'esprit, pour le purger de ses passions déréglées, les objets comme vrais et comme présents" ("Lettre sur la règle des vingt-quatre heures" 115). If the spec-tator should be caught off guard as a result of the author's work to "surprendre l'imagination du spectateur," the play would have achieved the goal of making "la feinte pareille à la vérité même." In the same vein Scudéry writes of the spectator's being "surpris par cette agreable tromperie" (*Observations sur le Cid* 74).

D'Aubignac's example of the perfectly naïve spectator is simply an example of the perfect spectator, but d'Aubignac has trouble remembering—as we all do, both seventeenth-century writers and twentieth-century readers—that the audience itself is called upon to play two remarkably different roles. During the tragedy, the audience is expected to behave as if what hap-pens onstage were *really* happening, "afin d'obliger l'esprit par toutes voies à se croire présent à un véritable événement et à vêtir par force dans le faux les mouvements que le vrai même lui eût pu donner" (Chapelain, "Lettre sur la règle des vingt-quatre heures" 116). Or, as d'Aubignac says, as far as the spec-tator in the theater is concerned, "tous les personnages doivent agir et parler comme s'ils estoient véritablement Roy, et non pas comme estant Bellerose, ou Mondory, comme s'ils estoient dans le Palais d'Horace à Rome, et non pas dans l'Hostel de Bourgongne [*sic*] à Paris" (38). In other words, the theoretical ideal of the spectator's relation to the world of the stage is to believe in the "truth" of the dramatic events, a truth that is cap-tured by the repeated use of the verb *to be* and the adjective *véritable*. On the other hand the spectator is also supposed to be able to reflect critically on the dramatic presentation and on the text (the poet's task is to create the tragic or comic fiction, which should be able to capture the audience's imagination whether it be performed onstage or read) in order to judge it as a work of art. Corneille, for instance, calls upon the readers of his *Discours* to remember their experience *as spectators* in order to be able to make subsequent judgments as critics in regard to the doctrine of "purgation" of passions.[3]

What d'Aubignac forgets when he imagines the naïve spectator is the distinction between these two audience roles, which are also two moments of the spectator's experience. Or rather, d'Aubignac sees the spectator's experience in sequential terms but fails to draw the bold conclusion that his example implies: verisimilitude does not exist in the theatrical experience. In the moment of the dramatic performance (or while reading a play), the audience of a successful tragedy believes in the *truth* of the events and characters. Only after this experience, and most of all, after repeated experiences of this sort, can the spectator transform the perception of the *véritable* into a judgment of *vraisemblance*. We recall the same theorist's comments about apoplexy in the plot: people die of apoplexy often in reality, but the playwright who uses such a death "pour dénouër une Piece de Theatre" would be considered ridiculous. Judgments about versimilitude are made in reference to plays and playwrights, and the spectator would only make a judgment about the lack of versimilitude if the play had released its hold on him or her sufficiently for such an intellectual judgment to be made.

Chapelain comes very close to a direct formulation of this disappearance of the verisimilar during the dramatic experience. Writing for the Académie française on *Le Cid,* he notes that verisimilitude affects spectators in such a way that "lors que le Poëte l'expose aux Auditeurs ou aux Spectateurs, ils se portent à croire sans autre preuve qu'il ne contient rien que de vray, pource qu'ils ne voyent rien qui y repugne" (*Sentimens* 364). Truth, on the other hand, is not the basis for epic or dramatic poetry because "le vray, qui pourroit estre si estrange et si incroyable qu'ils refuseroient de s'en laisser persuader et de suivre leur guide [le poète] sur sa seule foy" (365). The effect of truth, therefore, is what the play should produce in the audience, *not* an effect of verisimilitude. The verisimilar produces this effect of truth rather than the effect of the verisimilar—that is, the verisimilar disappears as such during the performance or reading. Truth, on the other hand, may produce resistance in the audience, awakening the audience to critical intellectual activity. Most theorists believed, as we saw in the previous chapter, that the most important quality of tragedy, its emotional impact, is lost when the audience is able to assume a dispassionate stance toward the actions onstage.

Sacrificing Verisimilitude for History and Pleasure

Corneille is the single important opponent of the idea that the tragic story should be verisimilar. It is a sign of how deeply he felt about this matter that his doctrine of the nonverisimilar tragic subject occupies about three-quarters of the long opening paragraph of his major theoretical text, the three *Discours sur le poème dramatique* (1660). Corneille also devoted the second of the discourses specifically to tragedy and "des moyens de la traiter, selon le vraisemblable et le nécessaire." Directly challenging prevailing views of verisimilitude, Corneille declares that Aristotle's comments on this topic were not understood:

> on en est venu jusqu'à établir une maxime très fausse, *qu'il faut que le sujet d'une tragédie soit vraisemblable:* appliquant aussi aux conditions du sujet la moitié de ce qu'il a dit de la manière de le traiter. Ce n'est pas qu'on ne puisse faire une tragédie d'un sujet purement vraisemblable . . . mais les grands sujets qui remuent fortement les passions, et en opposent l'impétuosité aux lois du devoir, ou aux tendresses du sang, doivent toujours aller au-delà du vraisemblable, et ne trouveraient aucune croyance parmi les auditeurs, s'ils n'étaient soutenus, ou par l'autorité de l'histoire qui persuade avec empire, ou par la préoccupation de l'opinion commune qui nous donne ces mêmes auditeurs déjà tous persuadés. (3: 118)

In demanding nonverisimilar *subjects* for tragedy, Corneille is not arguing that the tragedy as a whole should be without verisimilitude. He distinguishes between the "subject" and the "treatment" of the subject. Since the treatment concerns all that the playwright invents (dialogue and expositions concerning the characters' motivations, secondary plots, precise location of actions, timing, etc., where, as Corneille writes, "les moyens de parvenir à l'action demeurent en notre pouvoir" [3: 159]), this is an area in which the playwright should conform to verisimilitude. However, if the "subject" is the core of a story, the major event, then Corneille is essentially arguing for a non-verisimilar story, one of those "événements singuliers, qui servent de matière aux tragédies sanglantes par l'appui qu'ils ont de l'histoire, ou de l'opinion commune" (3: 168). It is worth noting that Corneille seems incidentally to confirm d'Aubignac's insistence that uncorrected public opinion cannot be trusted as the guide to verisimilitude. Corneille recognizes that there are nonverisimilar stories that will work as the basis of tragedy because "l'opinion commune" accepts them—so Corneille also distinguishes between verisimilitude and opinion. The difference between Corneille—and no doubt, in his practice, Racine—and the other theorists is that Corneille did not seek to "correct" nonverisimilar public opinion but to exploit it.

The attempts to define the verisimilar are only opening skirmishes before the main theoretical battles over the legitimate tragic story. In discussing actions in terms of frequency and infrequency or in denying the relevance of possibility as a determining factor in verisimilitude, theorists are taking positions that have practical consequences in the fight over the use of history as source of tragic stories. For Corneille historical subjects had many advantages over invented stories that were designed to fit the specifications of a pre-established grid of actions. The primary advantage of history is precisely its non-verisimilar quality. Corneille addresses the problem raised in an apparently accidental way by La Mesnardière: if everyone always behaves according to type, how can anything surprising happen, how can anything happen "contre les apparences," that is, contrary to expectation?

Corneille and La Mesnardière thus become unlikely allies against the Académie's preference for rigid formulaic stories. Because the nonverisimilar action occurs infrequently, it remains surprising and even striking. It is highly concrete and specific, it may not be known to the public, and it cannot be generated by the assumption that what will happen is what should happen. If pure verisimilitude were to triumph, if the "choses universelles" rather than the "actions particulières" were to dominate in tragedy, plays would revert to allegorical representations of vices and virtues, ages and classes, nationalities and emotional states ("l'amante passionnée"). It may seem a bit of a leap from verisimilar tragedy to allegory, on the basis of comments by d'Aubignac, La Mesnardière, and Chapelain, but such a logical outcome did appeal to one of the great classical scholars of the century, Dacier, who said of tragedy,

> Selon les regles d'Aristote une Tragedie est l'imitation d'une action allegorique et universelle, qui convient à tout le monde et qui par le moyen de la compassion et de la terreur modere et corrige nos passions. (6)

Dacier, an active opponent of the modernist current represented by Corneille, contrasted what he felt was the orthodox Aristotelian model of allegorical tragedy with the modern, particularist model:

> selon ces nouvelles regles la Tragedie est l'imitation d'une action particuliere, qui ne convient à personne, et qui n'est inventée que pour amuser le spectateur par le nœud et par le denouement d'une vaine intrigue et qui ne tend qu'à exciter et à remplir la curiosité, et qui allume les passions au lieu de les calmer ou de les éteindre. (6a)

This description of the new tragedy is particularly applicable to Corneille's work and responds to his defense of dramatic pleasure and to his emphasis on suspense.

Dacier's comments are especially important because they are the clearest statement of the timeless, abstract quality that opponents of Corneille sought to establish in opposition to a tragedy of history, theoretically and practically founded on the concept of time. The importance of time and history in seventeenth-century theoretical discussions is partially obscured for the twentieth-century reader by the use of the terms *vrai* and *vérité* to mean historically (or experientially) known actions. We might expect *vérité*, truth, to refer to the supratemporal structure behind appearance, in opposition to the "real" of everyday life. In the seventeenth century, however, *vérité* is synonymous with temporal reality and depreciated accordingly. D'Aubignac writes of the playwright:

> comme il ne s'arreste pas au Temps, parce qu'il n'est pas Chronologue, il ne s'attachera point à la Verité, non plus que le Poëte Epique, parce que tous deux ne sont pas Historiens. Ils prennent de l'Histoire ce qui leur est propre, et

> y changent le reste pour en faire leurs Poëmes, et c'est une
> pensée bien ridicule d'aller au Theatre pour apprendre l'his-
> toire. (68)

In *vrai-semblable* (often written in this hyphenated form), the
first term, *vrai,* is in fact the less important of the pair, a kind
of concession to the appearances that are required for passing
off the more important, changeless patterns that are above the
perception of the "vulgaire" but available to the learned critic
and poet. In this context Dacier's description of tragedy as the
"imitation d'une action allegorique et universelle" is one of the
most forceful and daring statements of the antihistorical group.
The verisimilar *is* the universal; real life, as recorded in history or as perceived by contemporaries, is defective to the extent that it falls away from this universal pattern.

From the Cornelian, prohistorical point of view, the univer-
sality of patterns that constitutes the verisimilar is exactly what
makes the verisimilar useless for tragedy. Predictable events
do not induce the intellectual and emotional response required
by drama. History, as the record of *broken patterns,* is already
a form of prototragedy. Corneille's reflection on history, traced
in the background of his theory of the tragic story, merits attention in itself. History is not merely what has happened but
rather a selection of events that should not have happened! Like
the academic theorists, Corneille keeps in mind a pattern of
conduct that constitutes the norm, but he uses that norm as a
filter to define the historical. Normal events do not figure in
history. History is instead the series of exceptions that were so
striking and so important as to merit separate treatment outside statements of the moral and religious law. In writing of
accidental parricides, Corneille observes:

> cette circonstance de tuer son père ou son frère sans le con-
> naître est si extraordinaire, et si éclatante, qu'on a quelque
> droit de dire que l'Histoire n'ose manquer à s'en souvenir,
> quand elle arrive entre des personnes illustres, et de refuser
> toute croyance à de tels événements, quand elle ne les marque
> point. Le théâtre ancien ne nous en fournit aucun exemple
> qu'Œdipe; et je ne me souviens point d'en avoir vu aucun
> autre chez nos historiens. (3: 156)

This image of history not *daring* to forget such an unusual murder underscores forcefully history's particular obligation to

record occurrences belonging to a type that is infrequently seen. In Corneille's formulation, this gleaning of the exception seems to have priority among the tasks of the historian, and the use of the verb *to dare* has a special resonance in the context of a theory of drama, for the historian would not dare omit what the academic tragedian would not dare include. History and academic tragedy are not merely different but symmetrical in their respective demands and prohibitions. The fine irony of Corneille's argument, however, pushes further into the relationship of tragedy and history through the paradigm of the perfect tragedy, the fetish of neo-Aristotelian poetics. *Oedipus* is the only example of such a story in ancient theater, and there are no examples of such an event in history. Sophocles's tragedy is thus a case of the type of parricide that (1) would necessarily have been recorded in "history" if it had happened, and (2) must not be believed if it is not recorded in history. Although Corneille does not adjudicate the question of whether or not Sophocles's subject is properly historical, he does declare that there are no other similar events recorded in history. *Oedipus* appears, therefore, as a kind of self-supporting nonverisimilar story that violates the requirements of the academic theorists as well as the demands of Corneille himself. It may be that both tragedy and history fail when they reach an exemplar such as *Oedipus,* where both discourses cross over into each other's territory and disappear into an imploded black hole, the point at which an event does not belong to an infrequent pattern but to no pattern whatsoever, the *hapax* of human conduct.

Oedipus is thus an extreme, toward which the playwright, in Corneille's theory, will always strive, though without reaching it. The Cornelian conception of tragedy is, in fact, always extreme and finds in history a kindred discipline of discerning extreme cases. D'Aubignac calls for purifying true events for tragedy, because "elles n'y sont receuës qu'autant qu'elles ont de la vray-semblance" (77). Corneille, on the contrary, finds his models in the nonverisimilar "grands crimes" of ancient tragedy (3: 118). While agreeing with the other theorists that the audience must not be incredulous during the dramatic experience, Corneille finds neither verisimilitude nor truth desirable in its own right. If the audience can be persuaded to accept a nonverisimilar story, so much the better for dramatic effect. Far from seeking, as the other poeticians do, to remove the implausible from historical events, Corneille argues that locating the singular, implausible historical event is a major advantage to the author of tragedy.

La Mesnardière's allowance of less verisimilar events to produce the "marvelous effects" of tragedy shows that the academic theorists had some awareness that verisimilitude could prevent tragedy from reaching one of its goals, the emotional manipulation of the audience. However, only Corneille followed this line of thought to the extreme of requiring, for the best tragedies, that the stories be implausible. It is difficult to fault Corneille's logic on this matter, for if academic tragedy represents the utopia of a world where things are as they should be, then it is hard to understand how any pathos can be generated. Yet Corneille's bold insight leads him to challenge not only Scudéry, Chapelain, and other contemporaries but Aristotle himself.

Corneille takes as his point of departure Aristotle's table of tragic outcomes according to what Aristotle considers two variables: whether or not the tragic deed (e.g., murder) is accomplished and whether or not the agent and the victim are related (*Poetics,* chap. 14): "Dans ces actions tragiques qui se passent entre proches, il faut considérer, si celui qui veut faire périr l'autre, le connaît, ou ne le connaît pas, et s'il achève, ou n'achève pas" [3: 152]). There follows a summary of the four combinations of recognized kinship and tragic act, with Aristotle's evaluation of each combination. One can,

1. Be aware of a close link to someone and kill him or her nonetheless (a bad tragedy, according to Aristotle);

2. Be unaware of the relationship to one's victim, kill that person, and then discover the relationship (a good tragedy, according to Aristotle);

3. Be unaware of a relationship to one's intended victim, discover the relationship in time, and abstain from the crime (the best tragedy, according to Aristotle);

4. Be aware of the relationship, attempt to kill the person nonetheless, and fail (according to Aristotle this plot is so bad that it is not even tragic).[4]

In rehabilitating this last of what we can call kinship ratios as the best kind of tragedy for a modern, seventeenth-century French audience, Corneille claims that this is "une espèce de nouvelle tragédie plus belle que les trois qu'il [Aristote] recommande" (3: 153). The reason for preferring this story is its lack of verisimilitude. It is contrary to the way things should be, contrary to the ideological quality of verisimilitude as the idealized "Nature des choses," for one family member to kill another. Even though domestic violence was undoubtedly as common in the seventeenth century as in the twentieth century, killing a family member was not part of things as "elles doivent estre." This kind of plot, corresponding to the first and fourth of the combinations Corneille attributes to Aristotle, was appealing to Corneille precisely because it belonged to the forbidden series of events that academic theorists declared should be wiped out of stories when they are transferred from history to tragedy. As d'Aubignac writes of such reworked historical subjects, the playwright

> n'a soin que de garder la vray-semblance des choses. . . . Il accorde les pensées avec les personnes, les temps avec les lieux, les suites avec les principes. Enfin il s'attache tellement à la Nature des choses, qu'il n'en veut contredire ni l'estat, ni l'ordre, ni les effets, ni les convenances; et en un mot il n'a point d'autre guide que la vray-semblance, et rejette tout ce qui n'en porte point les caracteres. (38)

In fitting thoughts to persons, the playwright eliminates such unseemly desires as the desire of son to kill father or mother to kill children. Such thoughts may belong to the world as we see it, but they do not belong to the "Nature of Things" as this is stated in the code of verisimilitude.

Corneille justified his "new" type of tragedy, the tragedy "à visage découvert" or tragedy with full awareness, by describing the great transgressions of supposed "natural" bonds and moral rules that such familial violence requires. While the academic theorists attempted to align the verisimilar with the legal and moral laws of seventeenth-century France, Corneille not only valorized the nonverisimilar, understood as embodied in exceptional and infrequent acts, but went further to promote representation of the most serious violations of social rules. In fully aware conflicts of close persons, the "sentiments de la nature" were set against "emportements de la passion" or the "sévérité du devoir" (3: 151). The analysis of the Italian playwright Ghirardelli's *Il Constantino* (which Corneille calls *La mort de Crispe* [1653]) demonstrates Corneille's insistence on increasing the transgressive quality of acts. Ghirardelli followed a procedure recommended by the French academic theorists, purifying the tragic story of historical facts, arranging events so that the hero's identity was unknown in order to attenuate parricidal and incestuous situations. While this arrangement promotes "agnition" (recognition), an ancient dramatic device, the hidden identity eliminates many "choses plus belles" derived from the characters' consciousness of the extremely forbidden acts in which they are tempted to engage:

> Les ressentiments, le trouble, l'irrésolution, et les déplaisirs de Constantin . . . et la qualité de fils, augmentant la grandeur du crime qu'on lui imposait, eût en même temps augmenté la douleur d'en voir un père persuadé. Fauste même aurait eu plus de combats intérieurs pour entreprendre un inceste, que pour se résoudre à un adultère, ses remords en auraient été plus animés, et ses désespoirs plus violents. L'auteur a renoncé à tous ces avantages. . . . (3: 155)

Incest is *better* than adultery for the purposes of tragedy. Far from diminishing the apparent crimes and emotional turmoil of the main characters, Corneille recommends aggravating them. He pointedly urges moving in the opposite direction from the verisimilar code promoted by Chapelain, Scudéry, and La Mesnardière.

The weakness of the two plots recommended by Aristotle—to attempt to kill an unknown person and to discover the intended victim's identity either in time to stop or too late to refrain from the deed—is that these plots are excessively verisimilar. There is nothing unusual about conflict between enemies or between neutral or indifferent persons. Such situations are entirely predictable, saturated as they are with verisimilitude; they occur with high degrees of frequency; they transgress moral and legal rules either not at all or without aggravating circumstance; and most of all, they do not produce the proper emotional conflicts. In judging the quality of tragic situations by the degree and kind of emotion generated both in characters and in the reader or spectator, Corneille was, as we will see, in complete agreement with the academic theorists. However, in his insistence that characters should transgress the limits of natu-

ral or moral law, Corneille distinguished himself from all his
contemporary theorists.

In the battle over verisimilitude, it is clear that this coded
term, so easily misunderstood to signify a reflection of life as
it normally appears, contains a heavy ethical and emotional
charge. The verisimilar is the lawful, not only in terms of
what the playwright is permitted to compose but in terms of what
the characters are permitted to do. When characters submit to the
verisimilar they surrender desire for conformity, pleasure for
duty, aesthetics for ethics. Corneille, alone among the theorists,
seized upon another term from Aristotle's poetics, *anagkaios*
(*le nécessaire*, "the necessary"), as the signifier of the subversive, desiring, aesthetic force that combats verisimilitude.[5] He
quotes Aristotle: "le poète n'est pas obligé de traiter les choses
comme elles se sont passées, mais comme elles ont pu, ou dû
se passer, selon le vraisemblable, ou le nécessaire" (3: 161).
Corneille's repetition of this last phrase has the effect of drawing
attention to the conjunction *ou,* suggesting that these two terms
are not joined in any relation of synonymy or equivalence but
rather are juxtaposed as radically different alternatives for tragic
plotting.

By locating this obscure term in Aristotle's text ("il répète
souvent ces derniers mots," writes Corneille, "et ne les explique
jamais"), the theorist is able to situate an escape from the verisimilar that bears Aristotle's authority but is without content
and thus available for whatever is the opposite of verisimilitude. Here is what Corneille pours into that empty vessel:

> le nécessaire en ce qui regarde la poésie, n'est autre chose
> que *le besoin du poète pour arriver à son but, ou pour y
> faire arriver ses acteurs.* Cette définition a son fondement
> sur les diverses acceptions du mot grec anagkaion qui ne
> signifie pas toujours ce qui est absolument nécessaire, mais
> aussi quelquefois ce qui est seulement utile à parvenir à
> quelque chose. (3: 170)

The "necessary" is thus all that is justified by the movement
of desire toward its object, all that is done to remove obstacles
to reaching the desired goal. Without doubt Corneille's most
important tactic is to create an equivalence between the writer's
goal and the characters' goals. In this way necessity does not
apply simply to the requirement that a plot be segmented into

five acts or that tragic actions be capable of being conveyed in words. Instead of this technical arrangement of the plot for the purposes of staging—a definition that would make this concept instrumental and extra- or para-textual—the necessary penetrates the fictive world of the tragic story to justify the actions of the characters. To say that the necessary is generated by the force of desire itself is fully justified by the examples Corneille gives. The characters' (*acteurs*) goals are different according to the role assigned by the plot:

> Un amant a celui de posséder sa maîtresse, un ambitieux, de s'emparer d'une couronne, un homme offensé, de se venger, et ainsi de suite. Les choses qu'ils ont besoin de faire pour y arriver constituent ce nécessaire, qu'il faut préférer au vraisemblable, ou pour parler plus juste, qu'il faut ajouter au vraisemblable dans la liaison des actions, et leur dépendance l'une de l'autre. (3: 170–71)

In some ways this list resembles the modular verisimilar characters presented at length by d'Aubignac and by La Mesnardière (which we will examine shortly)—and this resemblance is probably not fortuitous insofar as Corneille is countering academic theory with a theory from the other side of the looking glass (or from the other side of the Aristotelian "or"). However, the distinguishing feature of Corneille's examples of necessity is the extremely specific need. A lover is not described as being passionate, absentminded, solitary, or impulsive. He is, rather, recognizable by his desire alone, "celui de posséder sa maîtresse." Necessity is the path from desire to fulfillment. The tragic plot should follow this path rather than the stipulations of ideological verisimilitude. A lover should do what is required to possess his beloved, just as a man seeking vengeance should do whatever it takes, however unusual and however at variance from the things as "elles doivent estre."

The concept of the necessary bridges the distinction between the playwright and the character, since both have a stake in achieving some of the same goals. To be more precise, this "solidarity" works in only one direction—with the possible exception of certain metatheatrical texts like Corneille's own comedy *L'illusion comique*—the playwright has an interest in allowing certain of the characters to achieve their goals, though the characters do not share in the writer's goal of pleasing the audience within the rules of the art. In thus linking writer and character, Corneille actually makes a major statement about dramatic composition that sets him apart from most other theorists, and especially from La Mesnardière and Scudéry. The writer is encouraged to see the world from within the mind of the fictive character, or, in other words, the writer should identify with the character's desire before imagining any other characteristics, feelings, or actions of that character. This desire-based (or goal-based) approach to character differs strikingly from the modular characterization and plotting presented by the academic theorists. It explains why Corneille's Chimène, heroine of *Le Cid,* is unthinkable to Scudéry. The latter does not for a moment identify with the character's desire and cannot entertain the idea of all the transgressions of verisimilitude that such a desire entails.

La Mesnardière's approach, close to what Scudéry requires of *Le Cid,* does not start from the character's goal and build the character or the plot from that point. Instead, all that a character does is dictated by a table of characteristics, including appropriate actions, which are not hierarchically ordered in descending order from that point. It is rather difficult to imagine La Mesnardière's approach working—even setting aside any judgment of his practical achievements as a dramatist. La Mesnardière specifically envisions a dramatic world in which secondary characteristics come before the emotional drive assigned to the role:

> La Vrai-Semblance Ordinaire se tire encore d'ailleurs que des Qualitez naturelles, puis que les accidentelles en sont les principales sources: comme *la condition de vie, les divers attributs des âges, la nation, & la fortune;* choses qui sont aussi puissantes pour faire agir les personnes d'une certaine maniére, que leurs propres inclinations, si elles ne sont tres-fortes. (36)

Although he leaves himself an escape route in his last clause, La Mesnardière's system of priorities is evident and clearly opposed to Corneille's: class, age, nationality, and wealth are at least equal to individual passion.

For Corneille, necessity applies to the playwright's work even when he is not attempting to plot from within the fictive character's desire. In order to "plaire selon les règles de son art"

(3: 171), the playwright must make other choices that involve departures from the verisimilar and even from history itself in the name of necessity. Here we are back again with these three terms, none of which has much meaning unless it is played off against the other two. The necessary (within the characters' world) is the surprising, transgressive action aimed at achieving a goal. The necessary (within the playwright's world) is conformity to the physical requirements and customs of the theater. History is the record of actions that include transgressions of social expectations (and take no cognizance of stage conventions). The verisimilar is the absence of transgressions of social expectation. If the verisimilar represents the correction of real life according to social norms, the necessary represents the "correction" of the verisimilar according to the needs of characters and playwright.

Corneille explains the relationship between verisimilitude and theatrical convention by contrasting a play with nondramatic narrative, specifically with the *roman* (novel).[6] Assuming that a story can be represented in both dramatic and nondramatic form, Corneille proposes the novel as the genre in which all actions can be represented in a purely verisimilar way. By retelling the actions of a play as if they were in a novel, one can restore verisimilitude where the play removed it—in other words, one can detect points at which the play departs from verisimilitude:

> Cette réduction de la tragédie au roman est la pierre de touche, pour démêler les actions nécessaires d'avec les vraisemblables. Nous sommes gênés au théâtre par le lieu, par le temps, et par les incommodités de la représentation, qui nous empêchent d'exposer à la vue beaucoup de personnages tout à la fois. . . . le théâtre ne nous laisse pas tant de facilité de réduire tout dans le vraisemblable, par ce qu'il ne nous fait rien savoir que par des gens qu'il expose à la vue de l'auditeur en peu de temps. . . . (3: 163)

The narrator of a novel can pass from place to place at great distance in space, can return in time or move forward in time, and can show things that cannot (or should not) appear onstage. The consequence of this freedom, according to Corneille, is that the code of verisimilitude (apparently understood very much on the terms of the academic theorists) can dictate the correspondence of act to place and time; e.g., that high political secrets should not be confided in a public place.

In the choice of the term *reduction,* there may be a sense of passing from higher to lower; certainly the tragedy and the epic, genres both practiced and theorized in antiquity, have more prestige than the novel. In addition, however, the term contains an etymological trace of the Latin sense of *reducere* ("to bring back"). All poetics in the Aristotelian mode, including Corneille's, begin with the priority of the story. This is a priority both in value and in sequential order; the poet starts by finding the subject and then elaborates it into tragedy or into epic. Reducing a tragedy to a novel is a reversal of the sequence as well as a drop in value to the story in an unconstrained form, a kind of "blob" of narrative material. Corneille gives examples of this "reduction" of tragedy to the novel by reducing parts of his tragedy *Horace.* At the end of the first act, Curiace and his fiancée, Camille, go to join her family in a room where the whole group gets the news that her brothers, the three young Horaces, have been appointed to represent Rome in the combat against the Albans. Curiace congratulates the Horace brother to whom he is closest. In the "novel," Curiace would congratulate Horace on the spot, says Corneille; but in the tragedy, the two friends walk back to the large room (*salle*) in which Camille had been standing before she and Curiace went to see her family. The difference between the spontaneous congratulations right where the friends were standing and the movement back into the other room (that is, back onto the stage) is the difference between novel and tragedy, between verisimilitude and necessity.

This highly technical detail is more important that we might think, for it exemplifies the connection between the Cornelian *nécessaire* and the dominance of the aesthetic. When the two characters return to the stage, they are doing something non-verisimilar but necessary for the pleasure of the audience. They are exhibiting themselves to satisfy the audience's desire to see. Had they remained where they were, as they do in the "novelistic" rewriting, their conduct would be verisimilar and without any necessity whatsoever. Their action or inaction would simply belong to the concept of the character as dictated by assumptions about Roman life. The necessary is a kind of transcendent influence that makes characters do things that are completely inexplicable within the social fictions of their imaginary world. This influence is without moral purpose—morality is expressed through the verisimilar conduct of the characters—but it has a direct basis in the aesthetic shaping of the story. As a transcendent influence, the necessary is added, invisibly, to the events of the story. Corneille says that the necessary is preferable to the verisimilar, or more exactly it is there to "ajouter au vraisemblable dans la liaison des actions, et leur dépendance l'une de l'autre" (3: 171).

Drama exploits this tension between what characters should do according to an idealized, rational, atemporal schema called "the nature of things" and their conduct as it departs from this highly impersonal schema. When characters diverge from the predicted pattern for reasons of their own desire (Chimène's behavior toward Rodrigue as violation of the "virtuous daughter" paradigm), this is one form of necessity, one way in which the libido overrules social norms. When characters diverge from this pattern for other reasons, to satisfy requirements that are imposed by the playwright's desire to "plaire selon les règles de son art," this is another form of necessity. The two necessities have in common that they set pleasure over duty.

When Curiace and Horace walk back onto the stage, they are doing so for us. They do not "know" this, since they exist in a different world, but Corneille knows it. He therefore makes them do something they would not "normally" do for the pleasure of an audience that is invisible and unknown to them. This deviation from the verisimilar leads Corneille directly into collision with one of the major prohibitions of academic dramatic theory, a prohibition that has remained in force for most dramatic representation, including the cinema, well into the twentieth century: the acknowledgment of the audience. Characters are supposed to behave onstage as if they are not being watched. As d'Aubignac writes, the dramatic author "fait tout comme s'il n'y avoit point de Spectateurs . . ." (38). The invisibility of the audience permits action to unfold in complete conformity to the narrative patterns assigned to the types of character, the time, and the place while the audience pretends not to be there. Corneille's concept of the necessary reintroduces the presence of the audience, not into the thoughts of the characters but into certain aspects of their conduct. The necessary expresses the indirect control that audiences have over the characters who are there to bring them pleasure. To please us, the characters need to do things that may be bizarre by the standards of their world—they may, for instance, do things in the "wrong" place because it happens to be the place that is visible to the spectator.

Although Corneille does not so label the two kinds of necessity he describes, let us call the necessary actions of the characters as they pursue their objects ("un homme offensé, de se venger") *secondary necessity* as opposed to the necessary steps taken by the playwright to please his audience, which is the *primary necessity* of any play. Corneille theorizes that the verisimilar should have priority in the individual units of the plot but that the necessary should be preferred in the way these units are joined in sequence. Because the necessary is the linking forward of plot units without express verisimilitude, the necessary clearly disrupts or suppresses standard cause-effect relationships.[7] In commenting on two verisimilar events in *Cinna,* Corneille writes, "voilà une liaison nécessaire entre deux actions vraisemblables, ou si vous l'aimez mieux, une production nécessaire d'une action vraisemblable par une autre pareillement vraisemblable" (3: 166). To return to the earlier example of *Horace,* when Horace and Curiace are with the Horace family in their dwelling offstage, they are doing something that is purely verisimilar. When they are later standing onstage and Curiace congratulates Horace, they are doing something that is purely verisimilar. The fact that they have moved from one place to another between these two acts is not verisimilar; there is no reason for them to do it except to be present to the audience. The relationship between the necessary and *linking* ("une liaison") is apparent if we imagine Curiace walking onstage and standing on his head while Horace watches. This nonverisimilar action is not what Corneille justifies as necessary. Each action, each "tableau" we might say, should be verisimilar, but the sequence or "montage" may not have "le vraisemblable, qu'on doit toujours préférer au nécessaire, lorsqu'on ne regarde que les actions en elles-mêmes" (3: 165). In *Horace,* the linking between the scenes and the fictive action it requires is simply *necessary.* Moreover, it belongs to the category of primary necessity, since it corresponds directly to the playwright's aims but not to the desires of either character.

Distinguishing between the two types of necessity is important only when the playwright intervenes to frustrate the aims, or the apparent aims, of a character in order to achieve the greater pleasure of the audience. In fact such intervention may simply be a way of adding the force of two layers of nonverisimilar supplementation to prevent the verisimilar, normative, repressive, and predictable from occurring. *Le Cid* is such a case. The principal characters are driven by the desire to enjoy their love for each other. This desire leads in two contradictory directions: each must pursue a course of actions that proves their worthiness of the other (Rodrigue must fight Chimène's father; Chimène must in her turn seek to avenge her father's death by demanding Rodrigue's execution) while they aspire to be joined in a now-unthinkable marriage. However nonverisimilar this situation is, the outcome, by which the conflict in Chimène's own aims is overridden, is, by all standards, even less verisimilar. The ending of *Le Cid* is thus an example of the necessary in its purest, most open form as the nonverisimilar staging of desire, a plot construction that is required for the pleasure of the audience, a triumph of poetry over ideology.[8]

The denouement of *Le Cid* is another example of the necessary's role in linking actions that are themselves verisimilar but that do not form a verisimilar sequence. For Chimène to marry Rodrigue is in itself verisimilar; such a plan was, after all, the point of departure of the play. Yet the juxtaposition of Rodrigue's killing Don Gomès with this conclusion is not verisimilar. For Corneille, then, the sequential (or diachronic) order of acts in a play is the sphere of the necessary, the way in which desire and pleasure undo the static verisimilitude of individual moments.[9] In an interestingly contorted passage of the "Discours de la tragédie," Corneille seems to say that the links from action to action are best when they are both verisimilar and necessary, but he concludes by emphasizing the importance of the necessary—it's tempting to say the necessity of the necessary—as part of his overall devaluation of the verisimilar:

> cette liaison . . . est beaucoup meilleure, quand elle est vraisemblable et nécessaire tout ensemble. La raison en est aisée à concevoir. Lorsqu'elle n'est que vraisemblable sans être

nécessaire, le poème s'en peut passer, et elle n'y est pas de grande importance. (3: 165)

Corneille does not entirely fill in for us the conceivable reasons he mentions, but he gives us some clues. First of all, in saying that the play, the "poème," can do without verisimilar links, he supposes that any spectator can fill in verisimilar connections from the stock of preformed ideological situations. In fact, Corneille provides many examples of such ideological shortcuts in his plays and delights in subverting them at the same time. In *Le Cid,* Rodrigue and Don Sanche leave the palace to duel. One of them returns. Chimène borrows from the stock of plot motifs available in her society: the one who did not return must be lying dead on the field. This is a verisimilar link, but it is later shown to be a false one. Second, in saying that the play does not need a verisimilar link, he is alluding to the nonaesthetic quality of verisimilitude. The necessary is what is required by *art,* rather than by life or by that corrected vision of life that is the verisimilar. When the link between two actions can be taken for granted, this connection does not require the special attention of the spectator nor the creativity of the playwright.

The doctrine of the necessary allows Corneille not only to override verisimilitude, but even truth itself, that is, history. He classifies actions of the tragic plot in terms of their relation to historical truth and arrives at three patterns. Such actions either:

1. Follow history .... true, no need for verisimilar
2. Add to history .... sometimes verisimilar, sometimes necessary
3. Falsify history .... only when necessary
(3: 166)

When an action is simply transposed from a historical account to the plot of a play, the action need not be verisimilar, because the playwright can always defend himself by referring to the proof. If an action is added to the historical account, it can be either verisimilar or necessary (if verisimilar, it would seem, by the general tendency of Corneille's theory, to be less important and less artistic). If the action contradicts the historical account, it must be justified by the purposes of the play itself, by the aims of the playwright and the characters. The design of the tragedy as artistic construction directed at heightened emotional states is the strong justification for shaping stories into plots. Verisimilitude is a weak, secondary, merely "ornamental" concept that can be used as a kind of filler between the structural parts of the dramatic frame.

This position is quite different from that of the academic theorists. D'Aubignac says that in treating a factual story,

> les regles du Theatre ne rejettent pas les notables incidents d'une Histoire; mais elles donnent les moyens de les ajuster en telle sorte, que sans choquer la vray-semblance des Temps, des Lieux, et des autres circonstances d'une Action, ils puissent y paroistre, non pas, à la vérité, tels qu'ils ont esté dans l'effet, mais tels qu'ils doivent estre pour n'avoir rien que d'agreable. (29)

This insistence on the pleasant (*l'agréable*) is one of the principal differences between Corneille and the academic theorists, for Corneille's concept of the necessary, though it aims ultimately at producing pleasure, is always played against the idealized "nature of things" to create surprise, dissonance, and even pain.

Colors

Corneille's idea of the "necessary" is not the only strategy for linking plot elements that involves some manipulation of verisimilitude. D'Aubignac also ponders the relation between an idealized norm of actions and the demands of an audience seeking pleasure. He comes up with the doctrine of *couleur*, or pretense, and explains how various dramatic elements—a plot motif, a character's entrance or exit, or a speech—can serve at least two different purposes at the same time, one defined in terms of the story and one in terms of the performance in front of an audience.

To appreciate these "colors," we have to be acquainted with d'Aubignac's unusually extensive meditation on drama as representation. The art of painting, specifically narrative painting, provides d'Aubignac with his favorite comparison to clarify his thought about theatrical representation. When we see a play onstage we are not looking at "Horatius" or "Augustus" but rather at actors, speaking French, who, in some mysterious way, "stand for" those historical personages. Likewise, standing before a painting, what we see is first of all an object produced by a worker:

> Je prens icy la comparaison d'un Tableau, dont j'ay resolu de me servir souvent en ce Traitté, et je dis qu'on le peut considerer en deux façons. La premiere comme une peinture, c'est à dire, entant que c'est l'ouvrage de la main du Peintre, où il n'y a que des couleurs et non pas des choses; des ombres, et non pas des corps, des jours artificiels, de fausses élevations, des éloignements en Perspective, des raccourcissements illusoires, et de simples apparences de tout ce qui n'est point. La seconde entant qu'il contient une chose qui est peinte, soit veritable ou supposée telle, dont les lieux sont certains, les qualitez naturelles. . . . (34)

The opposition between "peinture" and "chose peinte" allows d'Aubignac to meditate on the fact that we simultaneously perceive the "representant" and the "representé"—a stage set and Auguste's palace, Floridor the actor and Horace the character. The painter, like the playwright, has to remember at all times during the creative process that both of these aspects of the very same "thing" will be perceived. A patch of color will be the face of a saint. D'Aubignac's description of a hypothetical painting of Mary Magdalene as penitent, taken from standard Renaissance iconography, illustrates his keen grasp of the entailments of this double nature of the work of art:

> s'il [le peintre] veut peindre la Magdeleine Penitente, il n'oubliera rien des marques les plus importantes de son Histoire, car s'il en usoit d'autre sorte ceux qui la verroient ne la reconnoistroient pas. Il la mettra dans une posture agreable, autrement on la regarderoit avec dégoust. Il y employera les plus vives couleurs; afin que l'œil y trouve plus de satisfaction. Il ne la jettera pas le visage contre terre, parce qu'il en cacheroit la plus belle partie, mais il la mettra à genoux. . . . Mais à l'examiner de l'autre maniere et comme une chose veritable, il fera que cette figure aura le tein pâle et defait, parce qu'il n'est pas croyable qu'il fust autre dans ses austeritez.

Il ne luy donnera pas devant elle une couronne, mais une
croix. Il ne la mettra pas sur un lict de velours en broderie,
mais sur la terre. . . . (37)

The "most important symbols of her story" refer to the "facts"
of the Magdalene legend. Though d'Aubignac does not give
this distinction any emphasis here, we should remember that
this concept of visual "symbols" could be used to describe a
painting of one historical incident that had happened at a specific time on a specific day. Instead, these symbols in the Magdalene painting refer to an idea, a commonplace, though one which
is here guaranteed as "true" by virtue of faith in the Roman
Catholic Church. Mary Magdalene was a penitent, and the
painting manifests this "truth" about her instead of referring
to a specific, attested moment within New Testament history
at which the saint was seen to perform the act represented in
this painting. The posture, clothing, flesh color, and location
of Mary Magdalene are drawn from that repertory of knowledge we recognize as the verisimilar.

Like Corneille, d'Aubignac divides his analysis of the work
of art into the verisimilar, which concerns a kind of immanent
logic of actions (that the Magdalene would kneel or prostrate
herself on the hard ground rather than on a soft bed is a motif
similar to the notion that Curiace would congratulate Horace
on the spot rather than move to another room to do so), and
another category that is directly concerned with the presentation of the work to an audience. This second, aesthetic category,
which Corneille calls the necessary, corresponds to d'Aubignac's
"Spectacle" or "simple Representation." D'Aubignac perceives
the tension between verisimilitude and representation, as Corneille does, and realizes that if verisimilitude alone were to
control the shape of a story, the construction of the artwork
would be quite different. In d'Aubignac's case, we could describe this clash as pitting semiotics against sensation.[10] The
Magdalene's posture and gestures must signify her history, her
emotion, her belief, and her resolve. This verisimilar aspect of
the painting conveys information that makes her recognizable
to the audience in her legendary or historical specificity. On
the other hand, the painting is meant to bring a much more
immediate, sensual (or at least sense-oriented) experience: hence
the insistence on using "les plus vives couleurs" for the plea-

sure of the eye. As Yoshiko Hagiwara says, the distinction between verisimilitude and representation coincides with—in fact, is simply a different name for—other dichotomies: between the intelligible and the sensorial, or between the verisimilar and the pleasurable, the *vraisemblable* and the *agréable*. On the other hand, it would be wrong to view d'Aubignac's distinction here as a split between the interpretable but absent and entirely imaginary scene, on one hand, and the entirely present, physical reality of the painting as object: pigment, oil, canvas, frame.[11] While the verisimilar, for d'Aubignac, does seem to belong entirely to the world of the story (in the case of the Magdalene, this is "une chose qui est peinte, soit veritable ou supposée telle" [34]), the *agréable,* pleasurable, or sensorial side of the painting belongs both to the physical reality of the painting as canvas and to the represented world, both to the idea of the Magdalene as a beautiful and sexual woman and to the pleasure of the color and balance of the painting.

D'Aubignac's problem can be stated in terms of a stock plot from modern thrillers: what to do with the body. The range of the *agréable,* bridging the distinction between color, line, and texture, on one hand, and the enjoyment of an apparent human "reality," simply overpowers d'Aubignac's attempt to make a direct contrast analogous to the signifier/signified opposition. While he does initially speak of the painting as "des ombres, et non pas des corps" (34), Mary Magdalene's physical beauty cannot somehow be eliminated from the aesthetic pleasure that the spectator will take from the painting. The painter "ne la jettera pas le visage contre terre, parce qu'il en cacheroit la plus belle partie, mais il la mettra à genoux. Il ne la couvrira pas toute entière d'un Cilice, parce qu'elle seroit sans grace; mais elle sera à demi nuë. Il ne la representera pas dans le fond d'un rocher, parce qu'elle ne pourroit estre veuë . . ." (37). Mary Magdalene's physical beauty, though it is part of the list of verisimilar attributes, seems to belong mostly to the pleasure of the representation for the spectator. D'Aubignac lists posture, partial nudity, and a high degree of visibility among the qualities necessary to the aesthetic success of the work, as a "peinture, ou un ouvrage de l'Art" (36).

The spectator of the artwork is deeply involved in the absent fictive "world" and not merely in the world of physically present objects. It is surely not a mere accident that d'Aubignac chose a hypothetical painting of Mary Magdalene to exemplify his theory of representation, for the pleasure that the spectator takes in this painting is deeply related to desire, to voyeurism, to some imaginary reconciliation between sanctity and prostitution, not merely the naïve and safe enjoyment of color and light. As Timothy Murray has so perceptively noted, d'Aubignac's theory "enhances the libidinal activity of the spectator" (176).[12] Like Mary Magdalene, the theater is an art that is both "fallen" and deeply linked to the Church. It gives pleasure, but it must provide moral improvement.

D'Aubignac's sensitivity to this change gave rise to what Hagiwara has described as an "internal" rather than an "external" concept of representation. In Hagiwara's view, d'Aubignac differs from other theorists (and especially from Castelvetro) in emphasizing that this dialectic between story and perception is internal to the experience of the painting. The Magdalene, along with all that signifies her penitence, is described in alternation with the spectator's pleasure in the color and light of the painting: "D'Aubignac oppose . . . la surface peinte du tableau dans son aspect sensible à ce qui est figuré ou représenté dans le tableau" (Hagiwara 25). For Hagiwara this new emphasis on the two levels of mimetic art breaks radically with the tradition of conceiving mimesis as a relation between model and copy, for here "la distinction ne s'établit pas entre l'œuvre, picturale ou dramatique, et un objet extérieur, représentée par celle-ci, mais elle traverse l'œuvre elle-même" (26). In certain respects, however, d'Aubignac's move away from a copy/model concept of the work of art does not depart from the main line of mimetic doctrine as understood in the seventeenth century. D'Aubignac, rather, adapted the notion of mimesis in keeping with the modern stress on verisimilitude—representation is no longer concerned with an *external* reality (*le vrai*) but with an intersubjective or communal universe of probabilities, demands, and relationships. The quasi-independent life and energy of Mary Magdalene as part of this verisimilar world is what d'Aubignac terms "une chose veritable," meaning that the Magdalene *within* the painting and not outside the painting in historical reality is what has the quality of truth. In this context, truth (*le véritable*) is used as the equivalent of the verisimilar, since the painter tries to avoid anything that would make the painting less "croyable." This transfer of the quality of the *véritable* from the "outside" world to the painted scene itself is what Hagiwara calls a confusion between the "objet représenté" and the "objet réel," but if we take seriously the ideology of verisimilitude there is no confusion. Instead, d'Aubignac must intentionally assert the veritable (that is, verisimilar) Magdalene as belonging completely to the process of making a story for an audience. There is no "real" Magdalene in Hagiwara's sense; there is only the Magdalene as she is painted in accordance with hagiography.

D'Aubignac's description of the Magdalene painting displays something that his dual terminology does not emphasize (and that Hagiwara's reading of the passage omits entirely): the pleasure the spectator takes in the likeness of the attractive, half-undressed woman herself. In his theory, the "agrément" of the painting comes from material qualities of the surface such as the color and the texture of the applied paint. Yet in the description of the painting and the hypothetical viewer's experience of it, d'Aubignac mentions the beauty of the saint's face and body. If her face were against the ground, we would be unable to see the most beautiful part of the painting. If she were covered by a hair shirt, the image would be "sans grace." So there is a second level of pleasure between the appreciation of the painting as crafted material object and a reading of the painting as a part of the story of the salvation of a sinner. In between, there is the simple pleasure of spectator (presumably male, like d'Aubignac) enjoying the sight of a beautiful, half-undressed woman—a woman, moreover, in some sense offering herself, though in this case she is offering herself on the mercies of her Savior.

When d'Aubignac says that one way to look at the painting is to see "des couleurs et non pas des choses," he pits colors against things, even though a color is also a thing. If we are looking at a color *as a color,* we are distracted in some way from the thing it represents in the painting. This opposition is the key to understanding dramatic color as a two-sided concept: one side is aimed at keeping the audience occupied while the other side is turned toward some other, less immediate purpose. D'Aubignac never provides a definition of color, but instead supposes that we understand the contemporary seven-teenth-century uses of the word. *Couleur* could, of course, mean simply "color," such as red, blue, and green, but it also meant a pretext or surface appearance under which something more real or substantial was hidden. Even in d'Aubignac's appeal to the painting analogy, color is more than a reference to the spectrum or painterly palette. When he writes, "il n'y a que des couleurs et non pas des choses; des ombres, et non pas des corps," d'Aubignac uses "colors" to show the difference be-tween *mere* appearance and the illusion of something more solid. The scores of occurrences of the term in *La pratique du théâtre* illustrate the broader usage, defined in Cotgrave's dictionary (1611), "A colour, hue; dye; staine; also, a pretext, pretence, cloake, shew, shadow, for a matter." Colors conceal something, and in the theater they exploit verisimilitude to cover the play-wright's deeper aims. As Hagiwara says, of color, "c'est . . . une technique de la vraisemblance" that "permet de rendre vrai-semblable et inoffensif . . . un fait potentiellement compromet-tant" (41).

The concept of color concerns the playwright's need to manipulate the audience's attention to conceal the deeper work-ings of the dramatic structure. For instance, color can be used to give some function within the plot structure to a part of the play that is actually created as a free-standing aesthetic ele-ment. If the playwright has created a speech or some poetry for a character to recite,

> Pour rendre donc vray-semblable qu'un homme recite des Stances, c'est à dire qu'il fasse des vers sur le Theatre, il faut qu'il y ait *une couleur ou raison* pour authoriser ce changement de langage. Or la principale et la plus commune est, que l'Acteur, qui les recite, ait eu quelque temps suffisant pour y travailler, ou pour y faire travailler. . . . (D'Aubignac 263; emphasis added)

Implicit in this arrangement is the notion that "stances" (met-rically different verse that stands out from the neutral alexan-drines that represent "normal" speech in tragedy) and certain long, highly polished speeches or narratives are ornaments in the play, created to dazzle the public or to exploit the celebrated declamatory talents of an actor or actress. In such cases the purely aesthetic potential of the stage is developed at the expense of the verisimilar conceptions of how characters behave and speak. Color is invoked to excuse this lapse into the purely aesthetic. So color is not synonymous with verisimilitude, because it appears at moments when the verisimilar has been neglected. Color is a kind of duplicitous verisimilitude, or verisimilitude with a bad conscience, very close to what Gérard Genette calls *motivation* in his study of another seventeenth-century text, Valincour's *Lettres à Madame la Marquise ***.* The writer resorts to colors when he realizes that he has something to conceal, usually something that is designed specifically for the audience's pleasure.

Color is generally forward-looking. It prepares a coming event, as in the case of the *stances.* An actor should not simply burst into poetry but should plan ahead, and the audience should be aware of the character's act of composition, at least after the fact. This leads to two important observations. First, the audience should be aware that the character who recites poetry has had time to prepare it, but the audience need not (in fact, had probably better not) know in advance that the character was working on the composition. Color is thus a mediation between the audience's delight in what is fully present on the stage at a given moment and the coherence of ongoing successive acts. Second, the time allowed for the character's composition of the *stances* is meant to conceal the *playwright's* composition. In this respect, color diverts the audience from any authorial intervention into the verisimilar, conceived as the autonomous working-out of entirely predictable, paradigmatic modules of behavior. Color is necessary when it becomes too apparent that we are in a theater, watching a play.

D'Aubignac addresses both of these issues in commenting on the need to divert the audience from what is going to happen later in the play:

> il y a certaines choses qui doivent servir de fondement pour en produire d'autres, selon l'ordre de la vray-semblance, et qui neantmoins n'en donnent aucune connoissance, non seulement parce qu'il n'y a pas de necessité que les secondes arrivent en consequence des premieres, mais encore parce que ces premieres sont exposées *sous des prétextes et avec des couleurs* si vray-semblables, selon l'estat des affaires

presentes, que l'esprit des Spectateurs est tout à fait arresté
et ne pense point qu'il en doive sortir aucun autre Incident
que ce qu'il connoist. (129; emphasis added)

The spectator is here meant to be entirely fixated on the present
by virtue of the colors that conceal the author's intention of
using an event as the first step toward another. D'Aubignac has
given an extremely useful insight into the mechanisms of verisimilitude; an action that is designed to assure the verisimilar
quality of a later action may be itself lacking in verisimilitude.
Long-range verisimilitude requires short-term betrayals of that
very concept, and another layer has to be supplied to cover the
plot structure itself. The covering arrangement consists of a
segmentation that is, paradoxically, required by the long-term
goal of making the play seem an inexorable chain of causes
and effects. In this case colors rivet (*arrester*) the spectator's
attention to the present, whereas in the case of the *stances* colors
do something quite different: they keep an act on the stage from
appearing solely and inexplicably present and reconnect that
act to the character's previous acts.

Color is a kind of patch or splicing device to fit together
segments of the plot in a way that increases surprise, permits
purely ornamental interludes, and yet assures narrative continuity. Because color is not in itself verisimilitude, it must assume a verisimilar guise—this is why the terms are repeatedly
linked by d'Aubignac ("couleurs si vray-semblables")—and it
must do this from within the world of the characters. We have
noted the resemblance between d'Aubignac's colors and "motivation." It is important to realize that there are significant qualifications to the relationship between these terms. As we view
the *Pratique* after having read Genette's influential essay, we
can see color as a subcategory of motivation. This subordina-
tion is due to the purely theatrical nature of d'Aubignac's field.
Genette gives great weight to the novel in exemplifying motivation. In the novel, motivation can be given at the level of
the narrator ("La marquise demanda sa voiture et se mit au lit,
car elle était fort capricieuse" [Genette 99]) or from within
the world of the characters either as action ("La marquise
demanda sa voiture et se mit au lit, *car elle se trouva mal*") or
as dialogue (". . . au lit, en disant 'Quelle migraine!'"). The
dramatic author has no recourse to explicit interjections of the

narrator's discourse but must create a self-explanatory and self-justifying world on the stage. When a specific passage of a dramatic text has colors, the playwright is acutely aware of his intervention into the actions to create a detour from the path they would otherwise follow. If he is successful, however, the spectators will never be aware that the passage is colored:

> Le Theatre est comme un Monde particulier, où tout est renfermé dans les notions et l'étenduë de l'action representée, et qui n'a point de communication avec le grand Monde, sinon autant qu'il s'y rencontre attaché par la connoissance que le Poëte en donne avec adresse. Mais il se faut toûjours souvenir que toutes les choses qui se disent et qui se font pour estre les préparatifs et comme les semences de celles qui peuvent arriver, doivent avoir une si apparente raison et une si puissante couleur pour estre dites et faites en leur lieu, qu'elles semblent n'estre introduites que pour cela, et que jamais elles ne donnent ouverture à prévenir les Incidens qu'elles préparent. (D'Aubignac 135)

It is clear that d'Aubignac's colors and Corneille's "necessary" have a good deal in common. Each is invoked when the playwright must make a rearrangement of the plot that departs from the verisimilar course of actions; moreover the departure from the verisimilar that is associated with colors and with the necessary is aimed at bringing pleasure to the audience and perhaps also (certainly, in Corneille's case) to the fictive characters. Like Corneille's necessary, d'Aubignac's colors have something to do with the way actions are linked to the preceding or following actions. There are significant differences, however. The necessary is the antithesis of the verisimilar, whereas d'Aubignac never mentions any possibility that the skilled playwright might make use of nonverisimilar colors. Colors are always the result of the author's need to compromise between the conditions of theatrical representation and his plans to affect the audience. They therefore resemble what we have called primary necessity in Corneille's doctrine. As far as the other kind of necessity is concerned in Corneille's poetics—what characters should do to reach their own goals—the less concealed the departure from verisimilitude the better, or so it would seem from Corneille's praise of the nonverisimilar tragic story. In d'Aubignac, on the other hand, this deliberate violation of the verisimilar on the part of characters is nowhere theorized, and color remains firmly attached to the playwright's concealed aims rather than the characters' overt ones.

Yet if we return to d'Aubignac's analogy to the Magdalene painting, we can see that there is a strong suggestion that the author of *La pratique du théâtre* is just as committed as Corneille to an emotional, libidinal, and perhaps transgressive participation by the spectator in the lives of the characters. For both theorists, pure verisimilitude would interfere with that pleasure. D'Aubignac uses the imagined painting to show how a merely verisimilar Magdalene would not provide the same *satisfaction* to the spectator's eye. The painter should use his brightest colors and make the Magdalene's face and half-nude body visible—this part of the artist's work is on the side of "des couleurs et non pas des choses"—but the concession to the story of the Magdalene, the verisimilitude that will make people see this figure as Mary Magdalene and not a painting of a pretty model, appears in the decision to depict her as pale and surrounded by wild animals. For Corneille, too, the purely verisimilar story would either fail to appear onstage (most things would take place out of sight, somewhere other than the single place chosen for the dramatic scene) or would not move the spectator's passions as do the "grands sujets qui remuent fortement les passions, et en opposent l'impétuosité aux lois du devoir, ou aux tendresses du sang" (3: 118).

The Verisimilar Character, or *Bienséance*

If the verisimilar is a corrected form of real life, cleansed of its messy and random detail and of all that is supposed to run against the expectations of a properly initiated audience, how far should that correction go? This question is especially acute in regard to ethical issues. When Rapin writes that "la vérité ne fait les choses que comme elles sont; et la vray-semblance les fait comme elles doivent estre," it is not entirely clear whether he means that verisimilitude stresses the major defining features of the world as opposed to stray and incomplete data or whether he means that verisimilitude improves and flatters the human models by making them behave better according to prevailing ethical ideas. These are, in any event, two sometimes

conflicting aims that appear in the poetics of tragic verisimilitude and in descriptions of characters (rather than of events),
and particularly of characters as *doers,* as agents.[13] While the
concept of the verisimilar in its broadest sense is only vaguely
defined and almost always in negative terms—in terms of what
is *not* verisimilar—the discussions of verisimilar characters are
often astoundingly specific and prescriptive.

The moral approach to verisimilitude was etched deeply into
French cultural history at the time of the Quarrel of *Le Cid,*
when Scudéry attacked a whole range of characters in Corneille's play for failings that were described as gross violations
of the moral order. The heroine, Chimène, was "impudique,"
a "fille desnaturée," and a "monstre," and Scudéry found that
the play as a whole became an apology for vice (Scudéry, *Observations* 80–81). This purely moral judgment became a
judgment concerning verisimilitude in Scudéry's observation:
"qu'il est vray que Chimene espousa le Cid, mais qu'il n'est
point vray-semblable qu'une fille d'honneur, espouse le meurtrier de son Pere. Cet evenement estoit bon pour l'Historien,
mais il ne valait rien pour le Poete" (75). Since the idea of
verisimilitude requires a correction of public opinion as well
as a correction of history, we find morality at issue in what the
Académie said about the theater audience. Implying that *Le Cid*'s
popularity was no indication of the play's verisimilitude, Chapelain wrote on behalf of the Académie that plays should not aim
to please people who "ne se soucient pas de voir violer les loix
de la Nature pourveu qu'ils se divertissent" (*Sentimens* 360).
Chapelain specifically joined the immoral behavior of characters and the public's equally immoral view of characters by
complaining that some spectators would be just as touched by
the misfortunes of the (evil) Clytemnestra as by those of the
(good) Penelope. Confirming this association of collective moral
norms with the verisimilitude of characters is Corneille's use
of the four-part table of kinship ratios. These ratios are basic
plots that are morally shocking in different degrees. For example, to kill a stranger and then to discover kinship to that
person requires the least transgression of a norm in which kinship is the basis of obligation and loyalty. On the other hand,
to recognize a kinsman and to kill him nonetheless seems to
be a deliberately transgressive act. Moreover, Corneille writes

of the dramatic impact of "la grandeur du crime" that Ghirardelli could have preserved in his tragedy *La mort de Crispe.*

It is easy to suppose that the demand of most theorists for verisimilar characters, in the context of a verisimilitude that is a "correction" of the defective reality of history, would lead to a moral purification of tragic character. Since a term often used for character verisimilitude is *bienséance* (or "decorum" in English poetics) it would be easy to suppose that characters, at least the principal characters, should be morally good. Scudéry's attack on *Le Cid* is centered on the moral failings of its characters, especially of its heroine. Because Chimène was a bad woman, his argument seems to go, the play is a bad play. This is an oversimplification, of course, for there is a second phase to Scudéry's assault: Chimène is a bad woman and she is not *punished* for her immoral behavior. As a consequence, Corneille's tragi-comedy "choque la raison et les bonnes mœurs" (Scudéry, *Observations* 77). Scudéry includes in his criticism just about all of *Le Cid*'s characters in terms that sound as if he is criticizing *people* instead of characters, as if he is making entirely moral judgments instead of dramatic or poetic ones. Scudéry's approach in this historically important and often paraphrased document skews our perception of character verisimilitude toward this moralizing habit. Because characters like the Infanta represent "la bien-seance mal observee" (86) and because the play as a whole "choque . . . les bonnes mœurs," it would be easy to suppose that character verisimilitude, or *bienséance,* is simply the requirement that characters follow the moral code considered normative in the world of the audience.

There is little doubt that theorists of the period often veer toward this assumption. However, with the exception of Scudéry in his highly polemical *Observations,* the authors of poetics of tragedy hold that verisimilitude requires many characters to be immoral or criminal. The term *bienséance* is often used to explain that character verisimilitude assigns priority to a character's fidelity to type, yet *bienséance* is itself ambiguous in seventeenth-century usage and may have exacerbated an already difficult merging of Aristotle's *Poetics* with French culture. Poetics takes up *bienséance* in the wake of Aristotle's discussion of "character" (*êthos*) in chapter 15 of his *Poetics,* where he presents four aims for dramatic characterization: that characters be good, appropriate, like (resembling known persons to whom they refer), and consistent. *Bienséance,* in seventeenth-century French, conveys, most of all, the second of these aims or requirements, but throughout the century goodness and appropriateness are mixed together. This mixture is what makes *bienséance* such an elusive concept. Yet, however elusive, it becomes the dominant term under which character is discussed, so that we often and properly consider *bienséance* to be a major concern of French classicism, and we rarely describe the French classical theorists as being preoccupied with character.

The duality of *bienséance* appears in the crisp terminology of Nicot's Latin glossary, *Le thresor de la langue françoise* (1606): "La bienseance & rapport des parties l'une à l'autre. *Convenientia rerum. Decentia.*" This definition shows how the term was used long before the French became preoccupied with using Aristotle's *Poetics* as a basis for their own in the late 1630s. The confusing double meaning of the word is not simply a reflection of the complexity of the philosopher's doctrine of character but shows, rather, that French usage prepared the later conflicts over tragic characters. There is a dominant sense from which the other grows: *bienséance* refers to a framework within which each thing finds its place, within which a thing "clicks" into its habitual association with the things around it. In the Latin translation that follows, this meaning is neatly conveyed by *convenientia rerum,* the fittingness of things. However, the second Latin term gives a derivative and much more narrow sense, the social or customary appropriateness of behavior that we call "decency" (*decentia*). The conflict between the broader and the narrower sense, between *convenientia* and *decentia,* becomes the schism that separates Corneille from his detractors and that makes *bienséance* an apparently contradictory requirement when La Mesnardière and others try to apply it to ancient tragedy. To give contemporary English terms for this dichotomy, we can turn to Cotgrave's dictionary (1611): "*Bienseance: f.* A comelinesse, becomming, seemelinesse, agreablenesse; also, congruitie, correspondencie. *Etre à la bienseance de.* To be fit for; as land & c."

Even Scudéry's comments on *Le Cid,* which stress so heavily the indecency of the conduct of all the characters in Corneille's play, contain traces of the requirement that characters' conduct should be measured by a flexible standard of fittingness rather than by some absolute and universal moral standard. The lack of *bienséance* in the Infanta is due to her specific social standing, preventing her from loving a subject "en une amour si peu digne d'une fille de Roy" (Scudéry, *Observations* 86). Chimène's conduct violates both absolute moral standards and her specific social standing ("il n'est point vray-semblable qu'une fille d'honneur, espouse le meurtrier de son Pere"), since Scudéry sees these ideal moral norms converging with character verisimilitude at the upper levels of society. In this view of *Le Cid,* both *decentia* and *convenientia* are lacking. The character has behaved badly, and the playwright has failed in his duty to conceal or correct that behavior by depicting the characters as they should have been:

> Fernand y auroit esté plus grand politique, Urraque d'inclination moins basse, Don Gomes moins ambitieux et moins insolent, Don Sanche plus genereux, Elvire de meilleur exemple pour les Suivantes, et cet Autheur n'auroit pas enseigné la vengeance, par la bouche mesme de la fille de celuy dont on se vange. . . . (Scudéry, *Observations* 82)

Scudéry is at least consistent in his thorough description of the *bienséance* of the highest social level, where all the women are modest and submissive and all the men are brave and magnanimous. However, in his view of the fitting, the verisimilar, as the good, Scudéry seems to have theorized a world in which tragedy could not occur because the characters' moral conduct and their skill at carrying out the duties of their station relegate any disruption of the social order to unforeseeable accident. This, as we will see shortly, runs against the prevailing seventeenth-century tendency to view tragedy as *crime.*

If for Scudéry *bienséance* seems to require moral goodness (and all other sorts of personal perfection), the majority of theorists saw *bienséance* as requiring imperfection and evil. The response of the Académie to Scudéry in its evaluation of *Le Cid* states this straightforwardly:

> comme plusieurs choses sont requises pour rendre une action vray-semblable, et qu'il y faut garder la bien-seance du temps, du lieu, des conditions, des aages, des mœurs et

des passions, la principale entre toutes est que dans le Poëme chacun agisse conformément aux mœurs qui luy ont esté attribuées, et que par exemple, un meschant ne fasse point de bons desseins. (Chapelain, *Sentimens* 365)

Here *convenientia* ("fittingness") is the meaning of *bienséance,* and this fittingness is further divided in regard to character into condition (rank), age, morals, and emotion. In addition the Académie emphasizes the most important aspect of character verisimilitude: consistency of the character's conduct. Significantly, the illustration chosen for this consistency is that a bad character should remain bad.[14] Chapelain elsewhere argues against the misunderstanding of *bienséance* as moral goodness, writing that *bienséance* is not "ce qui est honnête, mais ce qui convient aux personnes, soit bonnes, soit mauvaises, et telles qu'on les introduit dans la pièce" ("Discours de la poésie représentative" [second version] 130).

Certain characters, to fulfill the requirement of *bienséance,* should have defects of personality, some of which may have moral implications in the narrow sense. The good and bad qualities of characters are fixed by poetics and sometimes given in lists. For instance, La Mesnardière writes:

le Vieillard sera chagrin, avare, aisé à fascher, censeur rigoureux & injuste des plaisirs des jeunes gens, blasmera leurs occupations & les mœurs du siécle présent pour élever le temps passé. . . . un Asiatique est timide, un Africain infidelle, un Européen est sage, & un Americain stupide. Selon l'espéce des fortunes, un homme de basse naissance élevé aux grans emplois, & aux dignitez éminentes, est pour l'ordinaire insolent. (38–39)

When it comes to the major characters of tragedy, the heroes and heroines, seventeenth-century theorists have a tendency to be both highly moralizing and extreme. The verisimilar is not the world as it is, but the world as it should be. If evil is not simply eliminated from the tragic world, it should be shown to lead to unhappiness. This is a major difference between the world as it is (*le vrai*) and the world as it should be (*le vraisemblable*). According to La Mesnardière, "encore que dans le Monde les bons soient souvent affligez, & que les meschans prospérent," tragedy is "toujours obligé de récompenser les vertus,

& de chastier les vices" (107). D'Aubignac is even more emphatic about the centrality of the vice/virtue distinction in tragedy, though he does not require that vice always be punished:

> La principale regle du Poëme dramatique, est que les vertus y soient toûjours recompensées, ou pour le moins toûjours loüées, mal-gré les outrages de la Fortune, et que les vices y soient toûjours punis, ou pour le moins toûjours en horreur, quand mesme ils y triomphent. (8–9)

Rapin states that tragedy teaches men that vice never goes unpunished (23).

Poetic theorists see Aristotle as requiring the hero to commit an immoral act. *Hamartia,* the "tragic flaw" of chapter 13 of the *Poetics,* was seen, by all theorists—with the possible exception of Corneille—as being a moral failing rather than an error or accident. This "causal element productive of misfortune," as a modern scholar has called it, was usually called a *faute* or a *crime* in classical French poetics (Halliwell, in his ed. of Aristotle, *Poetics* 128). Almost all theorists of tragedy make gestures of respect toward Aristotle's demand that, as Chapelain says, "le poète imite les actions des grands dont les fins ont été malheureuses et qui n'étaient ni trop bons ni trop méchants" ("Discours de la poésie représentative" [second version] 130). Racine echoes this view in writing of Phaedra that she "n'est ni tout à fait coupable ni tout à fait innocente" and in explaining that Hippolytus's love for Aricie is added to the story to create an imperfection of character that would transform him from "un philosophe exempt de toute imperfection" to a son "un peu coupable envers son père" (preface to *Phèdre, Théâtre complet* 577).

The vocabulary of French dramatic theory makes it clear that tragedy was primarily a demonstration of the triumph of virtue over vice in a well-ordered, verisimilar world. Seventeenth-century poetics differs in the main from many other understandings of tragedy—and of Aristotle's *Poetics*—by emphasizing the polar opposition of moral goodness and badness rather than by concentrating on the middle. The theorists slide easily from token recognition of the isolated or moderate character of the hero's "fault," attributed to Aristotle's requirements of tragedy, into an extremist, dualistic tendency along the vice/virtue divide. Racine's preface to *Phèdre,* where he states in apparently moderate terms the guilt of Phaedra and Hippolytus, concludes with a crescendo of moral denunciation, with a vivid contrast between virtue and vice:

> je n'en ai point fait [de tragédie] où la vertu soit plus mise en jour que dans celle-ci. Les moindres fautes y sont sévèrement punies; la seule pensée du crime y est regardée avec autant d'horreur que le crime même; les faiblesses de l'amour y passent pour de vraies faiblesses; les passions n'y sont présentées aux yeux que pour montrer tout le désordre dont elles sont cause; et le vice y est peint partout avec des couleurs qui en font connaître et haïr la difformité. (*Théâtre complet* 578)

Discussions of tragic plots, and especially of the *peripeteia,* or reversal of fortune, veer frequently toward an extreme categorization of the tragic characters into depraved moral monsters or pure, innocent victims. It is this reversal

> qui touche l'esprit avec le plus de véhémence, et qui le met en un état où étonné par les disgraces qui arrivent à l'improviste, il admire et craint tout ensemble cette souveraine Justice qui punit rigoureusement les Personnes vicieuses, et ruinant des entreprises qui leur sembloient infaillibles, leur arrache l'Ame du corps, ou la Couronne de la teste, lors qu'elles se préparoient à opprimer les innocens. (La Mesnardière 55)

The tragic hero appears here as a vicious person, not a good person who has miscalculated, made a mistake, or briefly yielded to temptation, and the victims of this person's actions are not simply other people but *innocent* people. It is true that the adjective *vicieuse* can, technically, signify "having a defect" rather than "predominantly evil," but La Mesnardière's terms suggest the latter not only because of the vicious/innocent duality but because of the violence of divine Justice.

La Mesnardière in particular often writes in terms of emphasizing or enhancing the goodness of the virtuous and the evil of the vicious. Rather than devising plots to attenuate the evil nature of the hero and remind us that the hero should, in Aristotle's view "commett[re] une faute médiocre qui lui attire un grand malheur" (18), La Mesnardière proposes sharpening the distinction between the evil hero and other persons. One way to do this is to add particularly virtuous characters to heighten the contrast, "afin que la difformité d'un crime si odieux fasse naistre beaucoup d'horreur dans l'ame de ceux qui le voyent, et qui en doivent profiter" (La Mesnardière 99).

Since tragedy is the noblest dramatic genre in a society that links the social rank of the heroes with the aesthetic and moral quality of the text, tragedy must represent the most aristocratic and most perfect individuals:

> Comme le Poëme tragique consiste à bien réprésenter une Action remarquable, et qu'il prend pour son Sujet celles des plus excellens hommes . . . ainsi que la Comedie imite les plus imparfaits . . . , le Poëte doibt prendre garde à figurer ses Héros les meilleurs qu'il sera possible, à l'exemple des grans Peintres, qui flatent toujours leurs pourtraits, et leur donnent des agrémens que les naturels n'ont pas. (La Mesnardière 46)

While terms like "excellens" and "meilleurs" are not very specific and might allow for high intelligence and courage linked to great moral imperfections (this is, in fact, Corneille's approach to the problem of heroism), La Mesnardière continues after the passage just quoted to get deeper and deeper into the paradox of tragic evil. He admits that the tragic plot "demande que ses principaux Personnages soient plustost meschans que bons" but argues that "il suffira que ces Gens soient mediocrement mauvais" (here, of course, La Mesnardière takes a position radically opposed to Corneille's choice of heroically bad characters, heroes of evil, in plays like *Rodogune* and *Attila*). The main characters of La Mesnardière's ideal tragedy are thus evil rather than good, yet they are not only the most excellent of humans but they are embellished by art beyond natural perfection. What is even more striking is the facile equation of the low rank of comic characters with the imperfection of the people who serve as the models for comic imitation. When we consider that tragic crimes often include incest and parricide, we must find a way to understand how the best of humans can commit these crimes that are not attributed to the most imperfect of humans represented in comedy.

Caught between the demand, on one hand, to represent the best of humans and to improve them beyond their natural perfection and the need, on the other hand, to make them bad in some way, La Mesnardière exemplifies a major tension of seventeenth-century theory. The theorists on the whole have such a strong commitment to the representation of a world that is far superior to the real everyday world known to the spectators that it becomes difficult to provide for the crime that is also required by their notion of tragedy. The doctrine of verisimilitude required that the events and characters of the tragic plot *not follow* the patterns of life as it is experienced but rather life as it should be. As understood in classical France, the doctrine of decorum (under the headings of goodness, appropriateness, likeness, and consistency) required that characters—at least the principal ones—be among the most excellent of humankind.[15] In the case of dramatic characters modeled on historical figures, the stage version of the person should not only be as morally good as the historic person but, as La Mesnardière points out, *improved* with "agrémens que les naturels n'ont pas."

This tension is created in part by the extremism of tragic theory, an extremism that cannot accommodate the Aristotelian "middle."[16] The insistence on the perfection of tragic characters is frequently juxtaposed with very energetic descriptions of the moral failures of the heroes. While Corneille, often improperly considered the least Aristotelian of theorists, insists on "un milieu entre ces deux extrémités, par le choix d'un homme, qui ne soit ni tout à fait bon, ni tout à fait méchant, et qui par une faute, ou foiblesse humaine, tombe dans un malheur qu'il ne mérite pas" (3: 145), this moderation is far from universal. Scudéry's insistence on the proper tragic denouement pushes the characters and their actions to ethical opposites, far outside the range of moderate weakness: "vertu recompensée," "vice tousjours puni," "meschans," "gens de bien," "innocens," "coupables," "vice," "vertu" (*Observations* 80). La Mesnardière ties himself in knots trying to balance between an extreme vision of Oedipus's "crime" and his need to prevent contamination of the hero by the crime that he committed:

> *la merveilleuse Edipe,* qui nous représente un Heros parri-
> cide et incestueux, dont la sevére punition porte l'épouvante
> et l'effroy dans ces Ames dénaturées qui ont quelque dis-
> position à des crimes si éxecrables: Et cependant nous y

> voyons une innocence si claire, au moins pour la volonté,
> en ce miserable Prince, qu'encore qu'il nous semble horible
> par les forfaits abominables qui se rencontrent en lui, il nous
> fait beaucoup de Pitié . . . (84)

Parricide, incest, execrable crimes, abominable iniquity—these
are the terms La Mesnardière uses to describe the hero's act.
This is not a reading of Sophocles in which subtle nuances of
ethical requirements are applied to tragic acts. There are no
descriptions of excessive self-confidence, pride, rashness, mis-
judgment, unrestrained curiosity, and so forth, refined and
moderate descriptions of Oedipus's character to which
twentieth-century readers are accustomed. Instead La Mesnardière opts for a fully criminal denunciation of both Oedipus's
act and his person in a vocabulary worthy of fire-and-brimstone
pulpit oratory. He initially uses "parricide" and "incestueux"
as adjectives applied directly to the hero, not indirectly to Oedipus through his acts. Oedipus *is* incestuous; he has not inad-
vertently committed an incestuous *act*. Then La Mesnardière
finds himself obliged to distance Oedipus from these crimes
in order to permit one of the obligatory emotions of tragedy:
pity. To do this the critic must disassemble Oedipus, extracting the faculty of will from the character as a whole and at-
tributing pellucid innocence to that will. This is a complex and
extreme solution to the problem of fault, in which we find the
kind of dichotomy that appeared earlier in Scudéry—from
"forfaits abominables" we reach "innocence si claire" without any intervening term, such as the provision of what we
would call extenuating circumstances.

The Meleager fable and the story of Orestes provide La Mesnardière with another occasion to develop this drastic dualism,
protecting the heroes from guilt while giving forceful testimony
to the heinousness of their acts:[17] "Oreste a tué sa Mere;
Meleagre a tué ses Oncles. Ces crimes sont detestables; mais
ils ne sont point si grans qu'ils ne treuvent des excuses, lors
qu'ils seront considerez sans préoccupation d'esprit" (La Mesnardière 180). Again, we find the alternation between an extreme condemnation, one that forges a union between ethics
and emotion, and, on the other hand, a bizarre minimization
of the same crime. While La Mesnardière does provide an opening here to the argument from extenuating circumstances, he

does so only after a curiously double description of the same acts as "detestables" and "point si grans." At issue in this theoretical discussion is the extent to which Meleager can be considered worthy of our pity rather than our blame by reason of a violent, inhabitual, and unforeseeable emotion that prompted him to kill his two uncles at the end of the hunt for the Calydonian boar. La Mesnardière makes an excellent case for Meleager, who had given the boar's head to Atalanta as recognition of her success in giving the beast his first wound. His uncles interfere, ripping the head away from Atalanta. La Mesnardière gives a highly colored, highly partisan view of the scene. Meleager is flushed with pride at having finally killed the prey; he is charmed by Atalanta's beauty; he is the prince of the country and master of the hunt. The fault is essentially the uncles':

> En un état si sensible, y a-t'il lieu de penser que le genereux Meleagre souffre la rusticité de ces deux Oncles insolens? qui ne se contentent pas de condamner l'action que vient de faire leur Nepveu, en regalant la Princesse d'un present qui lui étoit deu; mais qui le menacent encore, et arrachent à sa Maistresse avec une impudence extréme la recompense de sa peine, et les glorieuses marques de la victoire qu'elle emporte et du Sanglier de Diane, et du Prince de Calydon? . . . Ses Oncles sont trop insolens pour n'en estre pas punis; et comme leur brutalité chocque tous les honnestes gens en offensant la Princesse, ils pardonnent volontiers cét excés de ressentiment. . . . (La Mesnardière 191)

What was to have been a presentation of extenuating circumstances turns out to be a full justification of Meleager's act. His uncles violated the rules of hunting, the political order, and the code of gallant politeness. The prince, menaced on his own territory, defends himself and the rule of law. Meleager would have failed by *not* punishing his uncles, "trop insolens pour n'en estre pas punis." Far from representing the vice and crime against which tragedy warns us, Meleager is upholding the civilization of the "honnestes gens."

La Mesnardière charges through the *juste milieu* and comes out on the other side, turning the crime needed by one branch of his theory into the virtue required by another. For Meleager has behaved in full conformity to the decorum, the *bienséance,* of his aristocratic and amorous station. He has become the exemplar of the *honnête* prince of the mid-seventeenth century driving back the rustic and violent who threaten civilization. This reversal of great crime into perfect civil exemplarity is far from an eccentricity of La Mesnardière's; Corneille performs the same turnabout in regard to Oedipus himself, the greatest, most authorized example of the flawed tragic hero. Oedipus does only a good, positively heroic thing in killing Laius, "il ne fait que disputer le chemin en homme de cœur contre un inconnu qui l'attaque avec avantage" (3: 145). Laius was at fault; he behaved without politeness, in fact, with insolence, in an armed encounter. It is important to remember that for seventeenth-century theory the moral obligations of tragic characters—and of real persons—goes beyond the kind of egalitarian prudence to which modernity so often reduces ethics. Oedipus and Meleager are princes, military leaders, enforcers of a civilization that mixed killing with polite gesture. As La Mesnardière and Corneille see their situation, the act of killing an *insolent* is not a privilege but a strict application of decorum. The poet who observes verisimilitude will make sure that *his* princes behave according to that decorum in a representation of life that improves princes, that makes each prince The Prince.

However, this drive to perfect the tragic hero and to protect him from vice creates an obvious problem, one that La Mesnardière notices. This perfect gentleman will be punished by death for his princely, magnanimous gesture. Now the theorist must rush to shore up the other part of the tragic structure. Having shown that Meleager is not too guilty, he must try to make him guilty enough so that his mother, Althea, who kills her son in outrage over the death of her brothers, can in her turn be considered safe from an excess of guilt. La Mesnardière hastily provides another view of Meleager, so that the *same* hero and the *same* act are evaluated in a completely opposite direction:

> A-t'elle donc si peu souffert pour le violent Meleagre, soit lors qu'elle l'a mis au monde, soit lors qu'elle a pris le soin de retenir par sa prudence une jeunesse impetueuse, bouillante et precipitée, qu'il ne doive pas souffrir en sa consideration une injure mediocre, qu'il reçoit de ses propres Freres? (194)

Meleager the *généreux* has become, retrospectively, Meleager the violent. The brutality that shocked all polite persons (*hon-*

nestes gens) has now become a slight offense. La Mesnardière continues:

> Non, non, il est trop coupable pour triompher superbement
> de la mort du Sanglier, et de celle de ses deux Oncles . . . le
> fils a été cruel dans les meurtres qu'il a commis . . . (195–96)

The Meleager fable exemplifies the duplicity of seventeenth-century theory, which needs to provide two competing views of the same act in order to satisfy the two extreme requirements of vice and virtue, which have much more cogent claims on the seventeenth-century aristocratic ideal than any appeal to the moral middle.

The disproportion of the flaw, or *hamartia,* and its consequences for the hero are frequently considered part of the Aristotelian theory of plot. In a verisimilar world, where things are as they should be, it is hard to justify the notion of disproportionate punishment. Racine's approach, as we have seen, is to attack the idea that there are small or moderate moral faults. In the tragic world of *Phèdre,* so often considered a projection of a Jansenist worldview into an ancient pagan framework, there is no significant difference between thought and action ("la seule pensée du crime y est regardée avec autant d'horreur que le crime même") or between love and incest. La Mesnardière tries defending this disproportion as a rhetorical figure before abandoning it in favor of didactic, proportionate punishment of the vicious:

> Cét excés des Punitions fait à peu prés la mesme chose dans
> les Ouvrages des Poëtes, que fait la trompeuse Hyperbole
> dans la bouche des Orateurs: et comme cette Figure s'éleve
> jusques au mensonge pour faire croire la verité, les Chasti-
> mens de Theatre passent jusqu'à la cruauté pour faire craindre
> la Justice.
>
> Mais possible le Philosophe permettra que les Heros
> soient absolument mauvais dans les Sujets odieux qui doivent
> produire la Crainte. (145)

La Mesnardière seems to admit defeat in attempting to adjust Aristotelian requirements to a modern tragic plot in which vice should be punished and virtue rewarded.

In examining the plots of Greek and Roman tragedy, the seventeenth-century authors did not find examples of moderate faults. Instead they located among the ancients extreme moral depravity that was a challenge to Christian, monarchical poetics. On one hand the faults attributed to princes in ancient tragedy ran directly against the idea of *bienséance* as rank-adjusted moral character. If Chimène was a monster, then what about Clytemnestra, Phaedra, and Thyestes? Secondly, the goal of correcting history to fit a proper, verisimilar world was challenged by the outcomes of tragedies in which order could only be restored by the death or punishment of the prince. Theorists of tragedy were explicit about the need for the modern, verisimilar tragic story to reject plots that suited the ancients.

Reformulating the decorum of tragedy presents a major challenge since the principal figures of these plays are now subject to the opposed requirements of tragic criminality and of Christian monarchical goodness. While tragedy permits the people "d'examiner toutes les actions de leurs Princes," writes d'Aubignac, the playwright is obligated to show that French kings, at least, do *not* fail. The writer must confirm this political and ethical concept for the people and "les entretenir dans cette pieuse croyance" (d'Aubignac, *Troisième dissertation,* in Granet 32). D'Aubignac sees this, rightly, as a major element of decorum in modern tragedy:

> il faut enseigner des choses qui maintiennent la société publique, qui servent à retenir les peuples dans leur devoir, et qui montrent toujours les Souverains comme des objets de vénération, environnés des vertus comme la gloire, et soutenus de la main de Dieu qui ne les défend pas moins des grands crimes que des grands malheurs. Et quand on met sur notre Théâtre des exemples de leur mauvaise fortune, il faut examiner quels en sont les accidents, il n'y faut rien mêler qui sente le déreglement des moeurs, il en faut retrancher toutes les circonstances qui peuvent faire mal penser de leur conduite, il faut empêcher que les peuples s'imaginent d'être châtiés pour les crimes d'autrui sans être les premiers coupables et ménager si bien les sentimens des Spectateurs en cela, que les précautions nécessaires au Théâtre paroissent naturelles, et tirées du fond du sujet sans l'artifice du Poëte. (*Troisième dissertation,* in Granet 33)

Ancient tragedy repeatedly shows kings and heirs to the throne engaged in parricide, incest, adultery, and even cannibalism. These failures of decorum are perfectly devised for plots in which the vicious must be punished, as Scudéry and others require of the tragic plot. However, the crimes of the ancient tragedies do not fit the "verisimilar" standards of the Christian monarchy in which a bad king (like the king in *Le Cid,* according to Scudéry's *Observations*) has no place. Four theoretical requirements of tragedy collide in the modern world: that the heroes of tragedy be kings and princes, that the hero commit a major crime, that the hero be punished severely, and that kings be represented as virtuous and without "déreglement des mœurs."

This apparently contradictory series of demands did not exist in ancient tragedy, think several of the seventeenth-century theorists, because the ancients delighted in seeing princes vilified and punished. Ancient verisimilitude is the opposite of the modern because of the different political regimes:

> Ainsi les Atheniens se plaisoient à voir sur leur Theatre, les cruautez et les malheurs des Roys, des desastres des familles illustres, et la rebellion les Peuples pour une mauvaise action d'un Souverain; parce que l'Estat dans lequel ils vivoient, estant un gouvernement Populaire, ils se vouloient entretenir dans cette croyance, Que la Monarchie est tousjours tyrannique. . . . (D'Aubignac 72–73)[18]

Corneille's view of verisimilitude in the tragic plot was globally different from that of the other theorists. When it comes specifically to character verisimilitude and the relation between the character's virtue and what happens to the character, however, Corneille arrives at some conclusions that are surprisingly close to those of La Mesnardière and d'Aubignac. Like them, Corneille avoids the moral middle for virtuous and vicious poles, and he makes this recommendation without the anguish that they seem to feel at contradicting Aristotle. Corneille writes, "j'estime qu'il ne faut point faire de difficulté d'exposer sur la scène des hommes très vertueux, ou très méchants dans le malheur" (3: 150). Corneille arrives at this view by a process of reasoning that is very different from that of the other theorists.

What could be called the "extremism" in La Mesnardière's view of character (the vicious versus the innocent) is anticipated by the extremism of Corneille's general statement about the best tragedies being based on nonverisimilar subjects.

Corneille links his exemplary nonverisimilar subjects with characters, such as Clytemnestra, who are held up as examples of evil in the poetics of the other theorists. His first mention of such implausible characters comes in the opening paragraph of his first *Discours,* a paragraph that begins with the reminder that the pleasure of the spectator is, according to Aristotle, the *only* goal of tragedy (3: 117). The nonverisimilar plot and the pleasure of the spectator are thus joined as Corneille proceeds to exemplify the pleasurable emotional turmoil caused by the nonverisimilar, criminal stories of Medea, Clytemnestra, and Orestes:

> Il n'est pas vraisemblable que Médée tue ses enfants, que Clytemnestre assassine son mari, qu'Oreste poignarde sa mère: mais l'histoire le dit, et la représentation de ces grands crimes ne trouve point d'incrédules. (3: 118)

These great "crimes"—note the same terminology that La Mesnardière uses—do not represent a problem for Corneille, even though he agrees with other poeticians that such crimes are not part of a verisimilar world. But what will Corneille do about the other extreme of character conduct, the extremely virtuous? Rather than use the same character to represent both poles, as La Mesnardière does with Meleager, Corneille distributes virtue and vice among a number of characters, completely eliminating (according to most modern readings of Aristotle) the tragedy of a moderate central character who, through a minor fallibility, suffers a stunning reversal.[19] Corneille shares with his contemporaries, including La Mesnardière, d'Aubignac, and Racine, a taste for the monstrous, the excessive, and the horrible. However, Corneille did not build a theory celebrating verisimilitude and then struggle to free himself from its constraints in order to explain the need for tragedy to represent vicious princes and the oppression of the innocent.

Of the four character requirements given by Aristotle (that the *mœurs* be "bonnes, convenables, semblables, et égales" [Corneille 3: 129]), the first is the one on which Corneille makes his most original comments. While La Mesnardière and Scudéry are trying to reconcile the two faces of tragic characters, their innocence and their odious criminality, Corneille disconnects "goodness" from virtue. These are dramatic characters, Corneille reminds us, and a *good* character for a tragedy somehow represents a character trait in its most vivid form, "le caractère brillant et élevé d'une habitude vertueuse, ou criminelle, selon qu'elle est propre et convenable à la personne qu'on introduit" (3: 129). The playwright need not have a guilty conscience if his characters are bad because that is the way they should be. Rather than try to make a character, like La Mesnardière's Meleager, both profoundly criminal and admirably virtuous, Corneille contents himself with including in his plays some characters who have a brilliantly evil nature and others who are highly virtuous. These moral qualities are merely aspects of characterization drawn from a broad repertory for constructing the population of the tragic world, a world that is not better or worse than the world outside the theater, but much more vivid, more brilliant, and more extreme.

Chapter Four

The "Unities" and the Classical Spectator

In the course of the century, dramatic theory progressively embraced the concepts usually called the *unités*. The three principal unities (of day, place, and action) were not all mentioned in Aristotle's *Poetics*—the French were very conscious that the Greeks never mentioned unity of place. However, the unity of place complemented the unities of day and action in the new French program of a *subjective* poetics, a theory of drama centered on the spectator. It is easy for modern readers to see these unities either as completely arbitrary or, on the contrary, as the purely mathematical working out of a set of axioms far removed from the spectator's imaginative experience of drama. Neither of these views fits what classical theorists had to say, though both reflect modern ways of appreciating French classical tragedy. Viewed as arbitrary constraints on the playwright, the unities can seem to increase the need for ingenuity and thus guide us toward the admiration of virtuosity and sheer technical skill. Viewed as the working out of certain axioms or postulates, the unities can allow us to think of tragedy as a dramatic counterpart to the mechanistic view of the world derived from Descartes's and Bacon's new science. This mechanistic relation appears, for instance, in the demand that no character travel a longer distance than can in practice be covered in the time represented.

The classical theorists of the unities, however, did not think of them as arbitrary constraints on the playwright nor as an accurate representation of the world around us. On the contrary, the unities are justified by appeals to an inward reality, the spectator's mind. The reason the stage cannot represent several places at once or actions lasting several weeks is that the spectator cannot believe these things. Mairet, one of the earliest to proclaim the importance of the unities in his preface to *La Silvanire,* confronts the question of why theater is subject to different limitations of time from narrative literature:

> que fera donc l'imagination? et quel plaisir pourra-t-elle prendre à la lecture des histoires et des romans, où la chronologie est si différente? . . . l'histoire n'est qu'une simple narration de choses autrefois arrivées, faite proprement pour l'entretien de la mémoire, et non pour le contentement de l'imagination; où la comédie est une active et pathétique représentation des choses comme si véritablement elles arrivaient sur le temps, et de qui la principale fin est le plaisir de l'imagination. . . . (485)

Even if the spectator's imagination could follow the changes of time and place ("les longs voyages"), argues Mairet,

> il est impossible qu'une telle supposition ne lui diminue beaucoup de son plaisir, qui consiste principalement en la vraisemblance. Or puisque l'on est d'accord que l'intention du comique [i.e., dramatic author or performer] est de contenter l'imagination de son auditeur, en lui représentant les choses comme elles sont, ou comme elles devraient être. (483)

The spectator's pleasure at the vivid experiencing of a scene as if it were present is the aim of dramatic art. Verisimilar representation is simply a means, not an end, for the spectator's imaginative pleasure is the goal of such art.

A key feature of Mairet's argument is the distinction between memory and imagination, for the latter faculty appears to him to offer great vividness or presentness and to demand less exertion. While reading or even listening to a narrative demands that the audience re-create the scenes and manage to keep in mind several different layers of time, the dramatic spectator can passively enjoy a sensation of action, for the work of representation has been transferred to the actors. This insistence on immediacy—both in the sense of "right now" and "without relays or barriers"—is linked to the spectator's perception of being directly related to the characters, of participating in the same world and within the same moral framework, as we saw in the previous chapter. Other theorists use different terms to convey this immediacy. Chapelain, for instance, uses the term *imaginative* roughly for Mairet's *mémoire* and the word *œil* for what Mairet calls *imagination,* but Chapelain, like Mairet, is convinced that representations of time and space should be structured to fit the spectator's mental abilities, to fit how the spectator's mind works, rather than to reflect an objective physical reality.

While all of the unities are theoretically related to the presence of the spectator, and even to the body of the spectator, there are many strange qualifications to this presence, limiting the spectator's direct access to the represented dramatic action for various reasons. In what follows we will describe the dramatic unities in terms of the theoretical spectator's experience, with emphasis on the newest of the unities, that modern unity, the unity of place.

Closure and Community

The unity of place is a concept based on the paradox that authorizes all "modern" theater: the audience and the characters in the play are physically present in the same objective space, but they are not in the same place. The characters are visible to the audience within an unchanging, ever visible, immobile space, but they are far removed in time and place from the audience that is watching them. Seventeenth-century theory pushes to an explicit extreme concepts of place that had previously been implicit or had been treated in ways that mitigated the rupture between the dramatic place—the place of the story characters—and the auditorium. In considering the unity of place in this chapter, we will introduce a number of theoretical characteristics of dramatic place that are sometimes thought to be independent of the rule demanding "unity" and yet depend on the concept of closure in space. For example, the idea of setting the dramatic action far away in time and place from seventeenth-century France is based on the theorists' demand for a dramatic place from which the audience is rigorously excluded.

Just as important as this rigid separation of the characters from the audience is the absolute theoretical continuity of the onstage space and the fictive offstage space required by the dramatic story. The fictive offstage space is in principle just as "real" as the fictive onstage space even though it is invisible to the audience (and to the actors), yet visible to the characters. Because tragedy depends on this offstage space as much as on the visible action onstage, narrative becomes a crucial element in drama. The audience, invisible to the characters, is present at an exchange of narratives concerning a space that is invisible to the audience.

The unity of place was apparently "created" or deduced from Aristotle's *Poetics* by Castelvetro, and can be dated, therefore, from the publication of his commentary in 1570. As a modern requirement, this unity suffered more than other concepts of drama from a sense of its lack of authority. Moreover, in a theoretical tradition that prided itself on its superiority to the merely practical concerns of the stage designer and the musicians, the unity of place seemed somehow deeply compromised with material considerations involving decor, machines, and the physical capacity of the audience. D'Aubignac's entry into his chapter on this unity demonstrates rhetorically his sense of being on an uncertain foundation. He gets several hundred words into the chapter, asserting that this unity "commence maintenant à passer pour certaine" (98) and that it is entirely indispensable for theatrical verisimilitude, before admitting,

> Aristote dans ce qui nous reste de sa Poëtique n'en a rien dit, et j'estime qu'il l'a negligé, à cause que cette regle estoit trop connuë de son temps, et que les Chœurs qui demeuroient ordinairement sur le Theatre durant tout le cours d'une Piéce marquoient trop visiblement l'Unité du lieu. (99)

This comment unites compellingly two major points on which seventeenth-century dramatic theory is sensitive to its divergence from antiquity, the omission of a concept from all ancient theoretical discourse and the importance of the chorus.

First of all, there is the theoretical status of the lacuna—is omission of a statement a stronger way of communicating a value or concept than the actual utterance of the statement? Or is Aristotle's silence on the unity of place an indication that the unity of place was simply not a concept recognized in antiquity? Good arguments can certainly be made to support the power of silence as an ideological statement—when an idea is so deeply rooted as to be entirely self-evident to speaker and audience such an idea is indeed beyond controversy and more potent than concepts and laws developed by exchange, argument, and consent. D'Aubignac is no doubt correct in believing that keeping the performed action in a single fictive place was taken for granted in antiquity, and we can see that the single place was as important a component of tragedy as metrical language. Yet the *practice* of the single dramatic place—the supposition that all that is said and done in the fictive world of the play is located in a single setting—is quite different from its *theory*. Therefore d'Aubignac is no doubt wrong in asserting that "cette regle estoit trop connuë de son temps" insofar as unity of place was not known *as* a rule. Corneille notes that there is "aucun précepte, ni dans Aristote, ni dans Horace" regarding the unity of place (3: 187). That this is a "merely" theoretical distinction is precisely the point—the seventeenth century insists on promoting rules in the place of practice precisely because of the resistance of modern practice to such rules.

A further implication of d'Aubignac's thesis that Aristotle's failure to mention the unity of place demonstrates the importance of this concept is that it could cause the complete implosion of the neo-Aristotelian theoretical value structure. If what is *not* mentioned is more firmly believed—or at least better known—than what is spelled out, the primacy of concepts such as verisimilitude, catharsis, and mimesis is violently shaken. D'Aubignac would therefore be suggesting implicitly a polemical reading of Aristotle (such as Corneille recognizes explicitly) in which the philosopher is proposing to his society new and controversial ideas about theater that are at variance either with the practice of the major dramatist or with the understanding of their audience or both. Since we have reason to believe that d'Aubignac thought of Aristotle as documenting established conceptions of drama, such a reversal of the explicit theoretical emphasis is apparently incompatible with d'Aubignac's relation to his fundamental textual authority. That d'Aubignac should place himself at risk of such an incompatibility, even unwittingly, shows how this innovation, the unity of place, troubled him and his fellow theorists.

More troubling still is a phantom from ancient tragedy, the chorus. The chorus, present in ancient tragedy and lacking in modern tragedy, leaves its trace in poetic theory. Even though writers on poetics know that they are giving advice for tragedies that will not have a chorus, many questions are resolved by reference to the Greek chorus of antiquity. Some adjustments are made, to be sure, and this idea of starting with the chorus and then solving the "problem" of its absence is a curious feature of seventeenth-century tragic theory. How will modern characters talk when they do not have the chorus to talk to? How will a modern audience relate to the stage characters without the intermediary of the chorus? Probably most important of all these adjustments of modern tragic theory is the concept of the unity of place.

In Greek tragedy the chorus claimed the stage for the community. Whether or not the chorus in any strict sense represented the audience or set forth the audience's values, doubts, or fears, the chorus did, indisputably, overcome the division between strictly private and strictly public space. Although many things happened within the palace or tent of the heroes and out of sight of chorus and audience, the play itself as spectacle was a place common to the tragic heroes and to the chorus. The chorus did not intrude into this place but had the standing to advise and question the highest political and religious authorities within their world. Therefore, what will later be thought of as a "public" place in the sense of a place that is unworthy of the highest issues of the state or the most intimate details of the heroic life was foreign to Greek tragedy.

The disappearance of the chorus, with the consequent reappropriation of place as a quasi-private area for the heroes and their intimates, is clearly tied not only to the immense difference in political and social structure between the urban democracy of fifth-century Athens and the postfeudal national monarchy of seventeenth-century France, but to the French reaction against Italian Renaissance theory that had conceded a greater place to community and, consequently, to the integration of "the people" into the tragic experience both as audience and as dramatic force. The characteristics of dramatic space are determined by the defensive posture that most French theorists assume toward what La Mesnardière calls the vile populace (H), which was free to pass through the streets, squares, or army camps in which characters of noble rank were seen transacting matters of the utmost delicacy. In ancient tragedy such passersby could be put to use representing the community that would inevitably be affected by any misfortunes or errors of their lords. In seventeenth-century France such a role is never assigned in drama to a low-born stranger, and only with some resistance granted to certain selected loyal servants in comedy, but not in tragedy. Thus the disappearance of the chorus splits the dramatic place into public and private spaces subject to the tight code of decorum or *bienséance* that determined the kinds of place that each type of character could occupy and the way each type could enter, use, and leave that place.

Although the disappearance of the chorus was related to the political and decorum issues that forced an elaborate theorization of dramatic place and its unity, the missing ancient chorus did not limit its "haunting" of poetics to the stratification of onstage relations. In addition, with the chorus gone, problems arose in describing the relation between the stage and the audience or *salle*. One topic that proved difficult for the seventeenth century was the *a parte* or dramatic monologue. Since there was no longer a permanent community presence on the stage, heroic characters had no one to whom they could expound their worries unless specific provisions were made within the plot. Thus the disappearance of the chorus and the creation of solitude had a ripple effect of requiring alterations in the plot and the creation of plausible reasons for the presence of an interlocutor, who would then have to appear in other scenes so that his or her simple functionality would not be painfully obvious.

Even though there was no chorus on the French stage, the French theorists still appeal to the logic of the chorus as a way of enforcing the immobility of the audience, which is the fundamental assumption about unities of place and time. The actors can come and go, but the audience remains (in *theory,* like the missing chorus) to guard the exposed scenic space and to assure that it does not change places:

> Que le Chœur engageoit encore le Poëte insensiblement et par necessité à garder l'unité du lieu de la Scéne; car puis que le Chœur reguliérement demeuroit sur le Theatre depuis qu'il estoit entré jusques à la fin de la Tragédie, il est indubitable que le lieu ne pouvoit pas changer, autrement il eust été ridicule que des personnes qui ne changeoient point de lieu, qui ne sortoient point de la Scéne, eussent passé d'Asie, en Europe. (D'Aubignac 209)

The unity of place is conceived by theorists who assume that the audience has the stage under permanent surveillance, an assumption that we find difficult to share because we are used to the practice of closing a curtain to release the audience from its attention to the spectacle and to allow time (and sometimes place) to change before the curtain is opened again. For theorists like d'Aubignac, on the other hand, anything that happens during the intermissions between acts must happen *offstage:*

> car enfin il n'est pas vray-semblable qu'elles y soient arrivées [onstage], si elles n'y ont point esté veuës: où tout au contraire il faut qu'on les y ait veuës, si effectivement elles y sont arrivées; autrement il faudroit supposer que ces choses auroient esté invisibles dans la verité de l'action pour les faire croire telles aux Spectateurs, ce qui feroit une assez froide et mauvaise invention. (104)

Necessarily, then, the intermissions occur when all the characters leave the stage and remain offstage until the following act. The action of a correct classical play must move completely away from the dramatic place four times. In this way seventeenth-century tragedy is a hybrid. On one hand the audience is supposed to behave like the chorus, always present and always watching. Yet the audience also is used to intermissions, time to be free of the stage and its fictions. So the dramatic characters are obliged to leave the stage in order to free the spectators from their role, the watching role of the missing chorus.

Place and Space

Various terms are used for what we commonly call the unity of place. The most common is *unité de lieu* (found in almost all the theorists—Scudéry, Corneille, d'Aubignac, etc.), but *lieu* is sometimes replaced with such other terms as *étendue* (La Mesnardière 419) and *espace* (Chapelain, "Lettre sur la règle des vingt-quatre heures" 117). La Mesnardière writes of "Unité de la Scéne" together with the "Simplicité du Lieu." In order to discuss dramatic "place" in the seventeenth-century theorists, and especially in order to mediate between the seventeenth-century and twentieth-century conceptions, it is useful to settle some terminological problems before going further. Both *scène* and *théâtre* are used to mean the stage, as in modern French. *Étendue,* or "extension," though in philosophical terms it can be used for all spatial quality, is generally used by authors such as La Mesnardière to mean "distance" in discussions of the furthest point that a character in a play can reach during the time allotted to the play's action. *Espace,* or "space," is usually used by the theorists as the most general term of volume or area, used to measure the limits of what can be shown to the audience and even what the characters can move through during the time of the play. Chapelain talks of space when he is justifying the *unité de lieu* in terms of the total capacity of human visual perception: "par la seule raison de l'œil qui ne saurait bien voir qu'une chose d'un regard et duquel l'action est limitée à certain espace . . ." ("Lettre sur la règle des vingt-quatre heures" 117). Although the term *space* is not used by all the theorists, in this chapter it will be used to describe a volume subject to division or arrangement as it is experienced visually or otherwise. Space contrasts with place in that place or *lieu* is not a quantity or volume but an individual area situated in space. Palaces may enclose similar spaces, but a palace in Toledo is in a different *place* from a palace in Trézène. As Chapelain writes, "la longueur du temps porte avec soi une inévitable nécessité de plus d'un lieu" ("Lettre" 123). Spaces have measurements and places have names. Each *lieu* has an individual character, and in seventeenth-century theory the consensus was that one such place is as much as a tragedy should represent—Corneille, in fact, presents an argument for what one could call the tragedy in less than one place (3: 189).

After this preliminary reflection on terms, we can begin to see that the theoretical discussions of this modern unity of place concern both place and space. In fact, how much space a "place" could occupy was a subject of some contention. Should a place be limited to the amount of space held in the volume bordered by the stage? Should a place contain many times that space and extend to the distance a character can walk within twenty-four hours? Should a place be all the space within a palace or only a single room within a palace?

The attention given to the unity of place varies greatly from one theorist to another. D'Aubignac devotes twice as many pages to this unity as he does to the unity of action and almost exactly the same number of pages as to the unity of time.[1] Chapelain's argument for the unity of time depends on his conception of the unity of space as presented in his celebrated letter to Antoine Godeau about the "règle des vingt-quatre heures." On the other hand Rapin simply mentions the unity of place in a list including the other unities and insisting that these unities are indispensable for establishing verisimilitude. The amount of text devoted to describing and defending the unity of place is no doubt proportionate to the degree of acceptance of this "unity" and of the rules in general at different moments in the century. D'Aubignac begins his chapter on place by speaking of the resistance to this rule among the "demi-sçavants." Thirty-five years later Rapin feels no explanation or justification is needed.

In the early discussions of the unity of place some important assumptions about theatrical space are set forth, sometimes explicitly and sometimes implicitly. Because both the actual and the theoretical relationship between the performance space—the stage or *théâtre*—and the spectator's space—the auditorium or *salle*—have changed in some respects since the seventeenth century and remained constant in others, we cannot always trust our modern sense of what goes without saying in regard to French classical drama. The most important variations between our assumptions and those made by contemporaries of Corneille and d'Aubignac concern the relation between performance and spectator space. Although the actors performed then as now on a raised platform above the heads of the largest group of spectators (the *parterre*), in many other ways the physical separation between the two spaces was much less marked than it was in the nineteenth-century and after. We know that unlike the twentieth-century image of "traditional" performance conditions, the seventeenth-century auditorium did not generally have a stage curtain that was opened at the beginning of each act and closed at the end of the act (see below).

Because the spectators could see the stage at all times, even during intermissions, a major resource for spatial flexibility was not available to seventeenth-century dramatists. Theorists apparently did not imagine this possible way of releasing the spectator's scrutiny of the performance space, because the stage curtain was not yet customary. This perpetual presence and openness of the scenic space seemed to prevent changes of place, though not modifications of the scenic space.[2]

Georges Védier has shown that the absence of a stage curtain, as we know it, would explain the acceptance of the unities. Our habit of seeing each act begin and end with the opening of a curtain—raised up above the stage or parted in the middle and pulled to each side—was unknown to seventeenth-century audiences. Ancient theaters had a form of stage curtain called by Romans the *auleaum,* which uncovered the scene by falling to the ground at the beginning of the spectacle. The curtain was then dragged away and did not reappear for the rest of the performance. Such a curtain was used in the Italian theater of the sixteenth century. As far as we know, it functioned only once during a performance, getting the play off to a start, and did not articulate the segments of action, symbolize the passage of time, or mark spatial changes. The late medieval stage used *mansiones,* that is, a series of sets of separate construction representing different, noncontiguous places. These mansions seem to have had curtains in two sections that were pulled apart to signal the beginning of a new scenic location and drawn together, perhaps, when the scene was finished (Védier 54–57). On the other hand the audience could see all the mansions, some with curtains closed, during the whole play, so that there was never a moment when the entire dramatic world was hidden. The recurrent opening and closing of a stage curtain (a *rideau d'avant scène*) reminding the audience of a sharp difference between its world and that in which the characters lived and moved was unknown in France before the eighteenth century (Védier 145). The line—or rather, plane—separating the two worlds entails a frame or border for the stage set as well as a curtain filling that border. Védier's patient historical account reminds us that prior to the seventeenth-century the stage was not framed by the proscenium arch that we know so well. Instead of this clear, forceful indication of where the auditorium stops and the opening to the fictive world starts, sixteenth-century audiences were accustomed to a gradual transition in which parts of the stage set projected out into the audience's space along the sides of the stage. Italian Renaissance achievements in perspective encouraged the construction of three-dimensional sets similar to high relief (*alto relievo*) using the edges of the stage to continue the architectural setting of the play. In the seventeenth century this high relief approach to sets gave way to the use of flat sets painted in perspective to give the illusion of depth. These flat sets did not need to jut out into the auditorium, for instead of real angles they had surfaces painted to look like the corners of buildings, roofs, and windows. Such sets were parallel to the front of the stage and required a frame to conceal their edges. This frame is our proscenium arch, similar to the gilded frame of paintings. In fact, the stage set had simply become a painting: "l'arche du proscenium, en fixant nettement au mur même de la salle de spectacle les bornes du monde réel, soulignait par là même le caractère fictif de ce qu'elle découvrait au delà" (Védier 39).

It is not surprising, then, that the two related innovations of a proscenium arch and a permanently installed stage curtain are first documented in France at the same theater, the Palais Cardinal, in 1640 and 1641 respectively. Even after the curtain was available, it was not used as it is today to interrupt the performance (Védier 63). Instead the curtain opened at the beginning of the play (or rather before the action of the play itself, so that the characters walked out onto the stage) and closed only at the end of the last act (Védier 106, 111–12, 147).

One of the important differences between onstage space and spectator space is that time passes at different relative speeds in one and the other (see below, p.185). Some other differences now seem routine to us but were so far from being accepted in the seventeenth-century that theorists had to campaign vigorously for them. It was an important and somewhat novel concept that scenic and spectator space were rigorously separate. According to almost all seventeenth-century theorists, the scenic space of tragedy is perceptible (visible and audible) to the audience, while spectator space is imperceptible to the characters. Therefore the characters should never address the audience (or vice versa). This important one-way vision marks a break with antiquity that confirms once more the seventeenth-century elimination of a shared community space in drama. The theorists' insistence on suppressing prologues and on integrating expository information into dialogue is a clear indication of the shift from a shared space to separate spaces. Corneille describes Euripides's prologues as being done "assez grossière-ment" (3: 137) and joins other theorists in appropriating the term *prologue* for the first act, eliminating any transitional contact between the stage and the auditorium. In Corneille's account this improvement, which remedies the "disorder" of Euripidean prologue, came in stages during the history of theater. Plautus improved on Euripides's clumsy prologue—in which a god or a character speaks directly to the audience—by having a separate character who does not figure in the play talk to the audience about events up to the time of the action. Terence kept Plautus's prologue structure but changed content, so that it became a literary apology or attack on critics. For giving exposition, "pour ouvrir son sujet," Terence used a separate set of characters who were not aware of the presence of the audience. These "personnages . . . protatiques" engaged in a dialogue from which the audience learned about the main characters. Corneille finds this construction "fort artificieuse"—a compliment—but for perfection he requires these characters to have some function later in the play to completely conceal any apparent attention to the audience (3: 138).

In his lengthy attack on the prologue, d'Aubignac is uncharacteristically direct and vehement in his criticism of Aristotle and of ancient practice. He calls prologues "des Piéces hors d'œuvre qui ne sont point du corps du Poëme" (163), thus insisting on their transitional or intermediate quality. For d'Aubignac and Corneille, this transition should be suppressed so that the world of the play can exist in apparently complete independence of the world of the spectator, and both the mechanism of the theater and the work of the playwright can be concealed. Corneille tightly links the prologue problem to the issue of dramatic space by moving directly on to monologues, which he permits under certain circumstances despite their similarity to prologues. In both cases, a character speaks to no one except the audience, but in acceptable dramatic monologues, according to Corneille, the character is not aware of speaking to anyone at all.[3] The insistence that the monologue not be addressed to the audience is universal among theorists who discuss the issue at all. Even brief asides (*a parte*) to the audience are unacceptable because the audience and the characters do not exist in the same world. As Charles Sorel (1671) says, "on demande quelle affinité ces gens-là peuvent avoir avec ceux qui les écoutent, puisqu'ils·ne sont pas des personnages de leur Histoire ny de leur Scene?" (192–93).

It is no accident that the spectators are not people from the story or scene on the stage. The dramatic theorists choose this difference and insist that the scenic characters not be confused with real persons. The practice of setting tragedies in distant countries or in a period centuries removed from the seventeenth century responds to a need to accentuate the independence of the story onstage from the world of the audience. D'Aubignac sees the distinction between characters and audience as an improvement on the ancient comic stage, an evolution from a time when comedians spoke directly to the audience. In this historical stage of theatrical development, corresponding to the Greek Old Comedy, plays referred directly to the reality around them, even using the names of real persons for the names of dramatic characters. In this way "la Representation étoit fort meslée avec la verité de l'action, elles estoient presque une mesme chose" (46). The direct political effect of drama in the Greek city was so unsettling that it was subsequently forbidden to use real names. The separation of players and audience thus results from political and social censorship:

> Ce qui reduisit les Poëtes à la necessité d'inventer non seulement les noms, mais aussi les avantures de leur Theatre. De sorte que la Comedie n'estant plus qu'une production de l'esprit, receut des regles sur le modelle de la Tragedie, et devint la peinture et l'imitation des actions de la vie commune. Alors la representation en fut entierement separée, et tout ce qui se faisoit sur le Theatre, estoit considéré comme une histoire veritable, à laquelle ny la Republique, ny les Spectateurs n'avoient aucune part. (47)

The entire separation of audience and players, their lack of interaction and the entire distinction of their places, is what paradoxically gives the play its status as a verisimilar autonomous object ("*comme* une histoire"). By giving up reference to the world of the spectators, the play advances in truth status, and this increases the importance of the closure of scenic space, preventing the confusion between the affairs of the audience and the affairs of the characters. D'Aubignac explicitly founds the geographic separation of the scenic place and the place of the audience on the political imperative to prevent direct and immediate reference:

> On choisissoit des avantures que l'on supposoit estre arrivées dans des pays fort éloignés, avec lesquels la ville, où se faisoit la representation, n'avoit rien de commun. On prenoit un temps auquel les Spectateurs n'avoient pû estre, les Personnages ne prenoient aucun interest dans les affaires de ceux qui les venoient voir. . . . Ainsi l'Action Theatrale et la representation n'estoient plus confondues, parce qu'elles n'avoient plus rien de commun. (47–48)

The unity of place with the closure of scenic space creates a disjunction in reference that appears literal but is also in a certain sense metaphorical. The characters do not speak to the public because they are not "there" in the same place, but they also avoid speaking to the public because there is no common point of reference. When a character refers to the "king," this word does not designate the figure that the audience knows as the king. The only characters who seem to speak to the audience, characters who give monologues, are not speaking to the audience since they are in a different place entirely. This spatial fiction serves to shift the reference of the character's words so that the audience is always, in theory, assured that these words do not refer to anyone or anything existing in the world of the audience.

Although they exist in radically separate spaces, characters and spectators share the ability to see all of the scene. The concept of unity of place was taken to imply complete openness of the dramatic place, and a visual scale that permitted characters on one side of the stage to see the characters on the other side. Neither one of these qualities—openness and limitation of distance—is surprising to a modern reader, but seventeenth-century theorists had the lucidity to see that such qualities should not be taken for granted. La Mesnardière uses the terms *nudity* and *simplicity* in evoking the most important qualities of scenic space: "La plus importante Régle qui concerne le Théatre, c'est *la Simplicité du Lieu,* ou autrement *sa Nudité*" (La Mesnardière 419). Historically, the unity of place was engaged in a struggle against the system of "mansions" or simultaneous multiple sets. In the "mansion" arrangement, the same space on the stage could in turn or even simultaneously represent several different places in the story. Theorists of the unity of place try to bring scenic space and fictional place close to a ratio of one-to-one. Everything that happens within the scenic space must be visible to the audience at all times:

> Que si on allégue que le Poëte monstre et cache ce qu'il luy plaist, j'en demeure d'accord quand il y a quelque vray-semblance pour faire qu'une chose soit veuë, et l'autre non; Mais il faudroit d'étranges couleurs et de merveilleux pre-textes pour faire que tantost on vist ce qui se passe dans un Palais, et que tantost on ne le vist point. . . . (D'Aubignac 106)

All characters onstage are considered to be within sight of all other characters, barring a physical obstacle, and such obstacles are strongly discouraged. The practice of having hidden characters spy on other characters (when this is shown onstage) may be a stock situation of tragi-comedy, but it is not encouraged by theorists, who consider overheard monologues to be particularly bad form (e.g., d'Aubignac 251–52). The scenic openness that permits the spectators to see the action must be shared by the characters and must obey a standard common to both characters and spectators (a standard of verisimilitude): "il faut encore que l'espace en soit présupposé ouvert dans la réalité des choses, comme il le paroist dans la representation" (103), and if the action is set in a city, the city must not be fragmented and shown separately in its parts, whether simultaneously or successively, but all of the city in which onstage action will occur must be visible at all times, without buildings that separate them (107). For d'Aubignac, this visibility is also what determines the extent of the place represented by the stage. A character on one side of the place should not be unable, for reasons of distance, to see a character on the other side of the place: "Je croy pour moi qu'elle ne peut estre plus grande que l'espace dans lequel une veuë commune peut voir un homme marcher, encore qu'on ne le puisse pas bien reconnoistre . . ." (105). In determining the distance from one extreme point on the stage to another, d'Aubignac's comment seems to indicate that the perfect equivalency of scenic space to fictional space

is not always required. If all characters onstage are recognizable to the spectators, and if the furthest distance between characters onstage can be supposed to be no further than the distance
of the farthest spectator from the stage, then only a fictional
expansion of space could make it seem that one character might
not recognize another character purely for reasons of distance.
Space in the theater, in d'Aubignac's view at least, enjoys a
flexibility comparable to that of time, whereby two hours of
performance can represent eight hours or even twenty-four hours
of fictional time. La Mesnardière, in contrast to d'Aubignac,
shows nostalgia for the more expansive dramatic space of the
mansion system, holding that characters can make *a parte*
comments not heard by the other characters provided that they
are in different parts of the stage labeled as different places.[4]

If the two principal elements of the unity of place are the
audience's separation from the characters and the immobility
of the place ("l'Avant-Scéne doit representer un Terrain immobile" [d'Aubignac 103]), the third overarching element is
that narrative must account for all aspects of scenic closure.
There may be changes in the aspect of the place as long as the
"place" is the same—a door can open to show the inside of a
palace and a mountain can appear where none was before provided that this is accounted for in the story, "ainsi que les Geants
porterent dans la Fable Pelion sur Osse. . . . Mais il faut, comme
j'ay dit, que le Sujet en fournisse toûjours des raisons de vray-
semblance: Ce que je répete souvent, tant j'ay crainte de ne
pas assez l'imprimer dans l'esprit du Lecteur" (103). For this
reason barriers to visibility or movement must not appear or
disappear unless they are placed or removed by acts within
the fiction. As an example of a violation of this principle,
d'Aubignac points to the wall that appears and disappears, as
in Théophile de Viau's *Pyrame et Thisbé* ("par quel moyen
supposé dans la verité de l'action, cette muraille devenoit visible
et invisible?" he asks [104]).

Narrative must account not only for the placement and removal of barriers onstage, but also for the type of place and
for movements into and out of that place. Although this principle concerns most of all the plot of the dramatic subject itself (e.g., Rodrigue and Sanche disappear from the stage so that
they can fight their duel), narrative accountability extends into

utterances of a lower rank (orders and other explanations) and even into the implicit accountability that is verisimilitude. Every character brings with himself or herself a set of plausible acts and a set of acts labeled implausible under the codes of the verisimilar. One consequence of this arrangement is that there is a mutual limitation of places and persons. If the plot requires that a king take counsel with his advisers, certain locations are eliminated as possibilities for the dramatic place. Corneille observes that in ancient tragedy the choice of a setting was much easier, since the division between public and private space was not as rigid, so that Greek playwrights could construct their plot, "faisant parler leurs rois en place publique" (3: 188). In modern theater, on the other hand, even private space is so carefully delineated and so bound by "verisimilar" codes attaching certain spaces to specific individuals with their limited possibilities of action that

> Nous ne prenons pas la même liberté de tirer les rois et les princesses de leurs appartements, et comme souvent la différence, et l'opposition des intérêts de ceux qui sont logés dans le même palais, ne souffrent pas qu'ils fassent leurs confidences, et ouvrent leurs secrets en même chambre, il nous faut chercher quelque autre accommodement pour l'unité de lieu. (3: 188)

The solution that Corneille proposes is, not surprisingly, a suspension of the rules of verisimilitude applied to place, which, in Corneille's description, seem particularly onerous. Place, in his vision, assumes an almost allegorical dimension in which each place is associated with only one party or set of interests and should not be contaminated with opposing viewpoints. Although he does not use the term in this connection, the polyvalent space he proposes for the theater seems like another instance of the opposition of necessity to verisimilitude:

> Mais comme les personnes qui ont des intérêts opposés ne peuvent pas vraisemblement expliquer leurs secrets en même place, et qu'ils sont quelquefois introduits dans le même acte . . . il faut trouver un moyen qui la rende compatible avec cette contradiction qu'y forme la vraisemblance rigoureuse. . . . Les jurisconsultes admettent des fictions de droit, et je voudrais à leur exemple introduire des fictions

de théâtre, pour établir un lieu théâtral. . . . une salle, sur
laquelle ouvrent ces divers appartements. (3: 189–90)

This "salle" would have two "privilèges": that each person who
spoke there would have the same "secret" as in his own room
and "qu'au lieu que dans l'ordre commun il est quelquefois de
la bienséance que ceux qui occupent le théâtre aillent trouver
ceux qui sont dans leur cabinet pour parler à eux, ceux-ci pussent
les venir trouver sur le théâtre, sans choquer cette bienséance"
(3: 189–90). Once again Corneille proposes, as in the cases we
earlier discussed (chapter 3) of necessity overriding verisimilitude, that the principles of aesthetics take precedence over other
regulations. Corneille's proposition of this scenic "fiction" has
the curious effect of returning the stage action to a potential
reality. That is, it seems conceivable that, in history, many secrets have been told by conspirators or partisans of different
parties within the same space. However, this potential reality
has been banished from the scene in the name of a verisimilar
corrected vision that allocates space so that only one faction's
secrets may be divulged in that place, using up the place, so to
speak, and making it unavailable for the secrets of the opposing side. Corneille would break down this verisimilar space-
allocation procedure to permit opposing secrets to be presented
at different moments in the same space. This fiction or convention of the theater would be a partial step back toward the
community space of ancient theater, except that there would
be no constant presence of a chorus. Instead of a public or community space, this Cornelian "salle" would be a shared private
space.[5]

Arranging a series of doors leading from apartments onto
the "salle" is Corneille's answer to part of the major spatial
problem raised by the unity of place: accounting for entrances
and exits. In the wave of texts advocating "regular" theater from
around 1640 until the end of the century, a major failing de-
cried in contemporary French drama is the random movement
of characters. In imposing the closure of the scene in conjunction with the unity of place, theorists declared that every movement across the boundary between the stage and the invisible
parts of the dramatic world should generate discourse. As we
will see below, the unity of place seems created precisely for

the purpose of amplifying and justifying the conversion of sight into sound, of action into narrative. This larger purpose is given a clear foundation in the accountability imposed on every movement across the scenic closure.

A reason for all characters' arrivals at and departures from the place of the action should be given to the audience, says d'Aubignac, "une raison qui les oblige à se trouver en ce moment plûtost dans ce lieu-là qu'ailleurs; autrement ils n'y doivent pas venir" (274). When characters leave, "il faut toûjours qu'ils se retirent, ou pour quelque affaire qui les oblige de se trouver ailleurs, ou par quelque consideration qui ne leur permette pas de s'arréter davantage dans le lieu de la Scéne; comme lors qu'un homme craint d'estre poursuivi par ses ennemis, ou qu'il conçoit de l'horreur d'un lieu qui luy remet en memoire quelque grand déplaisir . . . ." (275).

Offstage and Onstage

Perhaps the best-known distinction in Aristotle's *Poetics* is that between drama and epic, which differ in their mode of representation. Drama is mimetic—that is, the characters are seen and heard directly—whereas in epic, what the characters do and much of what they say is told by the poet (or narrator) using his or her own voice. This difference in mode—which we can also call a difference in enunciation, that is, in who is speaking—becomes a prominent issue for the seventeenth-century theory of dramatic place. The unity of place, by preventing the visual representation of more than one location, increases the need for narrative accounts of all that happens outside of that place. Concurrently, the unity of time increases the need for narrative accounts of all that has occurred and will occur beyond the two- to twenty-four-hour period that the dramatic story occupies.

The three unities together reinforce the difference between the highest narrative genre—epic—and tragedy. Epic stories can take years, tragedy takes only hours; epic stories can have many plots, tragedy only one; and, finally, the newest of the unities severely limits the number of places and the amount of space that tragic action can occupy. In the most limiting interpretation of the unity of place, a single room or the space in

front of a palace must contain all the action of the play. The
walls of that room or the visual limits of a single aspect of that
street become the tangible boundaries between tragic and epic
representation. This limitation affects the spectators more than
it does the characters, for the characters are allowed to move
beyond the limits of the spectators' sight. Once offstage they
can perform unspeakable—or more precisely, unshowable—
acts, and can travel to other places. The offstage characters are
still limited by the rules of the unity of place, but these rules
are looser, and allow a round-trip away from the stage and back
by foot or on horseback, a far greater space than the single room
that the spectators can see.

The rigid immobility of the spectators creates a situation
that we could almost describe as a combination of a dramatic
audience with epic characters, for the comings and goings of
the characters allow events to be filtered according to various
criteria that are not specifically spatial:[6]

> Aprés le choix du lieu, il doit examiner quelles choses sont
> propres pour estre veuës avec agrément, afin de les mettre
> sur son Theatre, et en rejetter celles qui n'y peuvent ou
> n'y doivent pas paroistre; mais qui doivent seulement estre
> recitées afin de les supposer faites en des lieux proches le
> Theatre, ou du moins qui ne soient jamais si éloignés que
> l'Acteur qui les recite ne puisse raisonnablement estre de
> retour sur le lieu de la Scéne depuis qu'on l'en a veu sortir;
> sinon il faut supposer qu'il estoit party devant l'ouverture
> du Theatre; car par ce moyen on le fait venir de si loin qu'on
> veut. . . . (D'Aubignac 110)

The characters range out through the city or the province, going
to battle or slaying monsters, and then return to tell us about
the things they have done or seen. The unity of place permits
the dramatist to override the opposition between epic narrative and dramatic action through dramatic narrative (what we
often call *récit*) of offstage events. As d'Aubignac says, the
choice of the dramatic place is paramount since it precedes and
organizes the entire discursive structure of the tragedy. Despite
d'Aubignac's description of this process as one in which the
discrimination between what should be shown and what should
be told follows the choice of place, we can presume that an

awareness of the requirements of decorum and of the staging possibilities precedes the final choice of a setting. Yet the rest of this account rings true in its explanation of how the unity of place furnishes a framework for a differential representation of certain events. Under the guise of a merely technical matter, in which aesthetic concerns are presented first (things "propres pour estre veuës avec agrément"), the playwright is allowed to reintroduce those things that are in some way forbidden, things that may belong to the category Chapelain evokes in saying that "toutes les verités ne sont pas bonnes pour le theatre" (*Sentimens* 365–66).

The unity of place partakes of a nostalgia for the freedom of the epic, and its greatest paradox is that this unity performs exactly the opposite function from what it seems to do. It extends the spatial, temporal, and ideological range of what can be represented rather than limiting that range. It justifies the shift from mimesis back to narrative—diegesis—and in doing so removes all practical limitation from the play's fiction. Hippolytus's monstrous death in *Phèdre* and Leocadia's rape in Alexandre Hardy's *La force du sang* can be represented in much more vivid detail through dramatic narrative than they could ever have if they were staged in a strictly mimetic fashion. The unity of place, by providing the means to "rejetter celles qui n'y peuvent ou n'y doivent pas paroistre," provided the return from mimesis to narration that the dramatic theorists privileged from the start. As La Mesnardière paraphrases Aristotle, "L'Avanture contient les choses que le Poëme doibt imiter . . . ; Le discours est l'instrument avec lequel il les imite . . ." (16).

Theory of dramatic place is also, therefore, a theory of mediated or graduated representation. In a suggestive and ambiguous passage of *La pratique,* d'Aubignac takes up the truism that drama should not represent certain things. While the most apparent purpose of his statement is to stress the importance of verisimilitude and to exclude the real from the theater, d'Aubignac also introduces a gradation of representation:

> C'est une Maxime generale que le *Vray* n'est pas le sujet du Theatre, parce qu'il y a bien des choses veritables qui n'y doivent pas estre veuës, et beaucoup qui n'y peuvent pas estre representées. (76)

One can read this passage with an emphasis on the opposition between *devoir* and *pouvoir,* between what *should* and what *can* (physically) be performed onstage. However, one can also, justifiably, note the movement from what can be *seen* and what can be *represented*. Both emphases dovetail perfectly, for the doctrine of verisimilitude is one of the factors controlling the borderline between onstage and offstage, seen and unseen. D'Aubignac's comment creates two classes of (true) things that are excluded from the visual space of the theater: the things that should not be seen and the things that cannot be represented. This leaves open the possibility that there are things that should not be seen but *can* be represented on the stage, unseen things (or events) represented verbally. Although theories of the unity of place promote vigorously the physical continuity and uniformity of onstage and offstage space, they also advance with equal force the radical perceptual, ethical, and psychological differences between onstage and offstage.

Ethically and psychologically, the offstage world can contain violent and criminal behavior that would not be tolerable onstage. These two qualities—the moral unacceptability and the psychological effect on the audience—are combined insofar as the audience is assumed to have a high degree of emotional revulsion for profoundly immoral behavior when it is displayed *visually* but the same audience can absorb and even derive some pleasure (e.g., Racine's "tristesse majestueuse qui fait tout le plaisir de la tragédie") from the same behavior when it is communicated in language, or even in nonlinguistic sound. La Mesnardière considers two of the three Greek tragedians at fault for their visual enactment of Orestes's parricide:

> Bien que le sensible Oreste eût grand sujet de punir l'insolence de Clytemnestre, je ne sçai pas si les deux Grecs [Aeschylus in *Choroephoroe* and Sophocles in *Electra*] qui ont traitté cette Avanture, ont merité des loüanges pour avoir fait que ce Heros l'ait poignardée en plein Theatre; puis qu'en fin elle étoit sa Mere, et qu'il ne la pouvoit tuer, quelque raison qu'il en eût, sans commettre un parricide, dont la veuë est desagreable. (211)

Euripides was wise to have Orestes kill his mother offstage, claims La Mesnardière, since this killing could not be eliminated entirely from the story: "il fait que ce parricide soit commis derriere la Scene dans un appartement secret, d'où on entend les parolles de Clytemnestre mourante" (211). La Mesnardière considers sound here as less affecting to the public than sight, yet he never explains why this is so. Is it self-evidently true that the angered or terrified last words of a woman being killed out of our sight are less disturbing than the visual reenactment? Is it clear that Euripides was aiming at such attenuation or did Euripides plan to increase the effect of the murder by removing it from sight? Earlier, La Mesnardière said that staging certain tortures made them ridiculous (205). The staging of certain deaths might similarly decrease the horror and subject the act to greater variations in effect dependent on the acting ability of the company, whereas the offstage words of the dying Clytemnestra—albeit, not the way they are spoken—remains in the control of the playwright. Corneille also took this position in discussing the ancient stagings of Clytemnestra's death, by saying that the major defect of such a staged crime was to lessen the spectators' belief. If the main action is too cruel or difficult to present onstage and might diminish the spectators' belief, then "il est bon de cacher l'événement à la vue, et de le faire savoir par un récit qui frappe moins que le spectacle" (3: 159).

Most of the spatial issues raised in the seventeenth-century poetics of the theater are closely connected to the unity of place in its control of the boundaries of the scenic space—the frontier between onstage and offstage and between the fictive world as a whole and the space of the auditorium. There are other spatial issues not directly implicated in the unity of place that should probably be mentioned, if only briefly, since they regard the spectators' place. This place outside the fictive world is required by the unity of place, which makes the side of the theater bordering the auditorium the *only* completely and permanently impenetrable boundary of the scenic space, since the scenic space can be arranged for characters to enter and exit in all directions except into and out of the audience. Dramatic theorists write about the visibility and the invisibility of the audience itself in its place.

When the audience is considered as visible, it becomes a spectacle in itself. Racine writes in the preface to his second tragedy, *Alexandre le Grand* (1666):

> je n'ai pu m'empêcher de concevoir quelque opinion de ma
> tragédie, quand j'ai vu la peine que se sont données certaines
> gens pour la décrier. On ne fait point tant de brigues contre
> un ouvrage qu'on n'estime pas; on se contente de ne plus
> le voir quand on l'a vu une fois, et on le laisse tomber de
> lui-même, sans daigner seulement contribuer à sa chute.
> Cependant, j'ai eu le plaisir de voir plus de six fois de suite
> à ma pièce le visage de ces censeurs . . . sans compter les
> chagrins que leur ont peut-être coûtés les applaudissements
> que leur présence n'a pas empêché le public de me donner.
> . . . je n'aurais jamais fait si je m'arrêtais aux subtilités de
> quelques critiques, qui prétendent assujettir le goût du public
> aux dégoûts d'un esprit malade, qui vont au théâtre avec
> un ferme dessein de n'y point prendre du plaisir, et qui croient
> prouver à tous les spectateurs, par un branlement de tête et
> par des grimaces affectées, qu'ils ont étudié à fond la *Poétique*
> d'Aristote. ("Première préface," *Théâtre complet* 70–71)

Racine describes the presence of a *cabale,* or literary-critical
conspiracy, among the public of his play, and he gives full weight
to the act of seeing as a statement rather than as a simple reception or consumption. In Racine's view *not* seeing for the second time a play that one dislikes is statement enough, a boycott.
We can infer that this act deprives the playwright of the pleasure of seeing a large audience of repeat spectators and helps
lower the receipts from paying *entrées.* Such an act would also
relieve the displeased spectators of the suffering of seeing a
failed tragedy several times. Instead, by returning to his play
more than six times in a row, the critics (*censeurs*) will increase
the paid audience and inflict on themselves a certain pain. As
a result the playwright is now the one who is in the position of
the spectator, having realized that there is a play going on in
his audience. Now Racine is the agent to whom the verb *voir*
("to see") applies as he views, not an "event" in the usual sense,
with a degree of spontaneity or unpredictability, but rather a
performance of disapproval that recurs with the same regularity as the play onstage and that includes planned gestures that
are meant primarily to be seen. These critics are therefore a
second set of players trying to draw the attention of the other
spectators to themselves and to their mimed commentary.

Bossuet also describes the spectators as forming a spectacle,
but one much like the sinful spectacle onstage rather than the
critics' elaborate dramatization of disgust that Racine describes.

In Bossuet's view of the spectators as performers, they are staging the play of concupiscence, which is exactly the failing for which Bossuet reproaches the drama onstage. In the Bishop's account of the effect of viewing a play, he not only emphasizes the communication of lust through the eyes, but makes the experience of viewing truly specular:

> Si les nudités, si les peintures immodestes causent naturellement ce qu'elles expriment, et que pour cette raison on en condamne l'usage, parce qu'on ne les goûte jamais autant qu'une main habile l'a voulu, qu'on n'entre dans l'esprit de l'ouvrier et qu'on ne se mette en quelque façon dans l'état qu'il a voulu peindre, combien plus sera-t-on touché des expressions du théâtre, où tout paraît effectif, où ce ne sont point des traits morts et des couleurs sèches qui agissent, mais des personnages vivants, de vrais yeux . . . ("Lettre au père Caffaro" 125)

Sexual representation, which for Bossuet is at the center of tragedy and comedy, both signifies and causes sexual desire. Significantly Bossuet locates one of the greatest dangers not in the eye as invisible receptor of depicted or enacted nudity but in the eye perceived as *object* or spectacle itself. There is a gradation of danger, which increases when we substitute drama for painting, from two-dimensional painted characters to three-dimensional living figurants. Following this progression, it is not surprising that the spectacle in the auditorium will be even more dangerous, for the spectators dress and groom themselves to be seen and to look at other spectators. The Fathers of the Church condemn:

> les passions excitées, la vanité, la parure, les grands ornements, qu'ils mettent au rang des pompes que nous avons abjurées par le baptême, le désir de voir et d'être vu, la malheureuse rencontre des yeux qui se cherchent les uns les autres . . . (Bossuet, "Lettre au père Caffaro" 135)

The most dangerous spectacle is the sight of the *eye itself,* not the visual display on the stage. In the context of seventeenth-century dramatic theory as a whole, it is clear that Bossuet is attacking the very concept of the division between stage and auditorium not only as far as the spatial division is concerned but in the very notion of fiction itself. The actors (and especially,

in Bossuet's view, the actresses) onstage are dangerous not insofar as they subordinate themselves to fictional roles but in their
quality as real people who may seek sexual partners and who
may be considered as sexual partners.[7]

To the critical audience and the sexual audience, seventeenth-
century texts of poetics add a third audience, the invisible audience
consisting of readers. This audience, outside the theater and
not present at a performance, guarantees the theoretical purity
of the dramatic work and authorizes purely textual models of
tragedy and comedy. By demanding that the dramatic text create
its full effect without the support of stage sets, architecture,
music, or actors, the authors of dramatic theory in the Aristotelian tradition could assert their superiority over the technicians of the visual arts. The isolated reader of a printed play is
supposed to experience the unity of place independent of perspective systems and machines. Freed from the constraints of
visibility, the reader may actually be the perfect audience to
fulfill the wishes of the dramatic theorists, fully enjoying the
barrier that the unity of place erects between characters and
spectators. The reader can see but not be seen, misses any imperfection of the sort that limited the staging of death to avoid
the displeasure or ridiculousness of sight, and most of all is
not part of the spectacle of the audience that is described by
Racine and Bossuet. The reader can be free to react without
limitation or shame. D'Aubignac writes of this freedom in the
specific case of religious tragedy:

> parce que celuy qui lit entre dans les sentimens de l'Autheur
> et ne voit rien alentour de luy qui porte sa pensée à la pro-
> fanation des choses sainctes; Il n'est point au Theatre, il est
> dans son cabinet; il n'entend point d'histrions qui recitent
> ces choses pour la necessité de leur mestier, et dont peut-
> estre la croyance n'est pas moins deguisée que leur personne;
> le livre luy parle sincerement et sans deguisement comme
> les autres ecrits de pieté; il n'est point environné de railleurs
> qui parlent contre le respect qu'ils devoient à ce qu'ils en-
> tendent; il est seul et personne ne contredit les mouvemens
> que cette lecture imprime en son cœur. (331)

The movements of the heart that are free in the reader's *cabinet* may not be solely the movements of religious emotion. The
cabinet (an almost untranslatable term, since it applies not only

to a reading room but to the private space of the aristocratic or comfortable middle-class individual) is the place of emotional release as well as the place of confidences and conspiracies. These functions are not implicit cultural generalities but are explicit formulations of texts of dramatic poetics. Therefore when we read La Mesnardière's amplification of Aristotle's assertion that a tragedy should be judged on the basis of its written characteristics, we can see that the addition of the term *cabinet* has shifted the emphasis from the purely textual quality of the poetics of tragedy to the *place* of the reader:

> j'estime avec Aristote, qu'un Ouvrage est imparfait, lorsque par la seule lecture faite dans un cabinet, il n'excite pas les Passions dans l'Esprit de ses Auditeurs, et qui'il ne les agite point jusques à les faire trembler, ou à leur arracher des larmes. (12–13)

The place of the reader, however, has a striking symmetry with the hidden offstage spaces of the dramatic place. The reader, as invisible spectator, shares with certain characters the deep emotional release that occurs out of sight of the theater audience and out of sight of the other characters. We arrive at the series

cabinet : audience :: onstage : offstage

where the extreme terms represent invisibility or escape from surveillance and the intermediate terms represent the controlled spaces of visibility. Some theorists of the unity of place do create a symmetrical structure in which the fictive world of the characters and the world of the spectators each have invisible depths surrounding the public space. This depth provides opportunities for emotional release. In demanding the removal of scenes of lamenting widows from the stage, d'Aubignac comments,

> Les Spectateurs sçavent bien qu'il est du devoir d'une femme d'honneur de soûpirer la perte de son mari; mais on devoit supposer les regrets faits dans son cabinet; il n'estoit pas necessaire de la mettre sur le Theatre, parce que les Spectateurs ne doutoient point de ses sentimens. . . . (337)

If we recall the death of Clytemnestra, it is worth considering that the "appartement secret" has some affinity with the "cabinet" in which the reader can test the emotional impact of a tragic subject (12). According to this previous description of the essence of the tragic text, the staging of the acts is irrelevant to theatrical poetry. In fact, the reader can experience much deeper pathos away from performance and from the company of other spectators. Likewise, Euripides moves toward restoring the purely verbal representation of death; we can hear Clytemnestra's *words* but we cannot see her except in our imagination.[8]

The relation between the unseen and narrative, between a place open to visual investigation and a supposed space beyond what can be seen, was of concern beyond the domain of dramatic theory—this should not surprise us given that poetics itself is a branch of philosophy. As La Mesnardière writes of Aristotle, "il a voulu que la Scéne assujettit ses Ordonnances aux Loix de la Philosophie" (113). Contemporaneous with Corneille's *Cid* and the debates it unleashed is Descartes's *Discours de la méthode* (1637). Corneille published his next tragedy, *Horace,* in 1641, the year in which Descartes also published his subsequent text, *Meditationes de prima philosophia.* Though there is no apparent causal force to these chronological coincidences, it is worth noting that both Descartes and Corneille are experimenting with the unity of place. In Descartes's work this unity is not only to be found where we might most expect it, in his formal study of optics (*La dioptrique*), but in his very conception of the work of the philosopher and, in the most literal sense, the *place* of philosophy. Descartes contrasts the isolation of his philosopher (the "I" or *je* of the *Discours*) at the moment of his deep and fruitful introspection with his earlier sterile peregrinations during which he had hoped to make discoveries in the "grand livre du monde" (Descartes 131). The *Discours* displays at length the contrast between these two spatial modes of exploration, giving clear and forceful endorsement to the meditative work done in a single, enclosed place.[9] At the same time, *Le Cid* shows that Corneille was eager to put to use the recently fashionable unities. Although the playwright finally chose to give priority to the unity of time—a move for which he was roundly criticized—the unity of place is observed to the extent that Corneille set his action within the area of a single city. Descartes also thought in terms of city space as analogous to the activity of philosophers and related that space to unity of time, observing that ancient cities that had grown little by little were usually very poorly organized compared to new cities planned by one person and built at a single time (*Œuvres et lettres* 133). Beyond these two mentions of space—first as instrument or condition of philosophical reflection and second as analogy for the result of this reflection—a third theme, space as object of study, appears in the *Discours* when Descartes finds that he can mentally conceive extension as quality even though that idea alone does not prove that space and spatial figures exist in the real world.[10] In all three of these spatial themes we find ideas that are relevant to the unity of place: a preference for an enclosed space and for a unified regular space designed and built in a single moment. Moreover, Descartes emphasizes the continuous uniform space of geometry, which can be divided in many ways without losing its uniform nature (it is the same on either side of the line that divides it).

The interplay between visual and verbal models for knowledge brings the philosophical interests of the years 1637–41 in contact with the establishment of unity of place in dramatic theory. By 1641 Corneille had advanced the unity of place to such a degree that the stage setting did not move at all, putting pressure on other theoretical requirements, notably verisimilitude (see chapter 3), in order to honor the newest of the unities. At the same time, in the *Meditations,* Descartes pushed further into the problem of dreams and illusions. At the end of the fourth part of the *Discours,* he had raised the problem of perceptions of things that are not known to be in the world outside the mind. In the *Meditations,* his examples include both images such as the chimera and figures—spatial representations—from the discipline of geometry. In the very terms in which Descartes raises this question we can see a potential analogy (which he does not make explicit) between the visualizations of the philosopher and the representations of the theater. In both cases something appears in visual terms as an extended figure, as if it existed in space, and in both cases we wonder whether this figure exists *elsewhere.* The problem of reality is framed in terms of an onstage and an offstage; truth will be proved by the ability of the figure to persist beyond the boundaries of its initial place of appearance.

Descartes also chooses, as his criterion of truth, the narrative, or *récit,* that becomes the standard for dealing with offstage reality in the theater of the unities. When characters leave the stage, they do not disappear but rather continue to move and act in a space that is similar to the space on the stage. Moreover, they are controlled by rules of time-space limitations that unite them to the characters who remain onstage—they cannot cover such a great distance as to make it impossible for them to return to stage during the five acts. It is extremely important that the characters' acts offstage be accounted for, since this is a guarantee of their reality. Rodrigue and Don Sanche suffer from this standard in *Le Cid* because they seem to do more offstage during the fifth act than "real" characters could do; the visible characters onstage do not accomplish as much as the two duelists offstage at the same time. Hence, Rodrigue and Don Sanche are weakened as credible persons by some doubt as to the verisimilitude of their acts when they are out of our sight (*Sentimens* 391). The characters of *Le Cid* do not seem to be human but rather "des Dieux de machine, qui tombe du Ciel en terre," according to Scudéry (*Observations* 77).

When Scudéry invokes the *Deus ex machina,* a cliché of technical criticism of plot construction, he accentuates the origin of this term as an appeal to the supernatural by alluding to the descent of the gods from heaven to earth. Descartes also finds supernatural (or demonic) apparitions difficult to remove from his rational account of the contents of his imagination. He tries to explain how he can tell the difference between a real person he has seen and a *spectre,* a preternatural or merely specious production of his mental activity. How can he tell whether the figure exists outside his mind or merely inside it?

> Et, en effet, si quelqu'un, lorsque je veille, m'apparaissait tout soudain et disparaissait de même, comme font les images que je vois en dormant, en sorte que je ne pusse remarquer ni d'où il viendrait, ni où il irait, ce ne serait pas sans raison que je l'estimerais un spectre ou un fantôme formé dans mon cerveau, et semblable à ceux qui s'y forment quand je dors, plutôt qu'un vrai homme. Mais lorsque j'aperçois des choses dont je connais distinctement et le lieu d'où elles viennent, et celui où elles sont, et le temps auquel elles m'apparaissent, et que, sans aucune interruption, je puis lier le sentiment

> que j'en ai, avec la suite du reste de ma vie, je suis entière-
> ment assuré que je les aperçois en veillant, et non point dans
> le sommeil. (*Œuvres et lettres* 334)

Descartes's solution to the problem of the specter, the enig-
matic character appearing as if in a dream, is to argue that specters are merely visible but they are without narrative continuity,
and hence without accountability (one might also say, verisimilitude). Specters come and go for no apparent reason, and
at times that are not precisely recorded. We do not know where
they come from nor where they go. These specters would make
very poor dramatic characters under the rule of the unity of
place, which requires that every entrance and exit be accounted
for and denies characters the freedom to wander in and out of
the scene without a stated reason. Even more important is the
requirement that narratives be furnished to assure the continued existence of specters when they are out of sight, offstage.
In Descartes's work, as in the theory of the unity of place, characters onstage need only be visible, but characters offstage must
be narratable. Their invisibility generates narration.

Since Descartes does not amplify the concept of narration
in this passage from the *Méditations,* we must consider carefully the evidence linking his plausibility test for exclusion of
specters with narration, on one hand, and with space, on the
other. The link, as was so often the case in the theoretical discussion of the unity of place, is time. Descartes argues that we
correct our errors of perception by comparing sensations across
a series of incidents spread through time. We verify our interpretation of a sensation of burning by comparing it to our memory
of earlier similar sensations. The case of the specter, however,
goes beyond this simple comparison of isolated sensation to
require not only that similar appearances have occurred before
but that both appearance and disappearance be connected. The
observer's short-term memory is called upon to keep track of
the place where the apparent person has come from and of the
place to which the person will go at the moment of leaving
the visual field. In the absence of such an account in memory
we determine that the visual appearance has no reality ("que
je ne pusse remarquer ni d'où il viendrait, ni où il irait") but
the availability of the account, characterized by strict continuity

("suite," "sans aucune interruption"), transforms our view of the apparent person into the conviction that what we see is no specter but a real person. In Descartes's description of the plausibility test to guard against specters, the immobile observer is the one who produces a narrative of comings and goings. This provides a rudimentary unity of place of the sort that would be available to the spectator of mime. In tragedy, the virtual narrative that spectators could provide of the comings and goings of stage characters is supported and even superseded by the characters' own more elaborate accounts of precisely what Descartes demanded: where did they come from and where are they going. The characters' explanations, which are sometimes only a sentence long and sometimes more than a hundred verses, also use time to assure continuity of spatial perception. Their *récits* guarantee that when they were out of sight they did not cease to exist and that their movements were compatible with the continuous space of which the stage space we see is only a sample.

It is important to stress the Cartesian requirement that the account of the appearance of a person, as opposed to a specter, must be linked "sans aucune interruption" with the rest of the observer's life. Although Descartes seems to assume a world in which the observer is also a participant and that the apparent person is capable of interacting with the observer—unlike the situation of the theater with its radical break between audience and characters—this requirement of seamless fit is precisely what is demanded by dramatic theorists for the spatiotemporal continuum of the stage world. There are two aspects to this assertion that Cartesian waking perception and the stage world as theorized under the doctrine of the unity of place are the same. First, the apparent person perceived by Descartes's observer must come into sight and leave the visible place without any observable difference from the way the other characters move in space (and time). That is, the person must not come out of the wall, must not appear in the middle of the place suddenly but must enter from a plausible entrance and move into the middle of the scene over a moment that coincides with the known properties of human movement, the same properties exhibited by all other perceived persons. Second, the apparent person perceived by Descartes's observer must appear, move, and disappear in accordance with what the observer knows about his own space; that is, Descartes is not allowing for the existence of two distinct spatiotemporal systems but only a single one in which all persons come and go in the same fashion. Despite the cleavage imposed between stage and auditorium by the unity of place, dramatic theory, like Cartesian meditation, requires that the observer and the apparent person, the spectator and the stage character, behave according to the *same* spatial properties. Rodrigue, Sanche, and Chimène, according to Scudéry, live in a place in which travel from one place to another takes just as much time as in the Paris of 1637. Any variation from this system is nonverisimilar for Scudéry, and for Descartes, is the sign of the specter.

The major difference between Descartes and the theorists of tragedy is that Descartes supposes an active thinker/observer who generates a number of hypothetical narratives and tests them against his observations. This alert and suspicious observer differs from the passive and limited theatergoer described by classical poetics. In connecting time and space, the playwright must be aware of the easily confused—and also easily duped—mind of the presumed spectator. In regard to the unity of time, the playwright's efforts to adapt the tragic story to the audience's limited imagination become even more central.

Time and the Eye's Memory

There are really two very different "unities" that are often called the *unité de temps*. One is the idea that in tragedy, unlike epic, the events represented take place in a single day. This became known as the *unité de jour* among seventeenth-century theorists and playwrights, though when twentieth-century authors write about it they often call it the *unité de temps*. This shift in terminology reflects a movement toward the second, very different conception of tragic time that evolved in the course of the century: the idea that the time of performance and the time of the tragic story should be the same length of time.[11]

Aristotle mentions time in distinguishing tragedy from epic: "whereas tragedy strives as far as possible to limit itself to a single day, epic is distinctive by its lack of a temporal limit, although in the early days poets of tragedy were as free in this respect as those of epic" (*Poetics,* chapter 5, Halliwell ed. 36). This Aristotelian concept offered many difficulties that were discussed at great length. Was a "day" twenty-four hours or eight hours? Was it the time from sunrise to sunset? Or could a tragic event happen after sundown and occupy a single night rather than a single day? Mairet's preface to *La Silvanire* (1631) describes *l'ordre du temps* as the third and most rigorous "condition" of comedy and tragedy. By *ordre du temps* Mairet apparently means the duration of the represented events:

> l'ordre du temps, que les premiers tragiques réduisaient au cours d'une journée et que les autres, Sophocle en son Antigone, et Térence en son *Heautontimoroumenos* de Ménandre ont étendu jusqu'au lendemain. . . . Il paraît donc qu'il est nécessaire que la pièce soit dans la règle, au moins des vingt-quatre heures, en sorte que toutes les actions du premier jusqu'au dernier acte, qui ne doivent point demeurer au deça ni passer au delà du nombre de cinq, puissent être arrivées dans cet espace de temps. (484)

Although the standard measure for the length of tragedy remained in theory a "day"—whether this was thirty hours, since Aristotle allowed a little more than a day (Corneille 3: 183); a *jour naturel* of twenty-four hours; a *jour artificiel* of twelve hours (Corneille 3: 183 and d'Aubignac 121); or even a shorter period like the six hours recommended by Scaliger (d'Aubignac 123)—the ideal formulated by d'Aubignac in his *Pratique* was three hours and by Corneille in 1660 was two hours. If the actions in the tragic story took two or three hours, they would match the time required for the standard dramatic performance (Corneille 3: 184).

Thus the one-day rule became a two-hour rule, a major transformation of tragic time. This transformation from one-day to two-hour unities of time reveals a shift from an event-based or story-based emphasis to a performance-oriented poetics in which the audience has more importance than the fiction (conceived as a separate, autonomous world). Even though the time taken by the events of tragedy is another time, usually far in the past, and separate from the world of the spectators, this separation is a fiction that covers the dependence of the tragic story on the expectations, mental agility, and even physical stamina of the audience. Nowhere does seventeenth-century poetic theory's preoccupation with the audience loom larger than in discussions of the time of tragedy.

It is important to emphasize this audience-centered character of the theory of the unity of time because even the most learned and informed scholar of seventeenth-century French theater did not perceive it. Jacques Scherer writes as if the unity of time were derived logically from the metaphysics of action, independently of the idea of literary or dramatic representation:

> Il ne faudrait pas en conclure que la règle de l'unité de temps est une règle extérieure, une pure condition de forme, qui n'aurait pas sa place dans une étude de la structure interne de la pièce de théâtre à l'époque classique. Si le nœud est action, et si toute action se déroule nécessairement dans le temps, la quantité de temps que se donne l'auteur dramatique est bien l'un des éléments premiers du problème qu'il se pose, un élément inhérent à la conception de l'œuvre et non à son exécution. (*La dramaturgie classique* 110)

Now, it is true that Scherer soon after notes that time is *also* required for the events to be presented to the audience, but he bases the need for the unity of time on the logical and ontological requirements of action: everything takes time. However, the reasoning behind the theories of a maximum duration of twenty-four hours or of two hours only incidentally concerns the objective requirements of action. As early as 1631, Mairet justified the one-day limitation on the grounds that the spectator's imagination is limited—though Mairet treats the limitation of time as if it were inseparable from the limitation of place. The ancients, he says,

> ont établi cette règle en faveur de l'imagination de l'auditeur. . . . il faut de nécessité que l'imagination soit divertie du plaisir de ce spectacle qu'elle considérait comme présent, et qu'elle travaille à comprendre comme quoi le même acteur, qui naguère parlait à Rome à la dernière scène du premier acte, à la première du second se treuve dans la ville d'Athènes. (Preface to *La Silvanire* 484)

In contrast to the small imaginative capacity of the theater spectator, Mairet attributes great ability to memory, the faculty that is active when we read or hear narratives. The reader of novels and romance can follow with pleasure stories that take years and cover large spatial distances:

> l'histoire [novel or story] n'est qu'une simple narration de choses autrefois arrivées, faite proprement pour l'entretien de la mémoire, et non pour le contentement de l'imagination; où la comédie est une active et pathétique représentation des choses comme si véritablement elles arrivaient sur le temps, et de qui la principale fin est le plaisir de l'imagination. (Preface to *La Silvanire* 485)

This distinction between memory and imagination resembles —though with reversed terms—the theory of ocular memory elaborated about the same time by the most outspoken and prestigious early advocate of the one-day rule, Chapelain. The weakness of the "memory of the eye" used by the theater audience obliges playwrights to limit the duration of tragic events.

Presented in his "Lettre sur la règle des vingt-quatre heures" (1630), Chapelain's creative and rather obscure doctrine of visual memory holds that we cannot remember a period lasting more than twenty-four hours if we have perceived that period primarily with our eyes. While readers (or, if it is recited or read out loud, listeners) can imagine periods ranging from several days to several decades, theater audiences cannot do so:

> pour les poème narratifs l'imaginative suit, sans contredit, les mouvements que le poète lui veut donner, étant particulièrement née à ramasser les temps en peu d'espace et suffisant d'entendre que l'on veut que les jours et les années soient passées en certain nombre pour s'accommoder à le croire et conformer à cette impression son indéfinie capacité . . . mais que pour les représentatifs [pièces de théâtre] l'œil, qui est un organe fini, leur sert de juge, auquel on ne peut n'en faire voir que selon son étendue et qui détermine le jugement de l'homme. (Chapelain, "Lettre sur la règle des vingt-quatre heures" 117)

The eye is somehow endowed either with a time-measuring faculty that is valid up to twenty-four hours or with a memory capacity that does not exceed that duration. The human imagination, when it receives information in nonvisual form, can, on the other hand, range freely through time. Chapelain insists on the relation between the one-day rule and memory, juxta-posing both the amount of time and the number of different events to the spectator's limited memory:

> je nie que le meilleur poème dramatique soit celui qui em-brasse le plus d'actions, et dis au contraire qu'il n'en doit contenir qu'une et qu'il ne la faut encore que de bien mé-diocre longueur; que d'autre sorte elle embarrasserait la scène et travaillerait extrêmement la mémoire. (120)

The correspondent to whom Chapelain wrote this defense of the twenty-four-hour limitation, Godeau, had apparently pointed out the arbitrary character of stage time—the fact that it is just as artificial to suppose that the three hours of the performance equal twenty-four hours as to suppose that they equal twenty-four days. Chapelain argues that it is easier to imagine three hours as representing twenty-four hours—"ne s'agissant que d'un petit espace au respect d'un autre qui n'est guère plus grand, je veux dire de deux heures au respect de vingt-quatre"—rather than two hours for ten years. The prob-lem of accounting for the missing twenty-one hours can be handled through the intermissions between acts, the "distinctions des actes, où le théâtre se rend vide d'acteurs et où l'auditoire est entretenu de musique ou d'intermèdes, doivent tenir lieu du temps que l'on se peut imaginer à rabattre les vingt-quatre heures" (121–22).

We can see that Chapelain's argument is far from the purely objective requirement that Scherer states as "toute action se déroule nécessairement dans le temps." The "Lettre sur la règle des vingt-quatre heures" does not center on the relation between action and time but on the capacity of the human imagination. This is an extremely important emphasis, one that should dis-pel any mistaken impressions that the unity of time is based on rational, quasi-mathematical construction of a hypothetical world in which the characters act. If there is any science in-volved in the theory of the unities, it is the psychology of per-ception. The playwright needs to build his tragedy in view of the perceptual limitations of the theater audience as opposed to the much greater resources of the audience of epic.[12] As a consequence of this emphasis on the psychology of the spectator, the treatment of time becomes deeply subjective, though

subjective in a collective sense—or "inter-subjective"—rather
than objective. The playwright who mistakenly believes that
each minute between the beginning of a performance and its
conclusion corresponds to an equal length of time within the
tragic story would be quite mistaken.

The writer's task, for Chapelain, is to modify reality in such
a way as to make it available to the limited imaginative capacity of the public within the rules of art. Both the amount of time
and the number of actions are calculated to "n'embarasser [*sic*]
pas la memoire" by containing more than "l'esprit n'en peut
regarder d'une veuë" (*Sentimens* 370). If historical or legendary topics are used in a tragedy, the time and circumstances
should be changed with these limits of perception in mind provided that the audience does not notice the changes:

> Quand [*sic*] à [la question] qui a esté proposée par quelques-
> uns, si le Poëte est condannable pour avoir fait arriver en
> un mesme temps des choses avenües en des temps differens,
> nous estimons qu'il ne l'est point, s'il le fait avec jugement,
> et en des matieres, ou peu connües, ou peu importantes. (371)

Chapelain, writing for the Académie, does not suppose that
events have any intrinsic logic or necessity requiring a certain
length of time to take place or certain pauses between events
or even a necessary succession. In no way does Chapelain respect the autonomy of events. This autonomous world beyond
the theater is the domain of the historians—Chapelain calls them
deprecatingly *Chronologistes*—whose obligations are foreign
to Aristotle's poetics and to the seventeenth-century theory
of tragedy (371).[13] The duration of the represented events in
tragedy depends solely on limitations in the mental capacity
of the spectator.

Although the spectator's limitations are the key to understanding the unity of day, in Chapelain's view, the spectator's
mental limitations are sometimes hard to separate into the categories used by neo-Aristotelian poetics. In defending the unity
of day for the Académie, Chapelain has a great deal of difficulty separating the amount of time covered by a tragedy and
the number and type of events assigned to that time. In *Le Cid*
Corneille had obeyed the unity of day, which is a rule imposed
by the poetic arts (*les regles de l'Art*), but had violated the rules

of "Nature," that is, he had represented "unnatural" and thus unbelievable, conduct on the part of the heroine, Chimène. This example concerns three different limitations in the spectator: first, the absolute limitation in the amount of time a theater audience can remember—what Chapelain later describes as ocular memory, but for which he did not have a name at the time of the Académie's censure of *Le Cid;* second, the audience's inability to believe actions so at variance with character types as Chimène's agreement to marry Rodrigue so soon after her father's death; and third, the audience's inability to keep track of a certain unspecified number of incidents. In *Le Cid,* Corneille *did* properly respect the limits of "ocular memory" in terms of the unity of day but failed to respect a rigid character verisimilitude. As a result, Chapelain comments with most energy on Corneille's failure to realize that the spectators of tragedy cannot understand a large number of events—and thus the faculty that is challenged by both the length of time and number of incidents is apparently the same: memory. The number of events in *Le Cid* is excessive for a tragedy, regardless of the amount of time that is supposed to pass. Thus Chapelain writes in the *Sentimens* that Scudéry's complaint about relation of time to incidents is beside the point:

> il veut que le Cid soit d'une grandeur excessive, parce qu'il comprend en un jour, des actions qui se sont faites dans le cours de plusieurs années, au lieu d'essayer à faire voir qu'il comprend plus d'actions que l'esprit n'en peut regarder d'une veuë. . . . Mais [nous estimons] que ce soit l'abondance des matieres, plustost que l'estendue du temps, qui travaille l'esprit et face le Poëme Dramatique trop grand. (370)

Although the events that occur in the tragic story are far removed in time and space from the theater audience, the quantity of action and the total duration of that action should be decided with a view to the mental characteristics of the audience, which is passive and pleasure-seeking. Mairet and Chapelain seem to concede that the theater audience *can* comprehend stage events that exceed twenty-four hours, but this activity is difficult and painful ("travaillerait extrêmement la mémoire," says Chapelain) and thus is not suitable to theater where the author aims to "contenter l'imagination de son auditeur" (Mairet, preface to *La Silvanire* 485). Oddly enough, the spectators for whom the limitation of time was imposed seemed quite content without the one-day rule. D'Aubignac complains that when he first spoke against these irregular plays (*des Poëmes si déreglez*), among the people who made fun of him were the spectators who "listened to them with pleasure" (118):

> Enfin cette regle du Temps sembla d'abord si étrange, qu'elle fit prendre tout ce que j'en disois pour les rêveries d'un homme qui dans son cabinet eust formé l'idée d'une Tragedie qui ne fut jamais, et qui ne pouvoit estre, sans perdre tous ses agrémens.

D'Aubignac is happy to report that the French audience gradually accepted this limitation, so that "[reason] a peu à peu surmonté les mauvais sentimens de l'Ignorance, et fait croire presque à tout le monde que l'action du Theatre devoit estre renfermée dans un temps court et limité" (118–19). D'Aubignac's argument, in other words, seems quite different from the one advanced by Mairet et Chapelain in that d'Aubignac does not conceive of the audience as having a pre-existent and fixed capacity or taste. Instead of limiting the duration of the tragic event to conform to the finite capacity of the ocular memory or of the imaginative faculty of the public, he implies that the public can learn to limit its expectations so that a shorter time seems to hold sufficient interest. On the other hand, d'Aubignac initially imposes the one-day rule, saying that the time limit is dictated by Aristotle, that is, by reason itself (118).

In fact, by a very roundabout argument, d'Aubignac also justifies a version of the one-day rule—recast as the ideal of a three-hour limit—on the basis of the audience's limitations. However, the limitation in question is not a memory-management problem. Instead, his theorized audience cannot forget the similarity between the situation of the dramatic characters and their own situation as audience. This similarity is at first vigorously and categorically denied but then reintroduced as d'Aubignac jettisons the twenty-four hour rule for the ideal of having the tragic events take only as much time as the performance itself.

D'Aubignac begins his chapter "Du Temps et de la durée convenables au Poëme Dramatique" by distinguishing between the time of the performance in the theater and the time of the tragic story. The audience's capacity should be taken into account in determining the duration of the performance but not of the tragic event. The performance duration "ne peut estre autre que ce qu'il faut de temps pour consumer la patience raisonnable des Spectateurs; car ce Poëme estant fait pour le plaisir, il ne faut pas qu'il dure tant qu'enfin il ennuye et fatigue l'esprit" (d'Aubignac 113–14). The appropriate length of time can be determined by observation, and the playwright can see that very brief spectacles leave the spectators feeling cheated, "de n'avoir pas été divertis suffisamment." On the other hand, the fringe of spectators with short attention spans—"certains Esprits inquietes [*sic*] qui se lassent incontinent de toutes choses"—should not drive down the length of the play. As a practical matter, then, three hours is the maximum of performance time and the minimum, for d'Aubignac, should not be much less (114). The time of the tragic event, on the other hand, does not depend on the audience at all and therefore cannot be determined by observation.

How can we discover the appropriate amount of time for the events of the tragic story? Unfortunately, Aristotle's authority, which is sufficient to establish beyond any argument the theoretical one-day limit, is not a reliable guide for a refined, modern theory. Aristotle did not explain himself very well ("Je souhaiterois qu'il se fust un peu mieux expliqué" [d'Aubignac 119]). Faced with this ellipsis in Aristotle's thought, d'Aubignac comes up with a truly unique theory about the time of the events in tragedy: his startling opinion is that *tragic events should only happen during the hours of normal daylight*. In other words, the one-day rule is quite literally and simply that tragedy take place during the period between sunrise and sunset. It is not enough, in d'Aubignac's view, that Aristotle be understood to limit the total duration to an "artificial" day of twelve hours rather than the "natural" day of twenty-four hours. In addition, the one-day rule *excludes events that happen after sunset* (121).

D'Aubignac's doctrine of the verisimilar as the elimination of the unusual leads him to the conclusion that ordinary events must be the basis of the tragic story. Since people *usually* sleep at night (or *should* sleep at night in a well-ordered state), they will not be awake and active at night:

> nous ne voyons point que regulierement les hommes agissent
> devant le Jour, ny qu'ils portent leurs occupations au delà;
> d'où vient que dans tous les Estats il y a des Magistrats
> establis pour reprimer ceux qui vaguent la nuit naturellement
> destinée pour le repos. Et quoy qu'il arrive assez souvent
> des occasions importantes qui obligent d'agir durant la nuit,
> cela est extraordinaire; et quand on veut establir des regles,
> il les faut toûjours prendre sur ce qui se fait le plus com-
> munément, et dans l'ordre. (121)

A thorough application of d'Aubignac's rule would eliminate tragedy itself (as Corneille, in demanding nonverisimilar subjects, saw clearly) because all the characters would be acting not only according to the most common pattern of human behavior but to the most "ordered" and law-abiding. In regard to the choice and duration of times for tragic events, d'Aubignac here implicitly rules out any "misuse" of time that would be repressed by the magistrates of the society represented in the tragedy. This could be interpreted to mean feast days and days chosen for public ceremonies, times that would seem to call for the same repressive vigilance as would curfews.

Having determined *when* tragic events should occur, using an argument based on verisimilitude as corrected reality, d'Aubignac pursues the question of the total duration of tragic events by using two near-contradictory arguments based on verisimilitude. Tragic time should be limited to the daytime because it is not "verisimilar" that people be awake and active at night— this claim interprets the verisimilar as a perfected reality where everything is in its place (a kind of "high" verisimilitude). He assumes that the spectator is willing to set aside the knowledge that people often do act at night, and that includes heroic military enterprises, crimes, or councils of state (material that is also not unknown in the tragic tradition), in order to consider tragedy limited to the ordinary, licit activities of a well-policed state. On the other hand, to prove that a tragic story should not take more than twenty-four hours—and finally to whittle it down to three—he uses the argument that the characters of tragedy are going to need to eat, sleep, and attend to other matters during the day of the tragic event. The audience will find it nonverisimilar that tragic characters can sustain purely heroic activities for the twenty-four-hour period (or even the three-hour period) of a tragic crisis. In other words, the same audience that can easily suppose that no one is active during the night cannot suppose tragic characters able to go without eating during the time of the tragic event. This argument is based on what we could call "low" verisimilitude; it supposes the inability on the part of the audience to set aside common knowledge about unperfected nature, whereas "high" verisimilitude supposes that the audience can easily set aside the knowledge of what happens at night.

Both of these arguments depend on the same premise: that the dramatic poem should be a representation of human life ("les Actions humaines dont il doit porter une image sensible" [d'Aubignac 121]) purged of the exceptional. Yet the application shows that the "exceptional" can take two emphases: the high verisimilar and the low verisimilar.[14] In the case of the high verisimilar, the spectator is expected to be able to believe that the image of a well-regulated civic life is absolutely required for tragedy and to ignore any nagging thought that ordinary life contains exceptions to this rule. In the case of the low verisimilar assumption, the spectator must set aside the thought that heroic characters at a time of crisis may manage, exceptionally, to get by with little food and sleep. In the case of the high verisimilar, the spectator has entire trust in the image of the world and has no difficulty suspending doubt; but in the case of the low verisimilar hypothesis, the spectator cannot get the troubling thoughts out of his or her mind: "Et quoy que le Poëte n'en parlast point dans tout son Ouvrage, cela ne laisseroit pas pourtant d'estre veritable et de choquer la pensée des Spectateurs qui ne pourroient s'empêcher de le concevoir ainsi" (121). Why should the spectators be thinking about eating, drinking, and their need to spend time "qu'ils s'employassent à beaucoup de choses" (121)? No doubt the audience cannot help identifying its own needs and appetites with those of the characters, and if the performance were to last more than three hours, these needs would become highly distracting.

There is a "missing link" to d'Aubignac's theory of tragic time, for the rigorous separation of performance and event that he makes is a mark of the modernity of French seventeenth-century theater. In antiquity the chorus, so important for the theory of unity of place, also provided representation of the audience within the staged tragic events. This is the decisive evidence to which d'Aubignac finally turns in his argument for a strict limitation of story time *and* performance time:

> Encore ne pouvons-nous pas oublier une raison particuliere aux Anciens, et qui est essentielle originairement à la Trage-die, sçavoir est que les Chœurs, dont ils se servoient, ne sortoient point regulierement du Theatre depuis qu'ils y estoient entrez; et je ne sçay pas avec quelle vray-semblance on eust pû persuader aux Spectateurs que des gens qu'on n'avoit point perdu de veuë, fussent demeurez vingt-quatre heures en méme lieu; ny comment on eust pû s'imaginer que dans la verité de l'action, ceux qu'ils representoient eussent passé tout ce temps sans satisfaire à mille besoins naturels non plus qu'eux. (122)

Although the chorus is gone from modern theater, it still haunts d'Aubignac's theory by providing this reminder of the *physical* limitations of audience, limitations that are attributed by verisimilar fiction to the characters within the tragedy. The unity of time, in d'Aubignac's *Pratique du théâtre,* is based on an empirical sense of the spectator's anatomical reality. The one-day rule, reduced to a three-hour rule, could be called the one-bladder rule.

The modern French theater, freed from the chorus, no longer needed to calculate time on the basis of the physical endurance of actors standing in front of an audience. D'Aubignac, like Chapelain and Mairet, creates a theoretical limitation in the absence of a practical one. The world of the dramatic characters was far away from the auditorium in space and time, and this staged world had an immense flexibility against which the poetic theorists rigged flimsy devices based on the supposed incapacity of the audience.

There is some theoretical recognition of the way this malleable stage time can be used to affect the spectators. Although Chapelain and Mairet use the audience's limited ability to keep track of time as an argument for a maximum of twenty-four hours of story time, the spectators' willingness *not* to add up the hours can be used to make time disappear. Disposing of "excess" time is a practice Corneille recommends in the 1660 *examen* of his first comedy, *Mélite:*

Je sais bien que la représentation raccourcit la durée de l'action, et qu'elle fait voir en deux heures, sans sortir de la
Règle, ce qui souvent a besoin d'un jour entier pour s'effec-
tuer: mais je voudrais que, pour mettre les choses dans leur
justesse, ce raccourcissement se ménageât dans les intervalles
des Actes, et que le temps qu'il faut perdre s'y perdît, en
sorte que chaque Acte n'en eût pour la partie de l'action qu'il
représente que ce qu'il en faut pour sa représentation. (1: 8)

In principle, each act (and therefore also, each scene) should
take the same amount of time onstage as the time that passes
in the auditorium during its performance. A meeting of Emperor
Augustus with his councilors that is supposed to take twenty
minutes would take twenty minutes to act out. Between the acts
time can drain away while the spectators are paying less attention
to the tragic story, even though the events are supposedly continuing out of sight.

Corneille gives the clearest, most positive recommendation
for discarding excess story time, but he is only making use of
something that the other theorists recognize a little more grudg-
ingly: the relationship between story time and performance time
is variable. During intervals—what we would call intermission—time could pass more quickly than during the acts themselves; this also means that time in the world of the characters
is passing more quickly than time in the world of the spectators. Chapelain promotes this device as a way of giving the
spectator the illusion of being able to watch in three hours events
that take twenty-four hours to happen.[15] D'Aubignac likewise
recommends the use of the intervals between acts to get rid of
various troublesome moments:

Le principal avantage que le Poëte peut tirer des Intervalles
des Actes est, Que par ce moyen il se peut décharger de toutes
les choses embarassantes, et de toutes les superfluitez de son
Sujet. . . . ces Intervalles qui luy fourniront un temps convenable pour tout executer. Mais il doit bien prendre garde de
tomber dans une faute tres-grossiere, et neantmoins tres-
commune aux nouveaux Poëtes, qui est, De supposer dans
l'Intervalle d'un Acte, une chose qui ne peut vray-semblablement avoir esté faite sans estre veuë; ce qui arrive quand
on suppose qu'elle a esté faite dans le lieu de la Scéne: car
estant ouvert et exposé aux yeux des Spectateurs, ils doivent

vray-semblablement avoir veû tout ce qui s'y passe, ou bien
il n'est pas vray-semblable que cette chose soit arrivée, puis
qu'ils ne l'y ont pas veuë. (238)

Although d'Aubignac's remarks are aimed at making sure that
difficult-to-stage and unpleasant incidents take place offstage,
he also mentions the constant visibility of the sole dramatic
place. If time is passing more quickly offstage between the acts,
then that same acceleration of time affects the constantly visible stage space during intermission. Since there is no movement onstage during the interval, the spectator loses awareness
of the passage of time, but theoretically time is passing more
quickly onstage than in the auditorium even though the two
spaces are contiguous and one is visible from the other. The
two spaces have very different properties in theory, so much
so that should a playwright make the mistake of having any
character enter the scene during the interval, that character
should move with extreme rapidity in keeping with the accelerated time pattern of scenic space—this is, of course, a *re-
ductio ad absurdum* of the doctrine of the variable relationship
between spectator and character time. The spectator is meant
to have the impression that time remains uniform in the world
of the story and the world of performance—and time is, objec-
tively, meant to be uniform in both worlds. What does change
is the *translation* (or scale) of time from one world to another.
Between acts time is passing at the same speed as it always
does within each world, but no longer does one minute of the
spectator's time signify one minute of the character's time.

The discrepancy between the "real" time of the spectator's
world and the time of the tragic story is not uniform, in Corneille's view. The playwright's virtuosity at time disorientation is particularly important, says Corneille, in the fifth act:

le cinquième par un privilège particulier a quelque droit de
presser un peu le temps en sorte que la part de l'action qu'il
représente en tienne davantage qu'il n'en faut pour sa représentation. La raison en est, que le spectateur est alors dans
l'impatience de voir la fin, et que quand elle dépend d'acteurs
qui sont sortis du théâtre, tout l'entretien qu'on donne à ceux
qui y demeurent, en attendant de leurs nouvelles, ne fait que
languir, et semble demeurer sans action. (3: 185)

Near the end of the play, then, the "scale" of equivalence between time in the characters' world and time in the spectators' world has been altered so that we are watching an accelerated scene, but we are not conscious of this acceleration as we would be in cinematic fast motion. On the contrary, Corneille sees that the spectators' emotional state is such that if time passed in the story at its previous, normal, rate, the audience would perceive the last act as being slower and longer than the others. Corneille does, however, state that this acceleration should be applied to actions that are out of the spectators' sight. The result is that time is passing at different rates of speed in different parts of the fictive world. He cites his own *Héraclius* and Terence's *Andria* for cases in which the visible action is slower than the offstage action.

The underlying principle of all theories of dramatic time in the seventeenth century is that *the spectator should be disoriented*. The spectators are to be distracted from the "objective" passage of time in both the fictive world of the characters and their own world as spectators so that the exact equivalence between these worlds is not put into question. While Chapelain uses this disorientation only to fit twenty-four hours of action into three hours of performance—so that the playwright, like the painter, can "obliger l'œil surpris à se tromper lui-même pour son profit" ("Lettre sur la règle des vingt-quatre heures" 117–18)—Corneille is more detailed and precise in showing how time can be manipulated without the spectator noticing. However, the one-day rule or unity of time is, in all the poetic writings of the French classics, based on the idea of using the spectator's inaccurate subjective perception of time to achieve aesthetic goals.

One Action:
From the Tragic Tableau to the Unity of Peril

The one-action principle is the least controversial of the three unities that distinguish tragedy from epic. Like the one-day requirement, the one-action feature is explicitly formulated by Aristotle, and no seventeenth-century writer argues that it is without importance. With a negative example that would be accepted, no doubt, by all contemporary theorists, d'Aubignac presents the difference in scale of action between epic and tragedy. He imagines a playwright staging the entire life of a hero rather than a single incident:

> il lui faudroit précipiter tous les Incidens, les accumuler les uns sur les autres, sans grace aussi bien que sans distinction, étouffer et perdre tous les endroits pathétiques, et enfin nous donner une figure monstrueuse et extravagante; comme ceux qui nous ont fait voir au premier acte d'une Tragedie, le mariage d'une Princesse; au second, la naissance de son Fils; au troisiéme, les amours de ce jeune Prince; au quatriéme ses victoires; et au cinquiéme, sa mort, ce qui pouvoit servir de sujet à plus de vingt Tragedies. (85)

The consensus that tragedy should concern a single action no doubt explains the relatively brief discussions of action in the works of the major theorists. Of d'Aubignac's chapters on the unities, the one on action is half as long as each of the others. However, this startling unanimity is matched by an equally amazing divergence when it comes to describing the single tragic action and to explaining why it is necessary. In fact, there is little practical guidance for determining what constitutes an "action" or for separating out "incidents" from the central action. Instead of concentrating on this challenging problem of definition, writers use the unity of action as a point of departure for fascinating reflections on the nature of tragedy and on the spectator's expectations. The three most complete treatments of action, in each case stated very concisely, are in d'Aubignac, La Mesnardière, and Corneille. The first creates a theory of what we can call the tragic tableau, the second closure through the mechanism of justice, and the third release from suspense.

The Tragic Tableau

D'Aubignac explains that there can be only one principal action in a tragedy just as there can be only one principal action in a painting. This analogy, which the theorist adopts apparently to simplify the concept for the reader, leads through a logical maze that is deeply confused and bizarre. However, it is worth trying to follow d'Aubignac through this maze since the outcome is a startling and unique way to unify time and action in the service of the transcendent goal of communicating tragic passion.

A painter cannot put more than one major action in a picture because "il faudroit qu'un mesme Personnage fust plusieurs fois dépeint"—d'Aubignac supposes that painting and tragedy alike are segments cut out from a longer narrative sequence with the same characters engaged successively in the first action, the second action, and so forth. A painting with several actions would therefore, like many paintings of the late medieval period, distribute the events in a character's life across the landscape. Continuity of space might be maintained, but at the cost of having many different moments visible simultaneously, thus violating the principle of representing one single time:

> ce qui mettroit une confusion incomprehensible dans le tableau, et l'on ne pourroit pas discerner quel seroit l'ordre de toutes ces diverses actions, ce qui rendroit l'histoire infiniment obscure et inconnuë; mais de toutes les actions qui composeroient cette histoire, le Peintre choisiroit la plus importante, la plus convenable à l'excellence de son art, et qui contiendroit en quelque façon toutes les autres, afin que d'un seul regard on pût avoir une suffisante connoissance de tout ce qu'il auroit voulu dépeindre. (83–84)

The painter has a choice of making several paintings—or even a large painting divided into different "quadres" as in a triptych—so that each painting or *quadre* contains one single time and one single likeness of the main character. The spectator's gaze would concentrate on each painting in turn so that one moment of viewing would correspond to one moment of narrative action and the spectator would not be confused. This is all fairly clear and logical, as far as painting is concerned. D'Aubignac simplifies the viewer's task in what could be called an analytic approach to narrative painting as opposed to the synthetic approach in which a single spatially continuous image contains multiple moments. However, it is obvious also that this analogy is awkwardly fitted to five-act tragedy, in which there really do seem to be five or more *quadres* in which the viewer can see successive actions of the main character without any confusion whatever about the order of occurrence.

What is really interesting, and unique to d'Aubignac, is that under the appearance of constructing an analytic tragic structure in which the passage of time is really important and the spectators are absorbed by the dynamic changes that occur from one moment to the next, d'Aubignac is actually proposing an almost static concept of tragic action in which sequence is only a background value, so to speak, and the single, richest, most pathetic moment consolidates the tragic action. The first clue as to where he is taking us appears in the instance of the painter selecting the action "qui contiendrait en quelque façon toutes les autres." Somehow succession is abolished here by the proper choice of a moment when all the actions are united into one that can be seen in a glance. The perfect painting is one that does not need to indicate the passage of time nor the one-to-one relationship of a multitude of subsidiary actions but contains *all the other* actions. In rhetorical terms, d'Aubignac is describing *metonymy,* the figure in which the effect, for example, can be used to represent the cause, or the container can be used to represent what is contained inside, or the instrument—the bloody knife—can be used to represent the deed.

Applying this to the tragic story, d'Aubignac recommends that the playwright

> choisira dans ces vastes matieres une action notable, et, s'il
> le faut ainsi dire, un point d'histoire éclatant par le bonheur
> ou le malheur de quelque illustre Personnage, dans lequel
> il puisse comprendre le reste comme en abregé, et par la
> representation d'une seule partie faire tout repasser adroite-
> ment devant les yeux des Spectateurs, sans multiplier l'action
> principale, et sans en retrancher aucune des beautez neces-
> saires à l'accomplissement de son ouvrage. (85)

The part of the story d'Aubignac is thinking of can be seen from the examples he gives of tragedies and comedies from antiquity. He always designates the *last* action in a series, and, in the case of the tragedies, the series consists of the illustrious actions in the life of the hero. So the choice of action comes down to one: death. Sophocles thus did not make a play out of all the exploits of Ajax but only "sa fureur qui fut cause de sa mort," and Seneca, in *Hercules Oetaeus,* did not show the hero's twelve labors but only his death. In an example from comedy, Terence's *Adelphoe* does not show "toutes les débauches d'Aeschinus, mais seulement la derniere d'où naist son mariage" (86). D'Aubignac, significantly, can only describe the perfect tragic and comic action by mentioning all the actions that are left out, or rather, all the actions that are somehow conveyed by one part of a series. Though he does not say so explicitly, the action that allows the spectator to understand "le reste comme en abregé" comes at the end or next to the end of the series. The examples given also sound like textbook cases of cause-effect or effect-cause metonymy. The final rage of Ajax shows in its effect the heroic life that led up to that moment.

It is not surprising that when d'Aubignac comes to the point when he should give an example of how a French tragedy would be constructed according to this model, he cannot produce one: "une seule action . . . toute entière avec ses dépendances, et n'y rien oublier des circonstances qui naturellement luy doivent estre appropriées, dont je ne croy pas qu'il soit besoin de proposer des exemples" (88). D'Aubignac's use of the painting analogy is so much a part of his thinking about theater that it seems as if the theorist is much more at home with static visual displays then with dramatic action and language. Following his thought to its logical conclusion would lead to a *tableau vivant* rather than to a tragedy. Yet his final painterly example of unity of action does reveal something about the priority of passion in his ideal tragedy.

D'Aubignac describes a tragic subject, the sacrifice of Iphigenia, but not in the form of a five-act dramatic tragedy. Instead he composes it as a painting:

> Celuy qui voudra peindre le sacrifice d'Iphigenie, ne la mettra pas toute seule au pied de l'Autel avec Calchas. . . . il y adjoûtera tous les princes Grecs avec une contenance assez triste, Menelaüs son oncle avec un visage extrémement affligé, Clytemnestre sa mere pleurant et comme deseperée, enfin Agamemnon avec un voile sur son visage, pour cacher sa tendresse naturelle aux Chefs de son armée. . . . (87)

Not only does this moment incorporate all the previous moments of struggle and resistance leading up to the decision to sacrifice Agamemnon's daughter, but each character is also the representative and the repository of a certain emotion. The Greek leaders, for instance, may be "assez triste" but they have also won, since they demand that Agamemnon pay the price for their safe passage to Troy, and Clytemnestra is not only sad but "deses-perée" or outraged at her own inability to control Agamem-non and the situation. This momentary assembly of overwrought characters makes a kind of collage or mosaic, emphasizing spatial composition over sequenced time and stressing emo-tion more than argument, principle, or the relation between cause and effect. The effect—the result—is shown, and it is an in-tensely pathetic one.

In concluding his section on the unity of action, d'Aubignac gives the playwright one piece of guidance on adding or sub-tracting incidents from a story to make it fit the tragic stage. The rule of thumb is to choose incidents in such a way as to increase the intensity and variety of emotions. If there is an existent story that has too many incidents, the playwright should omit the "moins importans, et sur tout les moins pathétiques." However, if there are too few incidents, the playwright should invent some, as did Corneille in *Horace,* where Sabine is intro-duced as Horace's wife and the sister of the Curiace brothers whom her husband will kill in battle. This "incident" (it is in keeping with d'Aubignac's metonymic, almost allegorical, imagi-nation that he has difficulty distinguishing incidents from char-acters) is valuable to the tragedy because it adds "toutes les passions d'une Femme" (88).

In short, d'Aubignac's approach to the unity of action is cen-tered on the final presentation of a spectacular—that is, visual, scenic—outburst of emotions on the part of the characters. Action should be simplified in order to avoid distraction from that goal:

> le Poëte doit toûjours prendre son action la plus simple qu'il luy est possible, à cause qu'il sera toûjours plus maistre des passions et des autres ornemens de son Ouvrage, quand il ne leur donnera qu'autant de fonds qu'il le jugera necessaire pour les faire éclatter. . . . Et tous ceux au contraire qui dans un méme Poëme, ont voulu méler plusieurs actions toutes fort illustres, en ont étouffé les beautez, en ne donnant pas assez de jour aux Passions. . . . (89)

Neither the historical significance nor the thematic interest of a subject is as important as this single-minded concentration on the emotions.

Closure and the Mechanism of Justice

Where d'Aubignac's model tragedy ends in an intense mosaic of passions, a moment that summarizes all that precedes, the closure of La Mesnardière's tragedy results from a simple two-part logical operation: a crime is committed and the criminal is later punished. Although the tragic ending is recognizable as the second half of the cause-effect pair, the tragedy itself, as aesthetic structure, must have three steps, for in between there is the lengthy, suspense-filled pause, when "l'esprit du Specta-teur [est] agréablement travaillé par l'impatient desir de voir à quoy aboutira la faute qu'il a vu commettre" (La Mesnardière 53). The tragic action, or *Avanture,* is defined by a one-to-one relationship of fault to punishment rather than by features like character development or condensation of a long series of acts into an act that implies or contains what precedes. Far more than d'Aubignac, La Mesnardière conceives of the tragic "ad-venture" in sequential terms and disengages the single staged action from all the possibly similar ones that precede—at least in the type of structure La Mesnardière recommends. He does mention the "simple" subject, defining it as a tragedy without sudden reversal or *chute.* The simple subject consists of a slow decline:

> le Héros devient malheureux peu à peu par la suite de ce Sujet, *sans qu'il y ait aucune Cheute qui semble le précipiter du bon-heur dans l'infortune, lors qu'il y pense le moins.*
> (La Mesnardière 53; italics in original)

It is not very clear here why the hero becomes unfortunate nor how the tragic adventure can be defined and limited, since the simple subject is defined as not being a complex subject, that is, one with a crime and a fall (or punishment) that results. However, La Mesnardière hastens to disown this type of tragic subject even though, he says, most ancient and modern trage-dies are of this type.

The perfect tragedy should be made out of a *Fable composée,* in which we see the hero suddenly "estre accablé de misères, & tomber, s'il faut ainsi dire, du faiste dans les abysmes" (La Mesnardière 54). Here the binary structure appears again "on the surface" and in such an extreme form that the spectator can immediately see the contrast. From extreme happiness, without intermediate stages, the hero plunges into extreme unhappiness. We can say that this contrast is on the surface to distinguish the material, phenomenal, or visible world from the metaphysical or noumenal world in which the balance between injustice and justice is maintained. The spectator identifies the visible misery of the hero toward the end of the play with the retribution that the invisible powers are exacting. If the hero just gradually sank into wretchedness, the audience could not recognize on the surface the two-part, right/wrong structure that lies behind the phenomenal world. For La Mesnardière the suddenness of the reversal and its completely unexpected quality are both necessary and deeply significant. For the spectator "est come frappé par la foudre d'un Accident impréveu, qui vient déterminer ses doutes en punissant le coupable lors qu'il s'y attendoit le moins" (54).

The expression "when he least expects it" is ambiguous. La Mesnardière in this context probably refers to the criminal hero's failure to foresee the oncoming consequence of his earlier action, but the audience is also surprised. A few lines later the theorist cites Aristotle's definition of *peripeteia* or *péripétie* as "un Evénement imprévu, qui dément les apparences, & par une Revolution qui n'était point attenduë, vient changer la face des choses" (55). La Mesnardière identifies this reversal with the hero's fall, saying that there can be only one peripeteia in a tragedy. The hero and the audience are both surprised, but with a difference—the audience does not know how the change will come about but is waiting impatiently and in suspense to see the just order snap back into place. This reflection on the structure of the single tragic action leads to an additional insight into the theory of the passions in tragedy, for *surprise* is the result of the reversal, a surprise that may perhaps belong to both characters and spectators: "on jugera dés l'heure mesme que le mouvement de l'Ame excité par cette surprise, est l'un des plus beaux effets que produise le Théatre." However, while the poet should increase and multiply the other emotions—because "le Théatre est le throne des Passions" (57)—this deep and transcendent surprise should happen only once. It would be no exaggeration to say that La Mesnardière defines the unity of action as the unity of surprise.

Rather than multiple reversals and surprises, the perfect tragedy of the "composed Fable" type has only one movement: from the hero's criminal prosperity to a sudden fall that the audience will understand as the consequence of the earlier act. The reversal cannot happen twice because it would destroy verisimilitude to have two such unforeseen events occur in a single day (58). From this comment we can infer that La Mesnardière sees the reversal itself as being on the very limit of the credible, but the audience is convinced that punishment is coming. This makes the reversal believable (or desirable—the audience described here really *wants* the criminal hero to suffer), and the careful establishment of worldly logical reasons why the early criminal act must lead to the later downfall is not a subject that gets much attention in *La poëtique*. La Mesnardière implies that the crime to punishment link is one that belongs to supernatural powers, to a huge but invisible cosmic structure rather than to the physical and social world that most recent interpretations and translations of Aristotle convey. In La Mesnardière's view, there is a deep mechanism to existence, one that breaks through the veil of appearances to express itself when we least expect it. In Sophocles's tragedy, Clytemnestra and Aegisthus are "accablez soudainement par la Justice de Dieu, qui fait arriver Oreste, dont ils célébroient la mort, pour venger celle de son Pere, & pour noyer la tyrannie dans le sang de ses meurtriers" (56). Once the divine justice has sprung forth, the single action of the tragedy is over.

The Unity of Peril

By far the most detailed and practical account of the single-action concept appears in Corneille's *Discours,* not only in the third discourse, which is specifically devoted to the unities, but throughout his three-part treatment of dramatic poetry. Corneille provides criteria for recognizing a suitable tragic action, for relating the sequence of the fictive action to the sequence of the stage performance, and for deciding when the action ends. Where d'Aubignac's theory provides little guidance in determining closure except to recommend the most highly wrought emotional moment and where La Mesnardière proposes closure based on the satisfying cosmic symmetry of crime and punishment, Corneille's approach is based on a bond between spectators and characters. He supposes that the spectators will be so concerned about each major character that they will not be satisfied until they know that no character is in any further danger. The singleness of the dramatic action is determined primarily in reference to the hero's (or heroine's) danger and safety. In a complete tragedy, the hero risks life or reputation in a way that affects the entire political community of the fictive world, and the action is ended when the hero can suffer no further from whatever caused that risk.

Although the *action* is defined in terms of the hero's risk, Corneille does more than define the completion of the action. He has in common with d'Aubignac and La Mesnardière the conviction that the completion of the action should be defined in terms of the spectator's satisfaction. None of the major theorists of the seventeenth century believe that an action can be defined as if it were part of an entirely autonomous world. The beginning and ending of an action can only be determined by a frame, a frame that is itself defined by reference to an audience. In La Mesnardière's poetics, for instance, the frame within which the action is located consists of a contract between spectators and the divinity according to which evil deeds are punished. This ideological foundation is crucial to the tragic author, who knows that a complete tragic action is one that shows this contract being carried out. Corneille likewise creates tragic actions with the intent to satisfy the spectator, but the Cornelian spectator is not looking for divine justice. Instead, Corneille's audience has a relatively benevolent curiosity about—and perhaps even empathy with—the characters.

This view of the spectators makes the completion of the action—the action used to determine completeness of the plot under the single-action principle—only a very basic minimal standard for success in writing tragedy. Audience curiosity goes beyond the hero to include the other major characters: "cette action doit être complète et achevée; c'est-à-dire, que dans l'événement qui la termine, le spectateur doit être si bien instruit des sentiments de tous ceux qui y ont eu quelque part, qu'il sorte l'esprit en repos, et ne soit plus en doute de rien" (Corneille 3: 125). Although both La Mesnardière and Corneille (unlike d'Aubignac) make suspense a central factor in tragedy, Corneille proposes a much broader and more varied emotional repertory.

His audience wants to know what happens to the characters and how they feel but is not looking specifically for punishment. In a sense, the Cornelian spectator's interest is centered on the characters rather than on the transcendent concept of retribution.

The end of the hero's peril is the focus of the action as the spectators see it, and around that focal point are arranged the completion of any impending business concerning the secondary characters. This formulation can be used to set up both tragedies with "happy endings" and tragedies that end with the hero's fall, since a dead or disgraced hero may have gotten all the way to the end of the specific danger that arose in the course of the play, "soit que son héros y succombe, soit qu'il en sorte" (3: 174). However, it seems as if Corneille's lifelong meditation on *Le Cid* leads him to a definition that works for happy endings in a way that La Mesnardière's requirement of a sudden fall would certainly not. The end of danger is enough for Corneille, even without any firm assurance of other benefits. Some people, he writes, "m'imputent d'avoir négligé d'achever *Le Cid,* et quelques autres de mes poèmes, parce que je n'y conclus pas précisément le mariage des premiers acteurs. A quoi il est aisé de répondre, que le mariage n'est point un achèvement nécessaire pour la tragédie heureuse. . . . c'est le péril d'un héros qui la constitue, et lorsqu'il en est sorti, l'action est terminée" (3: 126).

Corneille's definition of the "action" is precise and flexible, and most of all, it is very, very clever. The playwright controls the spectator's impression of completeness by using the characters as spokespersons with the authority to integrate a multitude of actions into the central peril. After all, it is the impact of events on the characters that makes these events either relevant or irrelevant. Consider the implications of Corneille's distinction between an apparently arbitrary ending and one that is based on events. The hero should not escape from danger simply because his opponent has a spontaneous change of heart—this kind of whimsy should not conclude any play, whether tragic or comic. Instead, a change of will should come about "par un événement qui en fournisse l'occasion":

Autrement il n'y aurait pas grand artifice au dénouement
d'une pièce, si après l'avoir soutenue durant quatre actes

> sur l'autorité d'un père qui n'approuve point les inclinations
> amoureuses de son fils, ou de sa fille, il y consentait tout
> d'un coup au cinquième par cette seule raison que c'est le
> cinquième, et que l'auteur n'oserait en faire six. Il faut un
> effet considérable qui l'y oblige, comme si l'amant de sa
> fille lui sauvait la vie en quelque rencontre, où il fût prêt
> d'être assassiné par ses ennemis, ou que par quelque acci-
> dent inespéré il fût reconnu pour être de plus grande condi-
> tion, et mieux dans la fortune, qu'il ne paraissait. (3: 126–27)

Any incident can become a legitimate part of the central action if it changes the way the hero is viewed by other characters. Corneille thus delegates to the characters the decision about
what events are important.[16] The father, in this case, might not
be convinced to accept the hero as son-in-law if the father has
been described as an ungrateful tyrant. Conversely, the hero's
participation in a conspiracy, though unsuccessful, might reveal
a political affiliation that the father finds highly congenial. The
unity of "action" can thus be a way of describing seamless
motivation.[17]

The decisive factor in determining the unity of action, from
Corneille's point of view, is in the mind of the spectator rather
than in the minds and motivations of the characters. If the spectator is in suspense, wondering about the possible consequence
of an action, then the overall action of the play is not complete.
The spectator must be in one of two states of mind: either in
suspense or without suspense. If the spectator is without suspense, the action is completed and the play should be over.
Otherwise, the spectator should be in a state of suspense, aware
of the possible implications of all incidents. Since the central
defining feature of the unity of action is the hero's risk, the hero
must be at risk up until the end of the play. The hero can be in
somewhat different dangers at different moments of the play,
provided that the resolution of the first danger necessarily places
the hero in another situation of danger (3: 174). Between the
hero's risk and the spectator's suspense, there is a clear link,
but suspense is more important. The hero might be out of danger while the play continues. What matters is that the audience
still be waiting for the news:

> Il n'y doit avoir qu'une action complète, qui laisse l'esprit
> de l'auditeur dans le calme, mais elle ne peut le devenir,

que par plusieurs autres imparfaites, qui lui servent d'ache-
minements, et tiennent cet auditeur dans une agréable suspension. C'est ce qu'il faut pratiquer à la fin de chaque acte
pour rendre l'action continue. . . . il est nécessaire que chaque
acte laisse une attente de quelque chose, qui se doive faire
dans celui qui le suit. (3: 175)

The unity of action is thus more psychological than logical. If
the spectator is not aware of a possible entailment of some
action, then that consequence, as a matter of dramaturgy, does
not exist. The unity of action, for Corneille, is thus a product
of adroit control of the audience's attention. In this way Corneille's theory of action overlaps d'Aubignac's theory of "colors," which is in part a way of directing the spectator's attention
toward one thing and away from others, "sous des prétextes et
avec des couleurs si vray-semblables, selon l'estat des affaires
presentes, que l'esprit des Spectateurs est tout à fait arresté et
ne pense point qu'il en doive sortir aucun autre Incident que
ce qu'il connoist" (d'Aubignac 129).

Corneille's insistence on defining the unity of action in terms
of the audience's forward-looking curiosity and concern for the
characters appears also in his treatment of Aristotle's apparently very abstract requirement that the tragic action must not
only be complete but must have a certain magnitude, "elle doit
avoir un commencement, un milieu, et une fin" (Corneille
3: 128). Corneille's brief consideration of this prescribed structure of the tragic action, in his *examen* of *Horace* and in the
Discours, justifies the division into three moments on the grounds
that the spectator must be prepared to accept the outcome. The
terms in which Corneille approaches the tripartite principle
reveal that for him Aristotle's comment was a problem to resolve, not an evident truth: "Ces termes sont si généraux, qu'ils
semblent ne signifier rien; mais à les bien entendre, ils excluent
les actions momentanées qui n'ont point ces trois parties"
(3: 128). Corneille thus first redefines the structural requirement into a time requirement, refusing legitimacy to events,
like Horace's murder of his sister, that occur "all at once" (*tout
d'un coup*). Then, in a way that is deeply revealing of Corneille's
dramatic values, he locates the time issue in the audience's world
rather than in the characters'. The audience needs to be prepared for what is coming. Horace's sudden violence "se fait

tout d'un coup sans aucune préparation dans les trois actes qui la précèdent" (3: 128). Whatever hints precede this incident are not enough "pour faire attendre un emportement si extraordinaire" (*Examen d'Horace* [Corneille 1: 840]).

Most of the theorists of the unity of action formulate their remarks to contrast the multiple actions that occur over many months or even years in epics with the action that occurs in one day in tragedy, but Corneille points out that this longitudinal or diachronic definition of the singleness of action is not complete. Such a longitudinal definition—the need to choose one event from a series of successive events—is what d'Aubignac implies when he describes the "monstrous" play in which the hero is born in the second act, goes courting in the third, and obtains military victories in the fourth. Corneille recalls that actions are not just strung together one after the other but also occur at the same time as other events. The playwright's concern with limiting the action does not end when he picks a moment out of the ongoing life of a hero. Instead the playwright must isolate the action onstage from other actions that are going on at the same moment. Corneille's attention to removing secondary but simultaneous actions is part of his concentration on the spectator's suspense. The characters may be doing many things on the day of the tragic event, but the audience's suspense must be directed toward a single linked series of incidents that apparently put the hero in danger and subsequently terminate that danger: "Il n'est pas besoin qu'on sache précisément tout ce que font les acteurs durant les intervalles qui les séparent [les actes], ni même qu'ils agissent, lorsqu'ils ne paraissent point sur le théâtre" (3: 175). Even if all the characters leave the stage and go to sleep, the "action" is not discontinuous in the theoretical sense, for Corneille defines action in terms of the spectator's concern for the hero. The characters' sleep between the third and fourth acts "n'empêche pas toutefois la continuité d'action entre ces deux actes, parce que ce troisième n'en a point de complète" (3: 175). The unity and continuity of action is not defined in terms of the totality of what the characters do during the time from the beginning to the end of the tragic day but rather in terms of the spectators' curiosity and concern—for the hero, most of all, and for the other characters as well.

Corneille's most overtly and proudly original contribution to the single-action concept is an entirely new rule requiring all the elements of dramatic suspense to be set out in the first act:

> [le premier acte] doit contenir les semences de tout ce qui doit arriver, tant pour l'action principale, que pour les épi-sodiques, en sorte qu'il n'entre aucun acteur dans les actes suivants, qui ne soit connu par ce premier, ou du moins appelé par quelqu'un qui y aura été introduit. Cette maxime est nouvelle et assez sévère, et je ne l'ai pas toujours gardée; mais j'estime qu'elle sert beaucoup à fonder une véritable unité d'action. (3: 135–36)

Corneille's new rule about introducing all the elements and the characters of the play in the first act has surely had a large influence on later ideas of a well-made play. He does not attempt to persuade the reader of the desirability of this rule, which must have seemed self-evident to its author. The sharp distinction between the first and the second acts that it implies (an important fact, intention, or character introduced at the beginning of the second act would be a violation); the assumption that the unity of the action is dependent on a highly knowledgeable, promptly informed audience; the apparent confusion among several desirable dramatic qualities (the unity of action per se is not necessarily identical with skillful exposition)—all of these possible objections are left unmentioned. Moreover it would be possible to follow this rule and still fail to have unity of action; two or more events could derive from a small set of characters and conflicts all presented promptly in the first act.[18]

Yet this rule about the first act (which Corneille variously calls the "prologue," the "parodos," and the "protase") is consistent with the author's view that unity of action is the same thing as unity of suspense. Since Corneille attaches little or no importance to the "objective" or abstract interrelation between incidents (he is not a strategist plotting all the conceivable repercussions of each event), he conceives action as the hypothetical spectator's curiosity about the outcome of each incident. An event that enters the play without warning—something that is merely *surprising*—does not belong to the audience's expectation and is therefore irrelevant, even distracting. Corneille supposes that the play and the "action"—the suspense—should coincide in duration. In other words, the audience should begin to be worried or hopeful about something that is going to happen to the hero or heroine right from the first act and should remain in such a frame of mind until the end of the last act. This does not always happen, usually because the hero is out of danger before act five ends.

D'Aubignac, La Mesnardière, and Corneille thus present a view of the single-action rule that is shaped by the prevailing conviction that a certain emotional state is the principal criterion for determining the beginning and end of the "action." For d'Aubignac the action is complete when the characters reach the point of greatest cumulative pathos. For La Mesnardière, the action is complete when the audience's suspense about the hero's punishment is relieved by arrival of the second part of the crime-punishment pair. And for Corneille, once the audience is satisfied that there are no further dangers to the hero, the action is ended. This action is a single action if each of the hero's resolutions of a danger makes him fall into another—or, put another way, if the audience never experiences a break in its suspense.[19] Of the three, Corneille's description—or, rather prescription— of the unity of action is both the most detailed and the most flexible in terms of the type of concern the audience feels for the hero. It may be primarily an intellectual curiosity or it may be some closer identification with the hero or heroine.[20]

Conclusion

If the dramatic theory of seventeenth-century France inaugurates a certain cultural modernity, it does so by disseminating the concepts of dramatic and literary criticism and by transferring authority from "authors" in the medieval sense to readers (Wood, "Authority and Boileau"). This shift, still obscured by reductive concepts like Bray's *doctrine classique,* can only be fully understood after a return to the theoretical texts of the seventeenth-century itself.

One way to look at the history of poetics in the seventeenth century is to see a *coup d'état* that failed, an attempt by theorists, encouraged by the state, to impose an authorized discourse of rules on the practicing writers of France. By the second half of the century, as E. B. O. Borgerhoff showed many years ago, literary practitioners and amateurs had decisively turned from the abstract, speculative, and overdefined poetics of La Mesnardière and d'Aubignac toward the *élan* of the artist (*The Freedom of French Classicism* 235). This may be a fairly accurate way of looking at the motives or feelings of the theorists of tragedy but it does not give us a good standpoint from which to consider the body of texts that they created. Borgerhoff's attempt, half a century ago, to dislodge the simplified vision of the "classical doctrine" perpetuated by Bray has had no impact on French critics and only partial success in America. One of the reasons for the persistence of the belief that there were "grandes règles du théâtre classique" and that these consisted of "nombre d'impératifs, de contraintes"[1] is that an approach such as Borgerhoff's lends itself to being perceived as a continued defense against the theorists' *coup d'état* and in favor of poetic freedom, even though he concludes that seventeenth-century France lived with both a high degree of authoritarian rationalism and a high degree of rebellious antirationalism (*The Freedom of French Classicism* 237). Thus the debate is framed in terms of being for or against freedom or for or against the "rules."

As long as the discussion is formulated in this way, even highly sophisticated readings of the plays of Corneille, Molière, Racine (and of Desjardins, Barbier, and other emerging playwrights of the period) will not correct rigid and simplified views of the theory of tragedy in the seventeenth century. Only attention to that theory itself can fill the lacunas in our knowledge of seventeenth-century culture and ideology.

There is another reason for not accepting the opposition of theory versus practice in the writing of tragedy. Neither authors of poetics nor authors of tragedy have the last word, for the real dynamism of the period is expressed in the growing role of the public, and the public is increasingly knowledgeable about both theory and tragedy. In addition to leaving a distinguished repertory of dramatic texts, the century left models of discourse about drama. These models are embodied in texts that do not have the immediate appeal of a Racinian tragedy, but they *do* constitute part of the "univers imaginaires du classicisme" (Pavel 371) and do propose fictional worlds that are different both from the real world of French society and from the tragedies that were actually written and performed during the reigns of Louis XIII and Louis XIV. These models propose a series of alternatives to the existing tragedies of their times and they appeal not only to contemporary and future playwrights but to a literate, French-reading public.[2]

The public, whether in Paris or in the provinces, was able to participate in the shift away from a relatively private discussion of the writing of tragedy among authors toward an increasingly developed public debate about this matter. Discussions for and against specific plays flourished, and these controversies left substantial written records, as in the case of the "quarrels" of *Le Cid, Horace,* and *La Sophonisbe.* However, these debates about individual works did not occur at random. They were outcroppings of more general discussions about social and political values and about the nature of tragedy.

The growing publicness of this general discussion belongs to the almost universal acceptance of one of the major contentions of the theorists of tragedy, even by those who on other points had little in common with such writers as d'Aubignac: tragedy—and other literary forms—can legitimately and usefully be discussed by people who do not write tragedy. In the early 1630s the public had already been drawn into discussion of these issues by texts such as Chapelain's "Lettre sur la règle des vingt-quatre heures" (1630), and seven years later the "quarrel" of the *Cid* erupted with the appearance of Scudéry's *Observations sur le Cid,* followed by a host of other publications within the space of a few months. Indeed the quarrel of the *Cid* was not only public but helped to define the "public" as a cultural concept (Merlin, *Public et littérature* 153–93), and the printed texts related to the quarrel brought examples of critical and theoretical debate to people who would not have access to such important sites of discussion as the salon of Catherine de Vivonne, marquise de Rambouillet, which was then at the height of its activity. Long before Donneau de Visé's periodical of social and literary discussion, the *Mercure Galant* (founded in 1672), helped promote a community of readers and critics for *La Princesse de Clèves* (DeJean, *Ancients against Moderns* 59–66), many publications on the poetics of tragedy had provided models for further debate. Thus, at least as early as 1630 the poetics of tragedy—that is, of *théâtre régulier,* which we can simply call "regularity"—provided what could be called an aesthetic forum, a general system of accountability and exchange that encouraged theater audiences, playwrights, and quasi-professional theorists to discuss not only individual dramatic works but also points of dramatic construction and effect that previously were reserved to a very small number of people, most of whom were practicing poets. As an aesthetic forum, regularity facilitated exchange among persons with very different degrees of practical involvement in theatrical writing and production by establishing a common vocabulary of terms such as *unité de temps, péripétie, sujet,* and *bienséance.* This terminology democratized literary and dramatic criticism while shaping it—one might also say, deforming it—according to the particular key features isolated by neo-Aristotelian scholars.

The fact that so many people had a common vocabulary and a focus on a limited number of issues does not mean that they agreed on a common set of "rules" for writing tragedy. Instead, the power struggle between the neo-Aristotelian scholars, or *doctes,* and the practicing playwrights produced a highly publicized discourse available to anyone who wanted to stake a claim to knowledge about tragedy. Regularity is not solely the quality of plays that observe rules derived from translations of Aristotle's *Poetics* but rather the practice of a community of writers, readers, and spectators who are engaged in analyzing the success of plays while confining themselves to a vocabulary that strains to describe contemporary taste within an Aristotelian model. Both Corneille, who practiced regularity by creating an ironic inflation of rules devised by himself, and Racine, who severely limited his intervention into the public discussion of tragedy and who ridiculed the "rules," are regular playwrights. Despite their opposition to *doctes* like d'Aubignac, Chapelain, and La Mesnardière, Corneille and Racine spoke the same language and knew the flashpoints of the debates.

Within the aesthetic forum of regularity, the public—those who are neither *doctes* nor playwrights—is assigned a pivotal and paradoxical role. On one hand the public now has unprecedented access to documentation about the theories of tragedy as well as possession of printed versions of the plays themselves, usually published within a year of the performance. The public can thus assume an informed, intellectual, distanced, critical, and even technical attitude toward dramatic writing. On the other hand, in its role as dramatic audience, the public is described in the theoretical texts as being deprived of the capacity to reason and as deliberately and gratefully deluded. The prohibition against a rational, self-possessed experience of tragedy appears in authors as different as La Mesnardière and Racine, who advance a view of the spectator as swept away in tearful passion.

This split function of the public appears as well in technical guidance concerning the unities and character motivation. Chapelain is typical in his account of the audience's relation to the passage of time during the performance of a tragedy. The audience of tragedy is inherently and naturally limited mentally in a way that the audience of epic is not. In other words, the audience does not conform to the institution of drama by becoming less able to comprehend the representation of actions lasting more than twenty-four hours or to sort out and distinguish moments widely separated. Instead, tragedy has been constructed by theorists and artists who understand the innate incapacity of audiences to manipulate information that is conveyed through the visual imagination. However, the audience's mental shortcomings may be an advantage in the tragic artist's creative endeavor. Knowing that the spectator cannot keep track of events and time, the playwright can recognize opportunities to augment the spectator's confusion when this is useful for the overall effect. Causing the audience to lose count of the number of hours that pass during intermissions is one example of the discrepancy in knowledge between playwrights and theorists, on one hand, and the theater audience on the other. Not only is the theater audience less intellectually aware of the details of the fictive world than is the playwright, but theorists recommend that the playwright avoid any reminders of the time structure that could help the audience become aware of the devices and decoys through which the playwright/audience hierarchy is kept in place.

Corneille and d'Aubignac also provide advice for keeping the audience in a state of pleasurable forgetfulness of the artistic devices. As d'Aubignac says about adding *couleurs* to conceal plot preparation, the writer must do this so that "esprit des Spectateurs est tout à fait arresté et ne pense point qu'il en doive sortir aucun autre Incident que ce qu'il connoist" (129). There is nothing remarkable about this artistic sleight of hand. We are quite accustomed to illusion and concealed mechanisms—indeed, the seventeenth-century "machine play" with its flying gods and monsters takes the concept of pleasurable semideception of the audience much further than the imperceptible plot preparation of a d'Aubignac's or Corneille's recommendation that time references be vague so that the audience loses track of the duration of the actions. What is worth noting as a defining characteristic of seventeenth-century literary culture is the way the public is cast in two radically different roles. On one hand, the public as dramatic audience is described theoretically as deprived of reason, as disoriented in time and space, and as convulsed with the requisite passion of tragedy. On the other hand, the public as potential reader of theoretical treatises, prefaces, and critical pamphlets or reports is given ample and detailed knowledge of the rearrangement of historical truth into plausible fiction, of the ways of heightening the spectator's emotional response, and of the specific alterations of the fictional world that are made with an eye to contemporary taste.

Corneille also sees the spectator as having a strongly emotive role during the performance and as having a critical and even theoretical capacity at a later time. In his *Discours,* as in the *examens* of individual plays, he invites his public to recall the reality of their experience in the theater and to generalize on that personal knowledge even to the point of questioning the commonplaces or received ideas of the learned authors of poetics.[3] Using the spectator's experience of tragic emotion, Corneille drives a wedge between the reality of modern tragedy and the abstractions of ancient and neoclassical theory. Yet rather than attack the critical and theoretical enterprise itself, Corneille emphasizes the right of any spectator to participate in this ongoing, modern, and newly democratized activity. On the other hand, Corneille's spectators as participants in salon discussions or even personal introspection are doing very different things. We might even call the former "meta-spectators," since they are no longer absorbed in the emotion of the tragic characters or even in their own immediate empathic emotion but are contemplating their *own* emotion as a source of knowledge about tragedy.

In general the public as audience is cast as inferior in imaginative and reasoning capacity to the playwright—Corneille's audience alone constitutes a possible exception.[4] The playwright can confront the shocking and untidy events of history and legend, exploring the more obscure events of the past for stories that are unknown to the less cultivated audience. When these events are transposed to the stage, they are reconfigured to eliminate or to conceal what is acceptable to the reader of history but intolerable to the spectator of tragedy. The theatrical audience is delicate and imaginatively limited, far from the robust audience implied for epic and even more for history. This relationship between audience and playwright also provides a shadow of the relationship between the playwright and the theorist, since the theorist stands above the tragic author as the latter dominates the tragic audience.

When the audience is not watching a performance or reading—in the fullest, most engaged sense (La Mesnardière's "lecture faite dans un cabinet")—the audience is offered the opportunity to shift into a mode of technical scrutiny. Not only do the general treatises, ranging from d'Aubignac's to Rapin's, provide the basis for such inquiry but the prefaces and *examens* of Corneille and Racine justify for the reader the adaptation of historical sources, features of characterization, and the organization of time and space.

The distinction between the involved audience and the reflective, critical public of connoisseurs is made both collectively and individually. The audience as a group appears mostly in the prefaces of La Mesnardière and d'Aubignac. In this context, in which the political and sociocultural usefulness of drama and especially tragedy is explained, the audience is defined, so to speak, from the bottom up. The theater, "qu'on peut nommer veritablement l'Ecole du Peuple" (9), is also useful, according to d'Aubignac, to occupy the excess leisure of those inclined to idleness and whose laziness "les porte ordinairement ou à s'abandonner à des débauches honteuses et criminelles, ou à consumer en peu d'heures ce qui pourroit suffire à l'entretien de leur famille durant plusieurs jours" (10).[5]

La Mesnardière has an antithetical view of the condition—we would say the class—of the audience of tragedy, though he also builds his description of the audience from below, denouncing the would-be spectator ("un animal si stupide" [Q]) who is below the threshold of tragedy. For the author of *La poëtique,* both tragedy and comedy are above the reach of the people in general. Not only would the common people ("la vile populace" or "multitude" [H, I]) not understand the profound thought or the refined language of tragedy, but such people would be left cold and untouched by the events of tragedy, thus failing to receive the primary benefit of such plays: fear. Only princes can be moved by the fate of other, unhappy princes. Yet this difference in the conception of the audience of tragedy does not prevent La Mesnardière from sharing the view that during the viewing of a tragedy, the spectator should be paralyzed ("transi") by the spectacle of a fate that could be his or hers. The absence of emotional identification and absorption during the performance produces a gross mock-connoisseurship on the part of the people, who interrupt the actors with ignorant approval and tumult—a state of affairs that shows the people to be ill fit both for the emotional experience of tragedy and for the intellectual experience of the critic.

Except for these prefatory comments on the aggregate of the theater audience—one that has limitations in the capacity to understand tragedy based on condition, "genius," and education—the theater audience is conceived in theory as made up of isolated individuals described as *le spectateur.* This spectator is the fixed point toward which theoretical comments and injunctions are aimed. For instance, La Mesnardière's insistence that the sacred person of a king should not be shown hanged or burned onstage describes audience emotion in the singular:

> cét excés de malheurs engendre aussi tost le murmure, le scandale, et le blasphéme dans l'esprit du Spectateur; qui est si puissamment chocqué par ces cruautez excessives, qu'il implore toutes les foudres pour en chastier les autheurs, et qu'il accuse le Ciel quand il ne les voit pas punir par un chastiment éxemplaire. (323)

La Mesnardière certainly expects identical feelings to occur in all the members of the audience but he does not describe this reaction as the result of a group revulsion in which an individual's feelings would be submerged in a specifically collective surge. This is not the reaction of a mob, nor is one spectator influenced by his or her neighbor. Instead, the spectator is directly influenced by the spectacle as if alone. This strange solitude of the tragic spectator is entirely in keeping with the insistence, on the part of almost all theorists, on treating the reader of tragedy as identical with the spectator.[6] Yet the solitary spectator, whom I have earlier called an "individual," is definitely not an individual in the modern colloquial sense of a unique person with qualities and feelings in some way different from everyone else's. None of the theorists thinks of the spectator in this way, since the tragic spectator has predictable reactions and feelings that theory claims to describe. Beyond those common parameters, the theory of tragedy does not venture. The solutions for the problems of dramatic construction have to work for each spectator, that is, for *the* spectator. D'Aubignac, describing dramatic narratives (*récits*), says that they should be coordinated sequentially with the actions off-

stage, "à mesure qu'elles arrivent: et s'il se trouve necessaire et plus agréable de le retarder, il y faut employer quelque adresse qui laisse au Spectateur le desir de les apprendre sans impatience; ou bien luy en oster l'attente, afin qu'il ne le desire pas avec inquietude" (289).

Bossuet is unusual in his insistence on the collective emotional activity of the audience as a group. Even though he does, like the other theorists, construct a theoretical singular spectator as the person on whom tragedy has its primary, and very dangerous, emotional impact, the Bishop pictures this seductive and perverting influence within an immediate group context. Not only does the theater have the long-term effect of undermining the morality of the individual Christian who may then induce others to sin, but the spectator is present in the same room with others whose complicity in sin is already evident from the very fact of being in that place. For Bossuet, then, the drama is always a double spectacle, one where each spectator is seeking out the eyes of potential partners.[7] However, the defining feature of this sinful assembly remains the aspiration to share the passionate feelings of the dramatic characters, and these feelings are conveyed to the absorbed individual spectator.[8]

Yet the same people whose limitations determine (in *theory*) the ways tragedy should be conceived and executed have access to the critical and theoretical debates concerning tragedy as well as other forms of writing during the seventeenth century. By their detailed treatment of certain poetic and moral questions, Racine's brief prefaces acknowledge that the reading public was interested in, and informed of, controversies in the poetics of tragedy, yet these same prefaces express reservations about the public's excessive engagement in poetics to the detriment of an immediate experience of the dramatic.

Although d'Aubignac, in describing spectators, says that "la pluspart ne sont pas d'un grand genie" (216), he expresses confidence that his own book about theater will be useful in helping those who are not playwrights understand the art of composing for the stage.[9] The hoped-for result of this educational enterprise will be to modify and increase the spectator's appreciation of the theater, even though this appreciation is based on considerations unavailable to the public during the performance.

While the audience should be, in the theater, completely absorbed in the fictive world before its eyes, the same audience may at another time consider how much work went into the production of these stage fictions.[10] In other words, the public of d'Aubignac's book must alternatively—and *not* simultaneously—belong to the happily abandoned audience that does not think of the playwright's constant manipulation and to the calm, clear-sighted, and never duped connoisseur of the techniques of dramatic writing.

This sustained ambivalence about the theatrical public in its partitioned, polar roles of emotional involvement and distanced, intellectual evaluation is a new and important characteristic of seventeenth-century French culture. It is a feature of that culture that we have difficulty remembering when we speak about French "classical" theater, confusing the cold rationality of the critical initiate with the pathos of the terrified and weeping spectator of tragedy. We may, of course, reject this polarity and may even dismiss the contemporary theorists of tragedy as deluded and irrelevant to the actual stage writing of their day. We risk a grave distortion of the cultural history of France, however, if we fail to acknowledge the complexity of a poetic doctrine that we too often reduce to four or five rules and an insistence on reason.

Notes

Preface

1. Makowiecka 125–26. See also the introduction to Russell Sebold's edition of *La poética o reglas de la poesía en general y de sus principales especies* and Luzán's "Proemio" (Luzán 123–24).

Chapter One
Regularity: Articulating the Aesthetic

1. "Cette pièce fut mon coup d'essai, et elle n'a garde d'être dans les Règles, puisque je ne savais pas alors qu'il y en eût" (Corneille 1: 5).

2. Jean Rousset, Raymond Lebègue, Imbrie Buffum, and many others have contributed to this view; and even Pierre Charpentrat, in attacking the concept of the "baroque," pays homage to the notion of baroque "illusion" in the title of his book *Le mirage baroque.*

3. In contrast to the articulated kind of rule that dominates the poetics of tragedy, there is another, unarticulated sense of "rule" that appears in Roger de Piles's use of the term for the plastic arts. In his *Cours de peinture par principes,* de Piles says that in antiquity Polyclitus gave the "rule" of the male nude. By this de Piles does not mean a list of qualities or a set of injunctions but rather a "standard": "Policlete . . . s'avisa de faire une Statue qui eut toutes les proportions qui conviennent à un homme parfaitement bien formé. Il se servit pour cela de plusieurs modéles naturels, et après avoir réduit son Ouvrage dans la derniere perfection, il fut examiné par les habiles gens avec tant d'exactitude, et admiré avec tant d'eloges, que cette Statue fut d'un commun consentement appellée la *Regle*" (133; emphasis added).

4. The *Regulae* were published posthumously in 1705. At the NASSCFL meeting in April 1996, George Hoffmann made an important contribution to our understanding of the *Regulae,* arguing, in an unpublished paper, that Descartes abandoned them in favor of a simpler and more resolutely sequenced procedure of thought.

5. Here, it should be admitted, La Mesnardière is stating a rule about the *stage (le Théâtre)* rather than about tragedy as a genre, though this is still typical of the somewhat unsettled priorities that appear in enumerations of "rules."

6. In a note in the Pléiade edition of Corneille's works, Georges Couton draws attention to a remarkable feature of this dedication. Corneille had it printed in subsequent editions long after Richelieu's death: "Assez normalement une épître dédicatoire n'est pas reproduite dans les éditions postérieures à l'originale; or Corneille maintient celle-ci jusqu'en 1657. . . . C'est d'autant plus remarquable que Richelieu était mort en 1642."

7. Note by Maurice Rat in his edition of Corneille's plays, 1: 655.

8. La Mesnardière's repetitious argument against happy endings (which are approved by Aristotle) and the scorn he heaps on the multitude are a reaction against Lodovico Castelvetro's populist theory of tragedy in his *Poetica d'Aristotele vulgarizzata e sposta* (1576).

9. Allen G. Wood examines many of the intricacies of the satirist's voice in literary satire. Wood notes that "satire is a shorter form, allowing less scope for the development of theoretical statements, which need room to develop, clarify themselves, and provide their own context. In contrast, the satiric tone purposefully disrupts the theoretical flow" (*Literary Satire and Theory* 77).

10. Boileau's *Réflexions critiques sur quelques passages du rhéteur Longin,* however, sheds less light on Longinus than on Boileau's long-standing polemic with Charles Perrault on the occasion of the Quarrel of the Ancients and the Moderns.

11. Boileau's poem was printed just a few months before the opening of Corneille's last tragedy, *Suréna, général des Parthes,* and one month before Racine's penultimate tragedy of Greek inspiration, *Iphigénie.* In short, *L'art poétique* coincides with the end of the Cornelian and Racinian "canon" of French classical tragedy.

12. As Wood notes, "the persona portrays himself as a reader advising the future poet, the addressee" (*Literary Satire and Theory* 73).

13. Likewise, the power of the reader appears in Boileau's preface to his French translation of Longinus: "Tout ce que le Lecteur n'entend point s'appelle un galimatthias, dont le Traducteur tout seul est responsable" (337).

14. In "De l'expérience," Montaigne wrote of the multiplication of laws: "Qu'ont gaigné nos legislateurs à choisir cent mille especes et faicts particuliers, et y attacher cent mille loix? Ce nombre n'a aucune proportion avec l'infinie diversité des actions humaines. La multiplication de nos inventions n'arrivera pas à la variation des exemples" (1066).

15. It is probably not entirely far-fetched to see in this replacement of many rules by a single, transcendent rule, a gesture no doubt familiar to Racine, the pupil of the Jansenists, by which the apostle Paul replaces law by the single commandment of love in the Epistle to the Romans.

16. "Le secret est d'abord de plaire et de toucher," writes Boileau in *L'art poétique,* which was printed in 1674 though apparently read in salons in 1672 (see Françoise Escal's note to the Pléiade edition, 989).

17. The strong distinction that Racine makes between "rule" and "rules" appears vividly in the letter to Henriette d'Angleterre that precedes *Andromaque:* "nous n'avons plus que faire de demander aux savants si nous travaillons selon les *règles.* La *règle* souveraine est de plaire . . ." (Racine, *Théâtre complet* 129).

18. The use of the term *rule* for the concepts of verisimilitude, unity of time, and so forth, has been so entirely accepted that skilled exegetes of the theoretical texts often overlook the distinction between verisimilitude as concept and verisimilitude as rule. Forestier writes, "Ce qu'on

appelle aujourd'hui l'*esthétique classique* est donc un ensemble de codes et de règles—issus du modèle antique et du modèle italien du XVIe siècle, qui ont été élaborés en France à partir de 1623. . . . Molière, La Fontaine, Racine affecteront même de mépriser les règles—affirmant que la grande règle est de 'plaire'—parce que ces règles auront été si bien intégrées dans leur travail créateur qu'elles leur sembleront naturelles" (*Introduction à l'analyse des textes classiques* 10–11). When is a rule not a rule? When is a theoretical statement an affectation and when is it a simple declaration? Does an "integrated" rule remain a rule, or does the concept "rule" not suppose some difference between spontaneous action, one that appears "natural," and an action that is deliberately non-natural?

19. Jean-Jacques Roubine writes of "Les 'règles' du théâtre" (15). In the glossary of their book, the authors of *Littérature française du XVIIe siècle* define *Règles,* "Directives données par la critique aux écrivains. . . . Les classiques, en les appliquant, les concilient avec le plaisir du public. Dans cette optique, les règles de bienséance et de vraisemblance jouent un rôle principal. Plus spéciales sont les règles des unités" (Zuber et al. 421). It is worth noting here, as a kind of revisionist stance toward Bray, that the rules are described as distinct from audience satisfaction so that the classical writers place themselves between the goal of pleasing the audience, on one hand, and the rules on the other. The rules are not a means for pleasing the audience, but rather constitute a difficulty that classical writers overcome, while at the same time avoiding overt violations.

20. "C'est donc en analogie avec un réel possible que se pense le concept de régularité du théâtre. . . . le théâtre, pour être pensé, induit en quelque sorte le domaine d'une expérience possible du théâtre: il requiert la présence d'une espèce de philosophie transcendantale permettant de penser les conditions de sa possibilité, sinon toujours de les connaître et de les arrêter sous forme de règles" (Kintzler 134).

For Kintzler, then, the regularity of the theater has little to do with what she calls "les trop fameuses règles des trois unités" and is centered on the construction of a world from which both audience and author are absent and that must function autonomously on the basis of its own history, space, and psychology. She describes quite well the theoretical struggle to isolate the stage from the audience, but she does so at the expense of actual theories, both those formulated explicitly by seventeenth-century authors and those implied by their polemical rejection of individual rules or of the rules as an aggregate, and she denies, in particular, that there is any conventional, or as she says, axiomatic quality to the theory of the theater: "C'est en effet dans le concept de nature qu'ils puisent la légitimité ultime de la régularité théâtrale; non pas une nature empiquement observable, mais une *nature légale,* pensée, soit en conformité rigoureuse (pour le théâtre dramatique), soit en analogie (pour le théâtre lyrique) avec la nature telle que la conçoit la science classique. Une nature de théâtre, fondatrice du théâtre, c'est alors une législation naturelle et théâtrale possible, elle doit pouvoir apparaître comme un représentable *a priori.* La régularité du théâtre classique se présente comme une physiologie pure du théâtre" (136).

21. Roubine in his *Introduction aux grandes théories du théâtre* (1990) shows the uneven degree to which theorists of the seventeenth century perceived and accepted convention, and notes that the theatrical public apparently was perfectly comfortable with dramatic convention (31).

22. Poetics for Kintzler, "c'est l'agencement des faits, le dispositif qui se déroule, non pas sous les yeux réels d'un public réel, mais sous l'œil théorique d'un lecteur attentif à la disposition dramatique" (15).

Chapter Two
Passion in the Age of Reason

1. Of course, one could make a utopian argument that if the subjects were all in perfect possession of their reason, they would recognize spontaneously the superiority of the monarchy as represented by the Cardinal. However, Senault does not envision a world where reason is equally distributed.

2. Timothy J. Reiss is one of the few recent critics to have written about the role of emotion in classical dramatic theory. Tracing a shift from a "baroque" theater of doubt to a "classical" theater of illusion and identification, he describes the goal of the classical theorists as being to eliminate psychical distance between spectator and character so that the character's emotions would control the spectator. However, most of Reiss's emphasis is on the epistemological issues raised by the creation of illusion rather than on the emotion itself (Reiss, *Towards Dramatic Illusion*). Tenacious is the view of classicism represented by V.-L. Saulnier's *La littérature française du siècle classique,* which abounds in formulas such as "il y a un beau éternel: c'est celui qui frappe la raison" (58) and "L'œuvre parfaite est accessible et claire: non pas la clarté de l'esquisse superficielle, mais celle que conquiert une lente analyse de la pensée et le raffinement artistique de la phrase" (61).

3. Even studies that seem to be entirely devoted to emotion in classical theater, like Octave Nadal's *Le sentiment de l'amour dans l'œuvre de Pierre Corneille,* displace their interest from the emotion of love to the objects or conducts that surround that emotion. A comment about love in an early play by Corneille is typical of Nadal's approach, "dans *La Place Royale* il l'entrevoit [l'amour] comme un conflit entre esclavage et liberté; il tient dès lors le plus original de sa psychologie des passions. Au même titre que l'ambition, le sentiment patriotique ou le désir de Dieu, l'amour impose une exigence" (23).

4. Biet's study demonstrates the importance of weeping in seventeenth-century French culture and the different approach to weeping in Corneille and Racine. However, Biet does not discuss in detail the extensive contemporary corpus of poetics of tragedy. Bayne's *Tears and Weeping* is another exception, though Bayne is primarily concerned with the representation of weeping and not so much the emotional impact on the spectator.

5. Spitzer, "Racine's Classical *Piano*" and "The 'Récit de Théramène' in Racine's *Phèdre*," in *Essays* 1–113 and 209–51.

6. DeJean gives an account of the replacement, toward midcentury, of "passion" by "sentiment" and "sensibilité" as the principal French terms for emotion (*Ancients against Moderns* 82), a change accompanied, in her account, by a shift from tragedy to novel as the major literary form. Such a dual shift makes even more apparent how central passion is to tragedy itself as a genre in the seventeenth century, for even three-quarters of the way through the century passion dominates Racinian tragedy as it does the ideal tragedy as theorized toward 1640.

7. La Mesnardière's vague thinking on this issue is shown by the divergence between his repeated and emphatic statements of the priority that should be given to terror and his less frequent, apparently pro-forma claim that tragedy should *moderate* terror, as in his direct quotation from Aristotle's *Poetics:* "l'imitation réelle des malheurs, et des souffrances, qui produit par elle-mesme la Terreur et la Pitié, et qui sert à modérer ces deux mouvemens de l'Ame" (8).

8. In showing that pity without fear cannot improve the spectator's conduct, Corneille remarks, "Quand ils [les personnages] sont innocents, la pitié que nous en prenons ne produit aucune crainte, et si nous en concevons quelqu'une qui purge nos passions, c'est par le moyen d'une autre personne que de celle qui nous fait pitié, et nous le devons toute à la *force de l'exemple*" (3: 148; emphasis added).

9. "Et il est d'autant plus aisé de conclurre qu'Aristote entend parler de la Terreur, qu'il veut que la Tragédie modere cette Passion, et qu'il ne peut desirer que l'Horreur soit adoucie par les spectacles de Théatre, puis qu'on n'en peut trop avoir pour les meschantes actions" (La Mesnardière 25). If this "moderation" of terror succeeds, then the major instructional value of tragedy will decrease, according to the logic of La Mesnardière's insistence on frightening the audience.

10. "[N]ous epreuvons que la Commiseration est infiniment plus douce, plus humaine et plus agréable que la terreur et l'effroy . . ." (La Mesnardière 19).

11. Dacier's edition of the *Poetics* is based on a profound ambivalence toward nature and history. In his preface he describes tragedy as an invention of the poets, who perceived that humanity had lost its original innocence and could no longer find pleasure in the direct expression of wisdom and prayer. Poetry in general is an attempt to entice humanity to attend to lessons of moral improvement with a pleasurable pretext. What is pleasing is not necessarily good, but what is good should also be pleasing. In the face of such a postlapsarian vision, it is puzzling to see Dacier also insist that poetic rules should not vary from one period to another, since nature has remained constant. Presumably he means that nature, since the Fall, has not substantially changed.

12. Voltaire: " *Le carnage et l'horreur,* termes vagues et usés qu'il faut éviter. Aujourd'hui tous nos mauvais versificateurs emploient le carnage et l'horreur à la fin d'un vers . . ." (142n).

13. On the other hand, the horrible is clearly connected to the influence of Seneca on Renaissance tragedy. See Ronald Tobin, *Racine and Seneca.* The important figure of Medea is conveyed to modern playwrights through Seneca, and Medea is crucial for the link of the "denatured" mother to horror. See Mitchell Greenberg, "Mythifying Matrix: Corneille's *Médée.*"

14. This is how La Mesnardière ends his discussion of the torments that *should* be represented to "bien émouvoir la Terreur" (99) by imitating the punishments of Ixion and Prometheus. Yet it is not clear why or whether the punishment of Prometheus is itself good and deserved.

15. Besides Corneille, who makes pleasure the basis of his poetics, we should recall Mairet. The latter used the increase of the spectator's pleasure as the major argument for the "règle des vingt-quatre heures" in his preface to *La Silvanire* (1631).

16. Beyond the issue of emotion, the broader implications of excess in Racine's theory and tragedy are treated by Richard E. Goodkin, *The Tragic Middle: Racine, Aristotle, Euripides.*

17. Franko proposes a very different reading of d'Aubignac as proponent of an "anti-illusionistic and intellectually mediated stage practice" (314–15).

18. In opposing reason to passion, theorists are not calling for the production of absurdity. This is an important point, for anything that appears absurd, rather than passionate, is thought likely to elicit unwanted audience reasoning. Thus La Mesnardière says, for instance, "il ne s'y doit rien passer qui puisse chocquer les yeux, comme font ces absurditez qui travaillent le Spectateur, & sont causes que sa Raison se révolte contre sa veuë" (271).

19. See also his comment on metaphor and emotion: "Les *Termes Metaphoriques* ont une merveilleuse grace dans le Langage Poëtique; mais ils ne me semblent pas propres pour dépeindre vivement le procedé naturel des mouvemens impétueux, où l'ame envisage les choses dans la premiere posture qu'elles se presentent à elle, et ne se donne pas le temps d'en chercher les plus beaux biais" (La Mesnardière 360).

20. "Pour rendre donc vray-semblable qu'un homme recite des Stances, c'est à dire qu'il fasse des vers sur le Theatre, il faut qu'il y ait une couleur ou raison pour authoriser ce changement de langage. Or la principale et la plus commune est, que l'Acteur, qui les recite, ait eu quelque temps suffisant pour y travailler, ou pour y faire travailler . . ." (d'Aubignac 263).

21. "[L]'on voit dans une Strophe quatre mesures différentes; un petit Vers entre deux grans, un grand entre deux petis, quatre petis & six grans, deux grans & quatre petis, & c." (La Mesnardière 402).

Chapter Three
The Tragic Story

1. Cf. d'Aubignac: "La Scéne ne donne point les choses comme elles ont esté, mais comme elles devoient estre" (68).

2. How La Mesnardière knows enough about these lost tragedies to judge their historicity or their likeness to truth is itself a tantalizing problem in verisimilitude.

3. In regard to the "purgation" of passions, Corneille writes, "Je m'en rapporte à ceux qui en ont vu les représentations: ils peuvent en demander compte au secret de leur cœur, et repasser sur ce qui les a touchés au théâtre, pour reconnaître s'ils en sont venus par là jusqu'à cette crainte réfléchie, et si elle a rectifié en eux la passion qui a causé la disgrâce qu'ils ont plainte" (3: 146).

4. Aristotle lays out the combinations rather differently from Corneille. Where the French version of this table shows the two plots of attempts to kill an ally or kin in first and fourth place (first to carry out the deed and fourth not to carry it out), Aristotle considers these to be variants of the same plot: "Of these cases, the worst is where the agent, in full knowledge, is on the point of acting, yet fails to do so; for this is repulsive and untragic (as it lacks suffering). . . . Not much better is for the deed to be executed in such a case" (*Poetics,* Halliwell ed. 46–47).

5. Aristotle, *Poetics,* chapter 7, Lucas ed. 1451a, "kata to eikos e to anagkaion." Corneille's use of this term is, to put it mildly, very different from what most modern readers of the *Poetics* understand by "necessity." As Halliwell (in Aristotle, *Poetics*) comments, "necessity . . . refers to complete certainty or inevitability, whether in a logical argument or in a relation between events" (100).

6. Corneille is not alone in equating the "subject" of a play with the *roman.* D'Aubignac defines the subject as what the ancients called "la *Fable*, et nous l'*Histoire,* ou le *Roman*" (65; emphasis in original).

7. One reading of this passage leads to the belief that Corneille contradicts himself and that the application of the "necessary" to the link between events is merely an attempt to conciliate the Aristotelians by maintaining some role for the verisimilar. Corneille early in the second discourse seems to accept—at least he does not criticize—the position that subjects should be treated in a verisimilar manner even though the best should, in themselves, be nonverisimilar.

8. This is a triumph over ideology that occurs only within the horizons of the very ideology that gives shape to the desire, since Chimène's and Rodrigue's love is explained as being the result of the aristocratic worldview that makes their marriage "unthinkable."

9. To understand the circumstances under which we should prefer the "nécessaire" to the "vraisemblable," says Corneille, we distinguish two things in tragic actions: (1) the actions themselves with their "inséparables circonstances du temps et du lieu" and (2) the link between the actions, "la liaison qu'elles ont ensemble." He adds, "En la première, le vrai-semblable est à préférer au nécessaire, et le nécessaire au vraisemblable dans la seconde" (3: 163).

10. In her important article on d'Aubignac, Hagiwara points to a dis-tinction between representation and imitation that, in her view, is a major advance of d'Aubignac's work over that of other theorists of this pe-riod: "la distinction ici ne s'établit pas entre l'œuvre, picturale ou drama-tique, et un objet extérieur représenté par celle-ci, mais elle traverse l'œuvre elle-même" (26). D'Aubignac's analysis of the Mary Magdalene painting concentrates on the arrangement of the scene as an aesthetic phenomenon and on the content of the scene as a supposed reality, "l'Histoire veritable ou que l'on suppose veritable" (35). Hagiwara con-trasts this approach with "le rapport omniprésent entre le modèle et la copie" among other theorists. Yet d'Aubignac's "Histoire veritable" is equivalent to the "modèle" just as the painting considered "comme une peinture" is the copy. This equivalency is possible because for d'Aubi-gnac as for Chapelain, Scudéry, and La Mesnardière, etc., neither the "Histoire veritable" nor the model is an "objet extérieur." The reality that is the point of departure for the work of painter and author is a reality that exists only in the world of ideas (or, at its most material, only in other paintings and texts). It is not any more or less external to the art-work in d'Aubignac's theory than in anyone else's. Although d'Aubi-gnac wrote one of the most lucid expositions of the application of general verisimilitude to the act of composition, he was not theoretically inno-vative in this domain.

11. Certain comments of Hagiwara's make it seem that she does at-tribute to d'Aubignac this split of the "support matériel à la chose qui est représentée en elle [la représentation]" (26) or of "la surface peinte du tableau dans son aspect sensible à ce qui est figuré ou représenté dans le tableau" (25).

12. Murray is writing about the role of color in d'Aubignac's *Pratique,* and while I understand *couleur* in a different way from that presented in *Theatrical Legitimation,* I fully concur with the general tenor of Murray's description of the libido in d'Aubignac's writings.

13. The distinction between the verisimilitude of events and of char-acters occasionally blurs in seventeenth-century French theory, though it derives from Aristotle's list (*Poetics,* chapter 6) of the six elements (or qualitative parts) of tragedy: plot, character, style, thought, spectacle, lyric. For the most part, events are the result of the actions of characters (e.g., it is not verisimilar that a father kill his son or that a king flee from a battle), but some events (e.g., a rival is killed by a lightning bolt) may not result from the actions of characters. Or the action of a character may be itself verisimilar but certain aspects, such as the rapidity with which the action is completed, may be nonverisimilar (e.g., that Rodrigue in *Le Cid* can complete a major military enterprise in a few hours) for reasons that seem independent of a character's will.

14. The four requirements of character in Aristotle's *Poetics* are, as Corneille cites them in his *Discours,* "qu'elles [les mœurs, ethos] soient bonnes, convenables, semblables, et égales" (3: 129).

15. Aristotle lists the four requirements of character in *Poetics,* chapter 15.

16. For the extensive study of the "middling" nature of ethics and tragedy, see Goodkin, *The Tragic Middle: Racine, Aristotle, Euripides.*

17. Meleager is mentioned by Aristotle in the *Poetics* (chapter 13) and cited by Castelvetro as an example of inconsistency in Aristotle's choice of tragic subjects. Castelvetro finds Orestes and Meleager's mother, Althea, fully guilty of premeditated parricide. La Mesnardière's discussion of Meleager is an attempt to absolve Meleager, Althea, and Aristotle.

18. Corneille echoes this sentiment: "ces républicains avaient une si forte haine des rois, qu'il[s] voyaient avec plaisir des crimes dans les plus innocents de leur race" (3: 161).

19. Modern tragedy, according to Corneille, is governed by a rule unknown to antiquity: to make the audience like (and sympathize with) the principal characters. This sympathy, rather than having a didactic purpose, should make playwrights avoid any intentional evil on the part of the hero.

Chapter Four
The "Unities" and the Classical Spectator

1. In Pierre Martino's edition, the chapter "De l'Unité du Lieu" is fourteen pages long (98–112), the chapter "De l'Estenduë de l'Action Theatrale, ou du Temps et de la durée convenables au Poëme Dramatique" is also roughly fourteen pages (113–27), and "De l'Unité de l'Action" is less than half of the others (83–89).

2. Although his remarks are somewhat obscure and may simply call for a complex but stable stage set, La Mesnardière seems, in fact, to advocate changes in the scenic space to help the spectator keep the story straight "& que les Distinctions de Scène empeschent que l'on ne treuve de la confusion en ces Lieux, qui embarrasse l'Auditeur" (413).

3. Corneille even casts doubt on whether the monologue character *is* speaking, within the fiction of the dramatic story. Casting doubt on interpretations of French classical theater in which characters' gestures can be read directly (i.e., when Don Gomès gives Don Diègue a slap in *Le Cid,* this is physically the same gesture, with the same meaning, as when one nobleman slaps another outside the theater), Corneille writes, "quand un acteur est seul sur le théâtre, il est présumé ne faire que s'entretenir en lui-même, et ne parle qu'afin que le spectateur sache de quoi il s'entretient, et à quoi il pense" (3: 138). In this view the character seems to be engaged in an interior monologue in which her or his lips move accidentally and unconsciously. Another character within the scene should not be able to hear what the character is saying: "ce serait une faute insupportable, si un autre acteur apprenait par là ses secrets" (3: 138).

4. La Mesnardière writes, "Nous permettons aux Dramatiques d'étendre en ces occasions [*a parte*] les bornes de leur Théatre, & de partager leur Scéne en plusieurs cartiers différens, pourveu qu'ils y fassent écrire, *Cét endroit figure le Louvre, & Cy est la Place Royale*" (270). Sorel also links the issue of the *a parte* to the unity of place: "on trouve aussi fort étrange qu'un des comediens estant d'un costé, et l'autre de l'autre sur le Theatre, ils parlent chacun à part comme s'ils ne se pouvoient entendre, et ils disent fort haut des choses secrettes qui devroient fascher chacun d'eux dès qu'ils les sçavent, quoy que cela ne les émeuve point" (193). But Sorel justifies this apparently unreasonable situation by an appeal to the stress of passion and by a practical comment that stages are not always big enough for the characters to be widely separated.

5. Corneille is, as far as I have found, the only theorist who establishes in such an explicit way this connection between the secrets of opposing sides and individual places. He gives no further justification of the sort that Chapelain gives for the unity of place on the grounds of what, paraphrasing Chapelain, we could call "ocular memory"—that is, the fear that the spectator will not be able to keep track of multiple places simulated alternately on the same stage. We could extrapolate from a combination of Corneille's and Chapelain's remarks the belief that the audience would use different places as tags to track opposing intrigues, just as cinema assigns alternative left/right positions to characters in field / reverse field shots.

6. The characters of tragedy are, of course, epic characters, as poetic theory since Aristotle had determined. They are of the same heroic group of individuals and families and pass from one genre to another, like Agamemnon, Medea, and Andromache. By insisting on the epic aspect of tragic characters in seventeenth-century theory, I want to stress not their rank but their freedom to act offstage and to report their acts in a mode that is also used for epic, the narrative form.

7. Bossuet is emphatic in decrying the presence of women on the stage, "elles que leur sexe avait consacrées à la modestie, dont l'infirmité naturelle demandait la sûre retraite d'une maison bien réglée? Et voilà qu'elles s'étalent elles-mêmes en plein théâtre avec tout l'attirail de la vanité, comme ces sirènes dont parle Isaïe . . ." ("Lettre au père Caffaro" 132).

8. In another (though post-seventeenth-century) testimony to the opposition between the *cabinet* and the visible audience, Granet prefaces his collection of texts from the *Cid* controversy by observing, "Un homme de Lettres examine dans son cabinet un livre nouveau, il en démêle tous les rapports, les beautés et les défauts; ce n'est, à proprement parler, que l'ouvrage de son esprit; mais une pièce de Théâtre qui a été représentée plusieurs fois, essaye la critique du Parterre et du Public; cette critique vole de bouche en bouche, et l'Auteur qui, dans un écrit imprimé, s'érige en censeur de la pièce, ne manque pas de profiter de ces observations;

ainsi il est en parti l'écho du Public, dont il atteste le goût aux siècles à venir" (ii–iii).

9. The earlier parts of the *Discours* alternate between open and closed spaces: the closed space of the school in part 1 is followed by the open space of travel (Descartes, *Œuvres et lettres* 131), and then travel yields to retreat into a space that is even more confining than the school at the beginning of part 2 (132).

10. Descartes writes, "m'étant proposé l'objet des géomètres, que je concevais comme un corps continu, ou un espace indéfiniment étendu en longueur, largeur, et hauteur ou profondeur, divisible en diverses parties qui pouvaient avoir diverses figures et grandeurs, et être mues ou transposées en toutes sortes. . . . je pris garde aussi qu'il n'y avait rien du tout en elles qui m'assurât de l'existence de leur objet" (*Discours, Œuvres et lettres* 150).

11. In what follows I will use the term *unity of time,* despite its anachronism, both to suit modern usage and to take into account the very wide-ranging questions about dramatic time that were in fact raised in the seventeenth century.

12. Chapelain does not make any allowances for the *reader* of printed versions of tragedy in order to extend the time allotted for the action. The reader of tragedy is presumably meant to reenact mentally the experience of viewing a play and thus to suffer the same imaginative and perceptual limits as the audience in the theater.

13. For the "official" view of history, as typified by Bossuet's *Discours sur l'histoire universelle* (1681), the study of history was primarily meant to help avoid *anachronism,* "c'est-à-dire cette sorte d'erreur qui fait confondre les temps" (41).

14. Despite the similarity in terms, I do not mean to refer to Northrop Frye's generic distinction between "high mimetic" and "low mimetic." The high and low verisimilar arguments apply equally to tragedy and comedy.

15. "Les distinctions des actes, où le théâtre se rend vide d'acteurs et où l'auditoire est entretenu de musique ou d'intermèdes, doivent tenir lieu du temps que l'on se peut imaginer à rabattre les vingt-quatre heures" (Chapelain, "Lettre sur la règle des vingt-quatre heures" 121).

16. Compare Halliwell's translation of this portion of chapter 7 of Aristotle's *Poetics:* "By 'whole' [action] I mean possessing a beginning, middle and end. By connection with a preceding event, but which can itself give rise naturally to some further fact or occurrence. An 'end,' by contrast, is something which naturally occurs after a preceding event, whether by necessity or as a general rule, but need not be followed by anything else. The 'middle' involves causal connections with both what precedes and what ensues. Consequently, well designed plot-structures ought not to begin or finish at arbitrary points, but to follow the principles indicated" (39).

17. This is a twist on Aristotle's separation of action and character: "without action you would not have a tragedy, but one without character would be feasible, for the tragedies of most recent poets are lacking in characterisation" (*Poetics,* chapter 6, Halliwell ed. 38).

18. Corneille in fact recommends as a standard dramatic structure that more than one action should be introduced explicitly in the first act. Then the playwright's task is to maintain the audience's curiosity about how those apparently separate actions will eventually fuse.

19. The case of two or more apparent "actions" beginning in the first act would leave the audience in continued suspense even if the hero escaped from the threat represented by one of the situations challenging him initially.

20. Georges May (*Tragédie cornélienne / Tragédie racinienne*) sees the spectator's intellectual curiosity as a central part of Corneille's aesthetic.

Conclusion

1. These terms are taken from Robert Horville, *XVIIe siècle* (1988) in the Hatier Itinéraires littéraires series (138–39), but they are typical of the almost universal pedagogical reduction of seventeenth-century poetics to a simple set of uncomplicated and harmonious principles.

2. This expansion of the critical audience—that is, of an audience that considers itself fully entitled to pass judgment on literary works—is a major theme of the seventeenth-century "Culture Wars" as described by Joan DeJean. For DeJean the audience's taste in matters of drama is only a preliminary to the more extensive and democratic participation in discussions of the novel (*Ancients against Moderns* 55, 64).

3. Of catharsis, Corneille writes, "Je m'en rapporte à ceux qui en ont vu les représentations: ils peuvent en demander compte au secret de leur cœur et repasser sur ce qui les a touchés au théâtre pour reconnaître s'ils en sont venus par là jusqu'à cette crainte réfléchie, et si elle a rectifié en eux la passion qui a causé la disgrâce qu'ils ont plainte" (3: 146).

4. I have discussed Corneille's view of the modern theater audience in "Corneille's *Discours* and Classical Closure."

5. It may seem that d'Aubignac is not specifically defining the audience of tragedy but the theater audience at large. However, his examples of the instructive use of the theater in these pages of the first chapter of book 1 of *La pratique du théâtre* include tragic subjects, that is, the dramatic embodiment of epic subjects: "ils y voyent la ruine de cette royale Famille de Priam. Tout ce qu'ils entendent de la bouche d'Hecube, leur semble croyable, parce qu'ils en ont la preuve devant les yeux" (9).

6. La Mesnardière writes, "j'estime avec Aristote, qu'un Ouvrage est imparfait, lorsque par la seule lecture faite dans un cabinet, il n'excite pas les Passions dans l'Esprit de ses Auditeurs, et qui'il ne les agite point jusques à les faire trembler, ou à leur arracher des larmes" (12). See also, in regard to the reader of the novel at the same period, Walter Benjamin's essay "The Storyteller."

7. Bossuet denounces "le désir de voir et d'être vu, la malheureuse rencontre des yeux qui se cherchent les uns les autres . . ." ("Lettre au père Caffaro" 135).

8. "Si l'auteur d'une tragédie ne sait pas intéresser le spectateur, l'émouvoir, le transporter de la passion qu'il a voulu exprimer, où tombe-t-il, si ce n'est dans le froid, dans l'ennuyeux, dans l'insupportable, si on peut parler de cette sorte?" (Bossuet, "Lettre au père Caffaro" 124).

9. D'Aubignac specifically says that he is not writing for theater professionals, "pour les avertir des choses qu'ils pratiquent tous les jours si heureusement." He says, to the contrary, "J'écris seulement pour faire connoistre au Peuple, l'excellence de leur Art, et pour luy donner sujet de les admirer, en monstrant combien il faut d'addresse, de suffisance, et de precautions pour achever des Ouvrages qui ne donnent à nos Comediens que la peine de les reciter, et qui ravissent de Joye ceux qui les écoutent" (18).

10. "[L]es Spectateurs penetreront dans toutes leurs beautez [des poèmes dramatiques], et considereront combien de Meditations, de Veilles, et de Reflexions elles ont cousté à ceux qui nous les donnent" (d'Aubignac 18–19).

Bibliography

Albanese, Ralph. "Le discours scolaire au XIXème siècle: Le cas Molière." *Continuum* 1 (1989): 31–49.

Alter, Jean. *A Sociosemiotic Theory of Theatre.* Philadelphia: U of Pennsylvania P, 1990.

Aristotle. *Poetics.* Ed. and trans. D. W. Lucas. Oxford: Clarendon, 1968.

———. *The Poetics of Aristotle.* Ed. and trans. Stephen Halliwell. Chapel Hill: U of North Carolina P, 1987.

———. *Rhetoric.* Trans. W. Rhys Roberts. *The Complete Works of Aristotle.* Ed. Jonathan Barnes. Bollingen Series. Princeton: Princeton UP, 1984. 2152–269.

Arnauld, Charles. *Les théories dramatiques au XVIIe siècle: Étude sur la vie et les œuvres de l'abbé d'Aubignac.* 1888. Geneva: Slatkine, 1970.

Baillet, Adrien. *Jugemens de savans sur les principaux ouvrages des auteurs.* Ed. Yvon Belaval. Hildesheim, Ger./New York: Georg Olms, 1971.

Balzac, Jean-Louis Guez de. *Œuvres.* Ed. Valentin Contrart. Geneva: Slatkine, 1971.

Barker, Francis. *The Culture of Violence: Essays on Tragedy and History.* Chicago: U of Chicago P, 1993.

Barnouw, Jeffrey. "Passion as 'Confused' Perception or Thought in Descartes, Malebranche, and Hutcheson." *Journal of the History of Ideas* 53 (1992): 397–424.

Barnwell, H. T. "Some Reflections on Corneille's Theory of Vraisemblance as Formulated in the Discours." *Forum for Modern Language Studies* 1.4 (1965): 295–310.

Batteux, Abbé Charles. *Principes de la littérature.* Paris: Saillant et Nyon, 1774–75.

Bayne, Sheila Page. *Tears and Weeping: An Aspect of Emotional Climate Reflected in Seventeenth-Century French Literature.* Études littéraires françaises. Tübingen and Paris: Gunter Narr and Jean-Michel Place, 1981.

Belardi, Walter. "Corneille, Racine e la catarsi tragica." *Scritti in onore di Giovanni Macchia.* Milan: Mondadori, 1983. 11–24.

Benjamin, Walter. "The Storyteller: Reflections on the Works of Nikolai Leskov." *Illuminations.* Ed. Hannah Arendt. Trans. Harry Zohn. New York: Schocken, 1969. 83–109.

———. *Origine du drame baroque allemand.* Trans. Sibylle Muller. Paris: Flammarion, 1985.

Berg, Elizabeth. "Recognizing Differences: Perrault's Modernistic Aesthetic in the *Parallel des anciens et des modernes.*" *Papers on French Seventeenth-Century Literature* 18 (1983): 135–45.

Beugnot, Bernard, and Roger Zuber. *Boileau: Visages anciens, visages nouveaux.* Montreal: Presses de l'Université de Montréal, 1973.

Biet, Christian. *Racine, ou la passion des larmes.* Portraits littéraires. Paris: Hachette, 1996.

Black, Cordell. *Corneille's Denouements: Text and Conversion.* Studia Humanitatis. Potomac, MD: José Porrua Turanzas, 1984.

Blum, Alan. *Theorizing.* London: Heinemann, 1974.

Boileau-Despréaux, Nicolas. *Œuvres complètes.* Ed. Françoise Escal. Bibliothèque de la Pléiade. Paris: Gallimard, 1966.

Borgerhoff, E. B. O. *The Evolution of Liberal Theory and Practice in the French Theater, 1680–1757.* Princeton: Princeton UP, 1936.

———. *The Freedom of French Classicism.* Princeton: Princeton UP, 1950.

Borowitz, Helen O. *The Impact of Art on French Literature: From de Scudéry to Proust.* Newark: U of Delaware P, 1985.

Borst, Arno. *The Ordering of Time, from the Ancient Computers to the Modern Computer.* Trans. Andrew Winnard. Chicago: U of Chicago P, 1990.

Bossuet, Jacques-Bénigne. *Discours sur l'histoire universelle.* 1681. Pref. Jacques Truchet. Paris: Garnier Flammarion, 1966.

———. "Lettre au père Caffaro." *L'église et le théâtre.* Ed. Charles Urbain and E. Levesque. Paris: Grasset, 1930. 121–41.

———. "Maximes et réflexions sur la comédie." *L'église et le théâtre.* Ed. Charles Urbain and E. Levesque. Paris: Grasset, 1930. 169–276.

Bouhours, Dominique. *Les entretiens d'Ariste et d'Eugène.* Paris: Max Leclerc, Librairie Armand Colin, 1962.

———. *La manière de bien penser dans les ouvrages de l'esprit.* Hildesheim, Ger.: Georg Olms, 1974.

Bourdieu, Pierre. *Outline of a Theory of Practice.* Trans. Richard Nice. Cambridge: Cambridge UP, 1988.

Bouwsma, William. "Anxiety and the Formation of Early-Modern Culture." Ed. Barbara C. Malament. *After the Reformation: Essays in Honor of J. H. Hexter.* Philadelphia: U of Pennsylvania P, 1980. 215–46.

Braden, Gordon. *Renaissance Tragedy and the Senecan Tradition: Anger's Privilege.* New Haven: Yale UP, 1983.

Braider, Christopher. *Refiguring the Real: Picture and Modernity in Word and Image, 1400–1700.* Princeton: Princeton UP, 1993.

Bray, René. *Formation de la doctrine classique en France.* 1927. Paris: Nizet, 1968.

Brenner, Jacques. "La Querelle du Cid." *Les critiques dramatiques.* Paris: Flammarion, 1970.

Brody, Jules. *Boileau and Longinus.* Geneva: Droz, 1958.

———. "What *Was* French Classicism?" *Continuum* 1 (1989): 51–77.

Brooks, William, ed. *Le théâtre et l'opéra vus par les gazetiers Robinet et Laurent (1670–1678) textes.* Biblio 17 78. Paris and Seattle: Papers on French Seventeenth-Century Literature, 1993.

Buci-Glucksman, Christine. *Baroque Reason: The Aesthetics of Modernity.* Trans. Patrick Camiller. New York: Sage, 1994.

Burns, J. H., ed. Assisted by Mark Goldie. *The Cambridge History of Political Thought.* Cambridge: Cambridge UP, 1991.

Bussy-Rabutin, Roger, comte de. *Correspondance avec sa famille et ses amis.* Ed. Ludovic Lalanne. Westmead, Eng.: Gregg International, 1972.

Caffaro, Father. "Lettre d'un théologien illustre par sa qualité et par son mérite." *L'église et le théâtre.* Ed. Charles Urbain and E. Levesque. Paris: Grasset, 1930. 67–119.

Caldicott, E. "Richelieu and the Arts." *Richelieu and His Age.* Ed. Joseph Bergin and Laurence Brockliss. Oxford: Oxford UP, 1992.

Calinescu, Matei. *Five Faces of Modernity.* Durham, NC: Duke UP, 1987.

Calzabigi, Ranieri de'. "Lettera all'autore sulle quattro sue prime tragedie." Preface. *Tragedie.* By Vittorio Alfieri. Ed. Luca Toschi. Vol. 1. Florence: Sansoni, 1951. 79–113.

Caput, Jean-Paul. *L'Académie française.* Paris: PUF, 1986.

Carel de Sainte-Garde, J. *Réflexions sur les orateurs et sur les poètes.* 1676. Geneva: Slatkine, 1972.

Carlin, Claire. "Racine, Mauron, and the Question of Genre." *Rocky Mountain Review of Languages and Literatures* 36.1 (1982): 26–33.

Castelvetro, Lodovico. *On the Art of Poetry.* 1570. Ed. and trans. Andrew Bongiorno. Binghamton, NY: Medieval and Renaissance Texts and Studies, 1984.

Cave, Terence. *Recognitions: A Study in Poetics.* Oxford: Clarendon, 1988.

Chantalat, Claude. *À la recherche du goût classique.* Paris: Klincksieck, 1992.

229

Chapelain, Jean. "Discours de la poésie représentative." *Opuscules critiques*. Ed. Alfred C. Hunter. Paris: Droz, 1936. 128–31.

———. *Lettres de Jean Chapelain*. Ed. Ph. Tamizey de Larroque. Paris: Nationale, 1880–83.

———. "Lettre sur la règle des vingt-quatre heures." *Opuscules critiques*. Ed. Alfred C. Hunter. Paris: Droz, 1936. 114–26.

———. Preface. *L'adonis*. Ed. E. Bovet. *Aus Romanischen Sprachen und Literaturen: Festschrift Heinrich Morf*. Geneva: Slatkine, 1980.

———. *Les sentimens de l'Academie françoise sur la Tragi-Comedie du Cid. La Querelle du Cid*. 1898. Ed. Armand Gasté. Geneva: Slatkine, 1970. 355–417.

Chappuzeau, Samuel. *Le théâtre français*. Ed. Georges Monval. Plan de la Tour (Var): Aujourd'hui, 1985.

Chartier, Roger, ed. *The Culture of Print*. Trans. Lydia Cochrane. Princeton: Princeton UP, 1989.

Clarke, David. *Pierre Corneille: Poetics and Political Drama under Louis XIII*. Cambridge: Cambridge UP, 1992.

Collas, Georges. "Richelieu et Le Cid." *Revue d'histoire littéraire de la France* 43 (1936): 568–72.

Conrart, Valentin. "Lettres à Félibien." *Valentin Conrart, sa vie et sa correspondance*. Ed. René Kerviler and Edouard de Barthélémy. Geneva: Slatkine, 1971.

Corneille, Pierre. *Œuvres complètes*. Ed. Georges Couton. 3 vols. Bibliothèque de la Pléiade. Paris: Gallimard, 1980–87.

Couton, Georges. *Corneille et la Fronde*. Publications de la Faculté des Lettres de l'Université de Clermont. Clermont-Ferrand: Bussac, 1951.

———. *Richelieu et le théâtre*. Lyons: Presses Universitaires de Lyon, 1986.

D'Aubignac, François Hédelin, abbé. *La pratique du théâtre*. 1657. Ed. Pierre Martino. Algiers: Jules Carbonel, 1927.

Dacier, André, trans. and ed. *La poétique d'Aristote*. Paris: Barbin, 1692.

Dandrey, Patrick. "Les deux esthétiques du classicisme français." *Littératures classiques* 19 (1993): 145–70.

Davidson, Hugh M. "Corneille interprète d'Aristote dans les trois discours." Ed. Alain Niderst. *Actes du Colloque Pierre Corneille*. Paris: PUF, 1985.

———. "Pratique et rhétorique du théâtre: Étude sur le vocabulaire et la méthode de D'Aubignac." Ed. Marc Fumaroli. *Critique et* *création littéraires en France au XVIIe siècle.* Paris: CNRS, 1977. 169–81.

De La Motte, Antoine Houdard, marquis de. "Discours de la tragédie." *Œuvres de théâtre.* Paris: Grégoire Dupuis, 1730. 1–208.

De Man, Paul. "Resistance to Theory." *Yale French Studies* 63 (1982): 3–20.

de Piles, Roger. *Cours de peinture par principes.* Paris: Jacques Etienne, 1708. Geneva: Slatkine, 1969.

———. *Les premiers éléments de la peinture pratique.* Paris: Nicolas Langlois, 1684. Geneva: Slatkine, 1973.

de Romilly, Jacqueline. *Le temps dans la tragédie grecque.* Paris: Vrin, 1971.

DeJean, Joan. *Ancients against Moderns: Culture Wars and the Making of a Fin de Siècle.* Chicago: U of Chicago P, 1997.

———. *Tender Geographies: Women and the Origins of the Novel in France.* New York: Columbia UP, 1991.

Deleuze, Gilles. *Le pli: Leibniz et le baroque.* Paris: Minuit, 1988.

Derrida, Jacques. *L'écriture et la différence.* Collection "Tel Quel." Paris: Le Seuil, 1967.

Descartes, René. *Œuvres et lettres.* Ed. André Bridoux. Bibliothèque de la Pléiade. Paris: Gallimard, 1953.

———. "Regulae ad directionem ingenii." *Œuvres complètes.* Ed. Charles Adam and Paul Tannery. Paris: Vrin, 1996. 349–488.

Desmarets de Saint-Sorlin, Jean. *Marie-Madeleine ou le Triomphe de la Grâce.* Paris: Sébastien Martin, 1673.

———. *Les visionnaires.* Ed. H. Gaston Hall. Paris: Didier, 1963.

Dryden, John. *Of Dramatick Poesie, an Essay.* Pref. Yuji Kaneko. Routledge/Thoemmes, 1996.

Dutertre, Eveline. "Scudéry et Corneille." *Dix-septième siècle* 146 (1985): 29–46.

———. "Scudéry et la Querelle du Cid." *Dix-septième siècle* 84–85 (1969): 61–75.

Ekstein, Nina C. *Dramatic Narratives: Racine's Récits.* Berne: Peter Lang, 1986.

Elias, Norbert. *The Court Society.* Trans. Edmund Jephcott. New York: Pantheon, 1983. Originally published in 1969 in German.

———. *Power and Civility.* Trans. Edmund Jephcott. New York: Pantheon, 1982. Originally published in 1969 in German.

Elkins, James. *The Poetics of Perspective.* Ithaca, NY: Cornell UP, 1994.

Emelina, Jean. "Le plaisir tragique." *Littératures classiques* 16 (Spring 1992): 35–47.

Félibien, André. *L'idée du peintre parfait, pour servir de régle aux jugemens que l'on doit porter sur les ouvrages des peintres.* London: David Mortier, 1707. Geneva: Slatkine, 1970.

Ferry, Luc. *Homo Aestheticus: The Invention of Taste in the Democratic Age.* Chicago: U of Chicago P, 1994.

Fidao-Justiniani, J.-E. *L'esprit classique et la préciosité au XVIIᵉ siècle.* Paris: Archives Nationales et la Société de l'École des Chartres, 1914.

Fogel, Herbert. *The Criticism of Cornelian Tragedy.* New York: Exposition, 1967.

Fontenelle, Bernard le Bovier. "Réflexions sur la poétique." *Œuvres complètes.* Corpus des œuvres de philosophie en langue française. Paris: Fayard, 1989. 111–59.

———. "Vie de M. Corneille avec l'histoire du théâtre françois jusqu'à lui." *Œuvres complètes.* Corpus des œuvres de philosophie en langue française. Paris: Fayard, 1989. 29–109.

Forestier, Georges. "De la modernité anti-classique au classicisme moderne: Le modèle théâtral (1628–1634)." *Littératures classiques* 19 (1993): 87–128.

———. "Illusion comique et illusion mimétique." *Papers on French Seventeenth-Century Literature* 11.21 (1984): 377–91.

———. *Introduction à l'analyse des textes classiques.* Nathan Université. Paris: Nathan, 1992.

———. "Théorie et pratique de l'histoire dans la tragédie classique." *Littératures classiques* 11 (1989): 95–107.

France, Peter. *Politeness and Its Discontents: Problems in French Classical Culture.* Cambridge: Cambridge UP, 1992.

Franko, Mark. "Act and Voice in Neo-Classical Theatrical Theory: D'Aubignac's Pratique and Corneille's Illusion." *Romanic Review* 78.3 (May 1987): 311–26.

Fredrick, Edna C. *The Plot and Its Construction in Eighteenth-Century Criticism of French Comedy.* New York: Franklin, 1973.

Garapon, Robert. "Le sens du mot 'raison' au dix-septième siècle." *Convergences: Rhetoric and Poetic in Seventeenth-Century France.* Ed. David L. Rubin and Mary B. McKinley. Columbus: Ohio State UP, 1989. 34–44.

Gasté, Armand, ed. *La Querelle du Cid.* 1898. Geneva: Slatkine, 1970.

Gellrich, Michelle. *Tragedy and Theory: The Problem of Conflict since Aristotle.* Princeton: Princeton UP, 1988.

Genette, Gérard. "Vraisemblance et motivation." *Figures II*. Paris: Le Seuil, 1969. 71–99.

Gethner, Perry J. "Jean de Mairet and Poetic Justice: A Definition of Tragicomedy?" *Renaissance Drama* 11 (1980): 171–87.

Gilbert, Allan H., ed. "An Essay of Dramatic Poesy." By John Dryden. *Literary Criticism, Plato to Dryden*. Detroit: Wayne State UP, 1962.

Girard, René. *La violence et le sacré*. Paris: Grasset, 1972.

Goodkin, Richard. "Racine en marge d'Aristote: *Phèdre* et le milieu exclu." *Poétique* 67 (1986): 349–70.

———. *The Tragic Middle: Racine, Aristotle, Euripides*. Madison: U of Wisconsin P, 1991.

Gordon, Daniel. *Citizens without Sovereignty: Equality and Sociability in French Thought, 1670–1789*. Princeton: Princeton UP, 1994.

Grafton, Anthony, and Ann Blair, eds. *The Transmission of Culture in Early Modern Europe*. Philadelphia: U of Pennsylvania P, 1990.

Granet, abbé François, ed. *Recueil de dissertations sur plusieurs tragédies de Corneille et de Racine*. Paris: Gissey, 1739.

Gravel, Pierre, and Timothy J. Reiss, eds. *Tragique et tragédie dans la tradition occidentale*. Special issue of *Études françaises* [Montreal] 15.3–4 (1979).

Greenberg, Mitchell. *Canonical States, Canonical Stages*. Minneapolis: U of Minnesota P, 1994.

———. *Corneille, Classicism and the Ruses of Symmetry*. Cambridge: Cambridge UP, 1986.

———. "Mythifying Matrix: Corneille's *Médée* and the Birth of Tragedy." *Corneille, Classicism and the Ruses of Symmetry*. Cambridge: Cambridge UP, 1986. 16–36.

Gross, David. *The Past in Ruins: Tradition and the Critique of Modernity*. Amherst: U of Massachusetts P, 1992.

Hagiwara, Yoshiko. "La théorie de la représentation dans *La pratique du théâtre* de d'Aubignac." *Études de langue et littérature françaises* 40 (Mar. 1982): 23–43.

Haight, Jeanne. *The Concept of Reason in French Classical Literature: 1635–1690*. Toronto: U of Toronto P, 1982.

Hall, H. Gaston. "Desmarets's 'L'Art de la Poésie': Poetics or Politics?" *Convergences: Rhetoric and Poetic in Seventeenth-Century France*. Ed. David L. Rubin and Mary B. McKinley. Columbus: Ohio State UP, 1989. 45–62.

Hanse, Joseph. "'Le Cid' et 'Les sentiments de l'Académie.'" *Les études classiques* 6.2 (Apr. 1937): 171–202.

Hardy, Alexandre. *Théâtre.* Ed. E. Stengel. Geneva: Slatkine, 1967.

Harth, Erica. *Cartesian Women: Versions and Subversions of Rational Discourse in the Old Regime.* Ithaca, NY: Cornell UP, 1992.

Hegel, G. W. F. *The Philosophy of Fine Art.* Trans. F. P. B. Osmaston. London: Bell, 1920.

Hjorte, Mette. *The Strategy of Letters.* Cambridge: Harvard UP, 1994.

Holtzman, Steven H., and Christopher M. Leich, eds. *Wittgenstein: To Follow a Rule.* London: Routledge, 1981.

Hooper, R. H. "Voltaire's *Commentaires sur Corneille.*" *Kentucky Foreign Language Quarterly* 10 (1963): 8–13.

Horville, Robert. *Itinéraires littéraires: XVIIe siècle.* Paris: Hatier, 1988.

Huet, Pierre Daniel. *Traité de l'origine des romans.* 1670. Ed. Hans Hinterhäuser. Stuttgart: Metzlersche, 1966.

Huguet, Edmond. *Dictionnaire de la langue française du seizième siècle.* Paris: Champion, 1925.

Jones, Thora Burnley, and Bernard De Bear Nicol. *Neo-Classical Dramatic Criticism, 1560–1770.* Cambridge: Cambridge UP, 1976.

Joos, Jean-Ernest. "La 'catharsis' et le moment historique de la tragédie grecque." *Tragique et tragédie dans la tradition occidentale.* Ed. Pierre Gravel. Special issue of *Études françaises* [Montreal] 15.3–4 (1979): 21–44.

Kern, Edith. *The Influence of Heinsus and Vossius upon French Dramatic Theory.* Baltimore: Johns Hopkins UP, 1949.

Kerviler, R., and E. de Barthélémy. *Valentin Conrart: Sa vie et sa correspondance.* Geneva: Slatkine, 1971.

Kintzler, Catherine. *Poétique de l'opéra français de Corneille à Rousseau.* Paris: Minerve, 1991.

Klenke, M. Amelia. "The Richelieu-Corneille Rapport." *PMLA* 64 (1949): 724–45.

Koch, Philip. "Horace: Réponse Cornélienne à la Querelle du Cid." *Romanic Review* 76.2 (1985): 148–61.

Kuizenga, Donna. "Once More with Feeling: Rhetorics of the Passions." *Cahiers du dix-septième* 5.1 (Spring 1991): 41–57.

Lafond, Jean, ed. *Les formes brèves de la prose et le discours discontinu (XVIe–XVIIe siècles).* Paris: Vrin, 1984.

La Mesnardière, H.-J. Pilet de. *La poëtique.* 1640. Geneva: Slatkine, 1972.

Lamy, Bernard. *Nouvelles réflexions sur l'art poétique.* Paris: André Pralard, 1678.

Landes, David S. *Revolution in Time.* Cambridge: Belknap–Harvard UP, 1983.

Lanson, Gustave. "L'idée de la tragédie en France avant Jodelle." *Revue d'histoire littéraire* 11 (1904): 341–85.

Larrain, Jorge. *The Concept of Ideology.* Athens: U of Georgia P, 1980.

Lawrenson, T. E. *The French Stage and Playhouse in the XVIIth Century: A Study in the Advent of the Italian Order.* 2nd ed. New York: AMS, 1986.

Lawton, H. W., ed. *Handbook of French Renaissance Dramatic Theory.* Manchester: Manchester UP, 1949.

Leblanc, Paulette. *Les écrits théoriques français des années 1540–1561 sur la tragédie.* Paris: Nizet, 1972.

Le Bossu, René. *Traité du poème épique.* 1675. Ed. Volker Kapp. Hamburg: Helmut Buske, 1981.

Le Moyne, Pierre. "Traité du poëme héroïque." *Saint Louys, ou la sainte couronne reconquise.* Paris: Augustin Courbé, 1658.

Lewis, Philip. *Seeing through the Mother Goose Tales: Visual Turns in the Writings of Charles Perrault.* Stanford: Stanford UP, 1996.

Lewita, Beatrix. *French Bourgeois Culture.* Trans. J. A. Underwood. Cambridge: Cambridge UP, 1994.

Lichtenstein, Jacqueline. *The Eloquence of Color: Rhetoric and Painting in the French Classical Age.* Ed. E. McVarish. Berkeley: U of California P, 1993.

Lichtheim, George. "The Concept of Ideology." *History and Theory* 4.2 (1965): 164–95.

Lioure, Michel. *Le théâtre religieux en France.* Que sais-je? Paris: PUF, 1982.

Litman, Théodore. *Le sublime en France (1660–1714).* Paris: Nizet, 1971.

Loukovitch, Kosta. *L'évolution de la tragédie religieuse classique en France.* 1933. Geneva: Slatkine, 1977.

Lucas, Frank L. *Tragedy: Serious Drama in Relation to Aristotle's Poetics.* New York: Collier, 1962.

Luzán, Ignacio de. *La poética o reglas de la poesía en general y de sus principales especies.* Ed. Russell P. Sebold. Textos hispánicos modernos. Barcelona: Labor, 1977.

Lyons, John D. "*Camera Obscura*: Image and Imagination in Descartes' *Meditations.*" *Convergences: Rhetoric and Poetic in Seventeenth-Century France.* Ed. David L. Rubin and Mary B. McKinley. Columbus: Ohio State UP, 1989. 179–95.

———. "Corneille and the Triumph of Pleasure, or The Four Axioms of Tragic Pleasure." *Papers on French Seventeenth-Century Literature* 19.37 (1992): 329–36.

Lyons, John D. "Corneille's *Discours* and Classical Closure." *Continuum* 2 (1990): 65–80.

———. "The Decorum of Horror: A Reading of La Mesnardière's *Poëtique*." *Homage to Paul Bénichou*. Ed. Sylvie Romanowski and Monique Bilezikian. Birmingham, AL: Summa, 1994. 27–41.

———. "Tragic Closure and the Cornelian Wager." *Analecta Husserliana* 18 (1984): 409–15.

———. "Unseen Space and Theatrical Narrative: The 'Récit de Cinna.'" *Yale French Studies* 80 (1991): 70–90.

Mairet, Jean de. Preface to *La Silvanire*. Ed. Jacques Scherer. *Théâtre du XVIIe siècle*. Bibliothèque de la Pléiade. Paris: Gallimard, 1975. 479–88.

———. *La Sophonisbe*. Ed. Charles Dédéyan. Paris: Droz, 1945.

Major, J. Russell. *From Renaissance Monarchy to Absolute Monarchy: French Kings, Nobles and Estates*. Baltimore: Johns Hopkins UP, 1994.

Makowiecka, Gabriela. *Luzán y su poética*. Barcelona: Planeta, 1973.

Mallinson, G. J. "Fiction, Morality, and the Reader: Reflections on the Classical Formula *Plaire et Instruire*." *Continuum* 1 (1989): 203–27.

Maravall, José Antonio. *Culture of the Baroque*. Trans. Terry Cochran. Minneapolis: U of Minnesota P, 1983.

Margitić, Milorad. "La Bruyère entre Corneille et Racine." *Cahiers de l'Association Internationale des Études Françaises* 44 (1992): 307–21

———, ed. *Corneille comique: Nine Studies of Pierre Corneille's Comedy*. Biblío 17 4. Paris and Seattle: Papers on French Seventeenth-Century Literature,1982.

———. "Sociological Aspects of 'La Querelle du *Cid*.'" *Homage to Paul Bénichou*. Ed. Sylvie Romanowski and Monique Bilezikian. Birmingham, AL: Summa, 1994. 59–74.

Marin, Louis. "La critique de la représentation théâtrale classique à Port-Royal: Commentaires sur le *Traité de la comédie* de Nicole." *Continuum* 2 (1990): 81–105.

Marshall, David. *The Figure of Theatre: Shaftesbury, Defoe, Adam Smith, and George Eliot*. New York: Columbia UP, 1985.

———. *The Surprising Effects of Sympathy: Marivaux, Diderot, Rousseau and Mary Shelley*. Chicago: U of Chicago P, 1988.

Masullo, Aldo. "Fine della tragedia e scoprimento del tragico." *Annali: Studi tedeschi* [Naples] 27.3 (1984): 98–106.

Maucroix, François de. *Œuvres diverses.* Ed. Louis Paris. Geneva: Slatkine, 1971.

May, Georges. "Corneille and the Classics." *Yale French Studies* 38 (1967): 138–50.

———. *Tragédie cornélienne / Tragédie racinienne.* Urbana: U of Illinois P, 1948.

Maynard, François de. *Les lettres du président Maynard.* Ed. Jean-Pierre Lassalle. Toulouse: Centre de Recherche, 1984.

———. *Œuvres poétiques.* Ed. Gaston Garrisson. Geneva: Slatkine, 1970.

McCabe, William, S. J. *An Introduction to the Jesuit Theater.* St. Louis, MO: Institute of Jesuit Sources, 1983.

McConachie, Bruce. "Theatre History and the Nation-State." *Theatre Review* 20 (1995): 141–48.

Menke, Anne M. "Authorizing the Illicit, or How to Create Works of Lasting Insignificance." *Esprit créateur* 35 (1995): 84–100.

Méré, Chevalier de. *Œuvres complètes du chevalier de Méré.* Paris: Fernand Roches, 1930.

Merleau-Ponty, Maurice. *Le visible et l'invisible.* Tel. Paris: Gallimard, 1964.

Merlin, Hélène. "L'auteur et la figure absolutiste: Richelieu, Balzac, et Corneille." *Revue des sciences humaines* 238 (1995): 85–96.

———. "L'*épistémè* classique ou l'épineuse question de la représentation." *Littératures classiques* 19 (1993): 187–98.

———. *Public et littérature en France au XVIIe siècle.* Paris: Les Belles Lettres, 1994.

Mesnard, Jean. "Vraie et fausse beauté dans l'esthétique au dix-septième siècle." *Convergences: Rhetoric and Poetic in Seventeenth-Century France.* Ed. David L. Rubin and Mary B. McKinley. Columbus: Ohio State UP, 1989. 3–33.

Moncond'huy, Dominique. "Poésie, peinture et politique: La place de Richelieu dans le cabinet de M. de Scudéry." *Dix-septième siècle* 165.4 (Dec. 1989): 417–36.

Mongrédien, Georges, ed. *Recueil des textes et des documents du XVIIe siècle relatifs à Corneille.* Paris: Centre National de la Recherche Scientifique, 1972.

Montagu, Jennifer. *The Expression of Passions: The Origin and Influence of Charles Le Brun's "Conférence sur l'expression générale et particulière."* New Haven: Yale UP, 1994.

Montaigne, Michel de. *Les essais.* Ed. Pierre Villey. 1922. Pref. V.-L. Saulnier. Paris: PUF, 1965.

Moore, Will. *The Classical Drama of France*. Oxford: Oxford UP, 1971.

Morel, Jacques. *Agréables mensonges: Essais sur le théâtre du XVIIe siècle*. Ed. Georges Forestier. Paris: Klincksieck, 1991.

Moriarty, Michael. *Taste and Ideology in Seventeenth-Century France*. Cambridge: Cambridge UP, 1988.

Morrissey, Robert. "La pratique du théâtre et le langage de l'illusion." *Dix-septième siècle* 146 (1985): 17–27.

Murray, Timothy. "Non-representation in La Pratique du Théâtre." *Papers on French Seventeenth Century Literature* 9.16 (1982): 57–74.

———. *Theatrical Legitimation: Allegories of Genius in Seventeenth-Century England and France*. New York: Oxford UP, 1987.

Nadal, Octave. *Le sentiment de l'amour dans l'œuvre de Pierre Corneille*. Paris: Gallimard, 1948.

Nancy, Jean-Luc, ed. *Du sublime*. Paris: Belin, 1988.

Nelson, Robert J. "French Classicism: Dimensions of Application." *Continuum* 1 (1989): 79–104.

———. "The Spirit of Corneille's Criticism." *Esprit créateur* 4 (1964): 115–34.

Nicole, Pierre. *Traité de la comédie*. Ed. Georges Couton. Paris: Les Belles Lettres, 1961.

Niderst, Alain. "Corneille et les commentateurs d'Aristote." *Papers on French Seventeenth-Century Literature* 14.27 (1987): 733–43.

———, ed. *Pierre Corneille: Actes du Colloque*. Paris: PUF, 1985.

Nietzsche, Friedrich. *The Joyful Wisdom*. Ed. O. Levy. Trans. Thomas Common. London: T. N. Foulis, 1910. Vol. 10 of *The Complete Works*.

Norman, Buford. "The Exile of Reason: Representation of Emotion in the *Tragédie Lyrique*." *Ars lyrica* 6 (1993): 65–74.

Ogier, François. *Apologie pour Monsieur de Balzac*. Saint-Etienne: Université de Saint-Etienne, 1977.

Olson, Elder. *Tragedy and the Theory of Drama*. Detroit: Wayne State UP, 1961.

Pascal, Blaise. *Pensées*. Ed. Philippe Sellier. Classiques Garnier. Paris: Bordas, 1991.

Pasquier, Pierre. "Les apartés d'Icare: Éléments pour une théorie de la convention classique." *Littératures classiques* 16 (Spring 1992): 79–101.

————. *La mimésis dans l'esthétique théâtrale du XVIIe siècle*. Paris: Klincksieck, 1995.

Pavel, Thomas. *L'art de l'éloignement: Essai sur l'imagination classique*. Folio essais. Paris: Gallimard, 1996.

Perrault, Charles. *Parallèle des anciens et des modernes en ce qui regarde les arts et les sciences*. Geneva: Slatkine, 1979.

————. "Le siècle de Louis le Grand: Poème." *Parallèle des anciens et des modernes en ce qui regarde les arts et les sciences*. Geneva: Slatkine, 1979.

Peyre, Henri. *Qu'est-ce que le classicisme?* Paris: Nizet, 1964.

Phillips, Henry. *The Theatre and Its Critics in Seventeenth-Century France*. Oxford: Oxford UP, 1980.

Pineau, Joseph. *L'univers satirique de Boileau: L'ardeur, la grâce et la loi*. Geneva: Droz, 1990.

Pizzoruso, Arnaldo. "Il Cid e i diritti della lectura." *Atti del convegno di studi su Pierre Corneille nel 30 centenario della morte*. Ed. Mario Richter. Introd. Mariano Rumor. Vicenza: Accad. Olimpica, 1988. 83–95.

————. "Il 'Cid' e i principi dell'arte." *Belfagor* 43.1 (Jan. 1988): 37–48.

————. *Éléments d'une poétique littéraire au XVIIe siècle*. Paris: PUF, 1992.

Poli, Sergio. "Tradition ancienne et récit baroque: Mythe et réalité dans l'histoire tragique." *Travaux de littérature* 5 (1992): 89–107.

Pure, Michel, abbé de. *Idée des spectacles anciens et nouveaux*. 1668. Geneva: Minkoff, 1972.

Racine, Jean. *Œuvres complètes*. Ed. Raymond Picard. Bibliothèque de la Pléiade. Paris: Gallimard, 1966.

————. *Principes de la tragédie en marge de la poétique d'Aristote*. Manchester: Manchester UP, 1978.

————. *Théâtre complet*. Ed. Jacques Morel and Alain Viala. Classiques Garnier. Paris: Garnier, 1980.

Rapin, René. *Réflexions sur la poétique de ce temps et sur les ouvrages des poètes anciens et modernes*. 1675. Ed. E. T. Dubois. Geneva: Droz, 1970.

Rat, Maurice, ed. *Théâtre complet*. By Pierre Corneille. Classiques Garnier. Paris: Garnier, n.d.

Reese, Helen R. *La Mesnardière's "Poétique" (1639): Sources and Dramatic Theories*. Baltimore: Johns Hopkins UP, 1937.

Régnier, Mathurin. *Œuvres complètes*. Ed. Gabriel Raibaud. Paris: Didier, 1958.

Reiss, Timothy J. *The Discourse of Modernism.* Ithaca, NY: Cornell UP, 1982.

―――. *The Meaning of Literature.* Ithaca, NY: Cornell UP, 1992.

―――. *Towards Dramatic Illusion.* New Haven: Yale UP, 1971.

Ricoeur, Paul. *Temps et récit.* Paris: Le Seuil, 1983–84.

Roney, Edmund. "La Querelle du Cid: Classical Rules or Political Expediency?" *Transactions of the Wisconsin Academy of Sciences, Arts and Letters* 61 (1973): 157–64.

Rorty, Amélie Oksenberg, ed. *Essays on Aristotle's "Poetics."* Princeton: Princeton UP, 1992.

Roubine, Jean-Jacques. *Introduction aux grandes théories du théâtre.* Paris: Bordas, 1990.

Rubidge, Bradley. "Catharsis through Admiration: Corneille, Le Moyne, and the Social Uses of Emotion." *Modern Philology* 95 (1998): 316–33.

Saint-Evremond, Charles de Marguetel de Saint Denis, seigneur de. *Œuvres en prose.* Ed. René Ternois. Paris: Didier, 1962.

Saulnier, V.-L. *La littérature française du siècle classique.* 1943. Que sais-je? Paris: PUF, 1963.

Scaliger, Julius Caesar. *Poetices Libri Septum.* Stuttgart-Bad Canstatt: Friedrich Fromann, 1964.

―――. *Select Translations from Scaliger's Poetics.* Ed. Albert S. Cook. Trans. Frederick Morgan Padelford. New York: Holt, 1905.

Schelandre, Jean de. *Tyr et Sidon, ou les funestes amours de Belcar et Melians.* Ed. Jules Haraszti. Paris: Sté Nelle et Edouard Cornély, 1908.

Scherer, Colette. *Comédie et société sous Louis XIII, Corneille, Rotrou et les autres.* Paris: Nizet, 1983.

Scherer, Jacques. *La dramaturgie classique en France.* Paris: Nizet, 1950.

―――. *Dramaturgies du vrai-faux.* Paris: PUF, 1994.

Scherer, Jacques, and Jacques Truchet, eds. *Théâtre du XVIIe siècle.* Bibliothèque de la Pléiade. Paris: Gallimard, 1975–92. 3 vols.

Scudéry, Georges de. *L'apologie du théâtre.* Paris: Augustin Courbé, 1639.

―――. *Observations sur le Cid. La Querelle du Cid.* Ed. Armand Gasté. 1898. Geneva: Slatkine, 1970. 71–111.

Searles, Colbert. "L'Académie française et 'Le Cid.'" *Revue d'histoire littéraire de la France* 21 (1914): 331–74.

————. "Italian Influences as Seen in the Sentiments of the French Academy on the Cid." *Romanic Review* 3 (1912): 362–89.

Sedgwick, M. "Richelieu and the 'Querelle du Cid.'" *Modern Language Review* 48 (1953): 143–50.

Segrais, Jean Regnauld de. *Œuvres*. Geneva: Slatkine, 1968.

Sellstrom, Donald. *Corneille, Tasso and Modern Poetics*. Columbus: Ohio State UP, 1986.

Senault, Jean-François. *De l'usage des passions*. Corpus des œuvres de philosophie de langue française. Paris: Fayard, 1987.

Sévigné, Marie de Rabutin-Chantal de. *Correspondance*. Ed. Roger Duchêne. Bibliothèque de la Pléiade. Paris: Gallimard, 1972–78.

Sherman, Nancy. "*Hamartia* and Virtue." *Essays on Aristotle's "Poetics."* Ed. Amélie Oksenberg Rorty. Princeton: Princeton UP, 1992. 177–96.

Smith, Barbara Herrnstein. *Poetic Closure: A Study of How Poems End*. Chicago: U of Chicago P, 1968.

Smither, James R. "Propaganda and Theater: Authorial Intent and Audience Response to Political Pamphlets, 1550–1650." *Cahiers du dix-septième* 5.2 (Fall 1991): 179–94.

Sorel, Charles. *De la connoissance des bons livres*. Ed. Lucia Moretti Cenerini. Rome: Bulzoni, 1974.

Spitzer, Leo. *Essays on Seventeenth-Century French Literature*. Ed. and trans. David Bellos. Cambridge: Cambridge UP, 1983.

Stanton, Domna C. "Classicism (Re)Constructed: Notes on the Mythology of Literary History." *Continuum* 1 (1989): 1–29.

Stegmann, Andre. "Corneille, théoricien de la tragédie et ses antécédents italiens." *La licorne* 9 (1985): 83–96.

Stendhal. *Racine et Shakespeare*. Paris: J.-J. Pauvert, 1965.

Sweetser, Marie-Odile. *Les conceptions dramatiques de Corneille d'après ses écrits théoriques*. Geneva: Droz, 1962.

————. *La dramaturgie de Corneille*. Geneva: Droz, 1977.

Thompson, John B. *Studies in the Theory of Ideology*. Berkeley: U of California P, 1984.

Tobin, Ronald. *Racine and Seneca*. Chapel Hill: U of North Carolina P, 1971.

Tocanne, Bernard. *L'idée de la nature en France dans la seconde moitié du XVIIᵉ siècle*. Paris: Klincksieck, 1978.

Toulmin, Stephen. *Cosmopolis: The Hidden Agenda of Modernity*. New York: Free, 1990.

Toulmin, Stephen, and June Goodfield. *The Discovery of Time*. Chicago: U of Chicago P, 1965.

Valéry, Paul. "Au sujet d'Adonis." *Œuvres*. Bibliothèque de la Pléiade. Vol. 1. Paris: Gallimard, 1957. 474–95.

Varga, Aron Kibédi, ed. *Les poétiques du classicisme*. Paris: Aux Amateurs de livres, 1990.

———. "La vraisemblance—problèmes de terminologie, problèmes de poétique." *Critique et création littéraires en France au XVIIe siècle*. Ed. Marc Fumaroli. Paris: CNRS, 1977. 325–32.

Vauquelin, Jean. *Les diverses poésies*. Geneva: Slatkine, 1968.

Védier, Georges. *Origine et évolution de la dramaturgie néo-classique*. Paris: PUF, 1955.

Venet, Gisèle. *Temps et vision tragique: Shakespeare et ses contemporains*. Paris: Service des publications Université de la Sorbonne Nouvelle, 1985.

Viala, Alain. "Qu'est-ce qu'un classique?" *Littératures classiques* 19 (1993): 11–31.

Vida, Marco Girolamo. *The De Arte Poetica*. Trans. Ralph G. Williams. New York: Columbia UP, 1976.

Vinken, Barbara. "The Concept of Passion and the Dangers of the Theatre: Une esthétique avant la lettre: Augustine and Port-Royal." *Romanic Review* 83.1 (1992): 45–59.

Virtanen, Reino. "Nietzsche and Corneille." *Symposium* (Fall 1957): 225–39.

Voltaire. Notes to *Sertorius*. 1764. *Œuvres de P. Corneille*. Vol. 8. Paris: Antoine-Auguste Renouard, 1817.

Weinberg, Bernard. *A History of Literary Criticism in the Italian Renaissance*. 1961. Chicago: U of Chicago P, 1974.

Wood, Allen G. "Authority and Boileau." *Actes de Baton Rouge* (16th Annual Conference of the North American Society for Seventeenth-Century French Literature, at Baton Rouge, LA, 27–29 Mar. 1985). Biblio 17 25. Paris and Seattle: Papers on French Seventeenth-Century Literature, 1986. 217–26.

———. "Boileau and Affective Response." *Cahiers du dix-septième* 1.2 (Fall 1987): 61–73.

———. *Literary Satire and Theory: A Study of Horace, Boileau, and Pope*. New York: Garland, 1985.

———. "The *Régent du Parnasse* and *Vraisemblance*." *French Forum* 3 (1978): 251–62.

Youssef, Zobeidah. *Polémique et littérature chez Guez de Balzac.* Paris: Nizet, 1972.

Zanger, Abby Elizabeth. "Classical Anxiety: Performance, Perfection and the Issue of Identity." *L'âge du théâtre en France / The Age of Theatre in France.* Ed. David Trott and Nicole Boursier. Edmonton, AB: Academic, 1988. 327–39.

Zebouni, Selma. "Rhetorical Strategies in *L'Art poétique* or What Is Boileau Selling?" *French Literature Series* 19 (1992): 10–18.

Zito, Marina. "Le teorie estetiche di Corneille." *Annali Istituto Universitario Orientale* 20 (1978): 279–97.

Zuber, Roger. *Les belles infidèles et la formation du goût classique.* Paris: Albin Michel, 1995.

Zuber, Roger, Liliane Picciola, Denis Lopez, and Emmanuel Bury. *Littérature française du XVIIe siècle.* Collection Premier Cycle. Paris: PUF, 1992.

Index

—Also of Interest—

Reading Boileau
An Integrative Study of the Early Satires
by Robert T. Corum, Jr.
Vol. 15, 170 pages, cloth, $36.95, ISBN 1-55753-110-2

Robert Corum dispels misconceptions about Boileau by focusing rigorous critical attention on Boileau's first nine *Satires* and the accompanying *Discours au Roy*, composed between 1657 and 1668. His reading takes into account many factors, including sources, genesis, relation to one another, coherence, and continuity of argument. This examination reveals Boileau to be a gifted poet, not just a talented versifier or a strait-laced mouthpiece for French classical doctrine.

Falsehood Disguised
Unmasking the Truth in La Rochefoucauld
by Richard G. Hodgson
Vol. 7, 192 pages, cloth, $33.95, ISBN 1-55753-063-7

Through close textual analysis of La Rochefoucauld's writings, Richard Hodgson studies the moralist's use of metaphors such as the mask as well as his very personal concept of what constitutes an *être vrai*, or genuine person. The study then traces the impact of La Rochefoucauld's ideas on thinkers from Vauvenargues and Chamfort to Nietzsche, Lautréamont, and Lacan. It concludes by suggesting reasons why La Rochefoucauld's concept of truth continues to have such enormous appeal to the modern reader.

Purdue University Press
West Lafayette, Indiana
For more information, call
(800) 933-9637.

—Purdue Studies in Romance Literatures—

Vidas im/propias
Transformaciones del sujeto femenino en
la narrativa española contemporánea
by María Pilar Rodríguez
Vol. 19, 1999, 268 pages, HC, $42.95, ISBN 1-55753-164-1

Kingdom of Disorder
The Theory of Tragedy in Classical France
by John D. Lyons
Vol. 18, 1999, 272 pages, HC, $38.95, ISBN 1-55753-160-9

The Gendered Lyric
Subjectivity and Difference in
Nineteenth-Century French Poetry
by Gretchen Schultz
Vol. 17, 1999, 256 pages, HC, $38.95, ISBN 1-55753-135-8

Fictions du scandale
Corps féminin et réalisme romanesque au
dix-neuvième siècle
by Nathalie Buchet Rogers
Vol. 16, 1998, 324 pages, HC, $36.95, ISBN 1-55753-123-4

Reading Boileau
An Integrative Study of the Early Satires
by Robert T. Corum, Jr.
Vol. 15, 1998, 170 pages, HC, $36.95, ISBN 1-55753-110-2

Conflicts and Conciliations
The Evolution of Galdós's
Fortunata y Jacinta
by Geoffrey Ribbans
Vol. 14, 1997, 352 pages, HC, $42.95, ISBN 1-55753-108-0

Calderón y las quimeras de la Culpa
Alegoría, seduccíon y resistencia en
cinco autos sacramentales
by Viviana Díaz Balsera
Vol. 13, 1997, 288 pages, HC, $36.95, ISBN 1-55753-098-X

Plotting the Past
Metamorphoses of Historical Narrative in
Modern Italian Fiction
by Cristina Della Coletta
Vol. 12, 1996, 280 pages, HC, $38.95, ISBN 1-55753-091-2

The Subject of Desire
Petrarchan Poetics and the
Female Voice in Louise Labé
by Deborah Lesko Baker
Vol. 11, 1996, 272 pages, HC, $39.95, ISBN 1-55753-088-2

Cervantes's *Novelas ejemplares*
Between History and Creativity
by Joseph V. Ricapito
Vol. 10, 1996, 176 pages, HC, $33.95, ISBN 1-55753-078-5

Cruzados, mártires y beatos
Emplazamientos del cuerpo colonial
by Mario Cesareo
Vol. 9, 1995, 213 pages, HC, $37.95, ISBN 1-55753-075-0

André Gide dans le labyrinthe de la mythotextualité
by Pamela Antonia Genova
Vol. 8, 1995, 226 pages, HC, $34.95, ISBN 1-55753-067-X

Falsehood Disguised
Unmasking the Truth in La Rochefoucauld
by Richard G. Hodgson
Vol. 7, 1995, 190 pages, HC, $33.95, ISBN 1-55753-063-7

Tournier élémentaire
by Jonathan F. Krell
Vol. 6, 1994, 240 pages, HC, $39.95, ISBN 1-55753-056-4

Machado de Assis, the Brazilian Pyrrhonian
by José Raimundo Maia Neto
Vol. 5, 1994, 248 pages, HC, $40.95, ISBN 1-55753-051-3

Feminism and the Honor Plays of Lope de Vega
by Yvonne Yarbro-Bejarano
Vol. 4, 1994, 344 pages, HC, $40.95, ISBN 1-55753-044-0

After Machiavelli
"Re-writing" and the "Hermeneutic Attitude"
by Barbara J. Godorecci
Vol. 3, 1993, 224 pages, HC, $40.95, ISBN 1-55753-045-9

Kinship and Polity in the *Poema de Mio Cid*
by Michael Harney
Vol. 2, 1993, 300 pages, HC, $45.95, ISBN 1-55753-039-4

Writing and Inscription in Golden Age Drama
by Charles Oriel
Vol. 1, 1992, 200 pages, paper, $21.95, ISBN 1-55753-074-2

Purdue University Press
West Lafayette, Indiana

For more information, call
(800) 933-9637.